NEW YORK

ENCOUNTER

GINGER ADAMS OTIS

New York Encounter

Published by Lonely Planet Publications Pty Ltd
ABN 36 005 607 983

Australia	Head Office, Locked Bag 1, Footscray, Vic 3011
	☎ 03 8379 8000 fax 03 8379 8111
	talk2us@lonelyplanet.com.au
USA	150 Linden St, Oakland, CA 94607
	☎ 510 250 6400
	toll free 800 275 8555
	fax 510 893 8572
	info@lonelyplanet.com
UK	2nd fl, 186 City Rd
	London EC1V 2NT
	☎ 020 7106 2100
	fax 020 7106 2101
	go@lonelyplanet.co.uk

This title was commissioned in Lonely Planet's Oakland office and produced by: **Commissioning Editor** Jennye Garibaldi **Coordinating Editor** Nigel Chin **Cartographer** Brendan Streager **Coordinating Layout Designers** Yvonne Bischofberger, Nicholas Colicchia **Assisting Editor** Stephanie Pearson **Managing Editor** Liz Heynes **Managing Cartographer** Alison Lyall **Managing Layout Designer** Celia Wood **Cover Researcher** Naomi Parker, lonelyplanetimages.com **Internal Image Researcher** Sabrina Dalbesio, lonelyplanetimages.com **Thanks to** Mark Griffiths, Trent Holden, Lisa Knights, Gina Tsarouhas

ISBN 978 1 74179 709 1

Printed by Hang Tai Printing Company, Hong Kong
Printed in China

Acknowledgements New York City Subway Map © 2010 Metropolitan Transportation Authority. Used with permission. New York City Bus Map © 2010 Metropolitan Transportation Authority. Used with permission.

HOW TO USE THIS BOOK
Colour-Coding & Maps

Colour-coding is used for symbols on maps and in the text that they relate to (eg all eating venues on the maps and in the text are given a green knife and fork symbol). Each neighborhood also gets its own colour, and this is used down the edge of the page and throughout that neighborhood section.

Shaded yellow areas on the maps denote 'areas of interest' — for their historical significance, their attractive architecture or their great bars and restaurants. We encourage you to head to these areas and just start exploring!

Send us your feedback We love to hear from readers — your comments help make our books better. We read every word you send us, and we always guarantee that your feedback goes straight to the appropriate authors. The most useful submissions are rewarded with a free book. To send us your updates and find out about Lonely Planet events, newsletters and travel news visit our award-winning website: *lonelyplanet.com/contact*.

Note: We may edit, reproduce and incorporate your comments in Lonely Planet products such as guidebooks, websites and digital products, so let us know if you don't want your comments reproduced or your name acknowledged. For a copy of our privacy policy visit *lonelyplanet.com/privacy*.

GINGER ADAMS OTIS

As a working reporter in New York City, Ginger is intimately acquainted with all the nooks and crannies of the five boroughs, and often winds up riding the subway or walking the streets alongside visitors who are using her books. Thanks to the vagaries of being a print and radio reporter, Ginger gets to experience the city anew each day, getting pushed into off-the-beaten-track locales and coming into contact with new groups of people through her assignments. When she's not busy working for Lonely Planet, Ginger likes to travel in Latin America, where she has also done extensive reporting.

GINGER'S THANKS

Working for Lonely Planet in NYC is a dream gig. My sincere thanks to all the LP editors who contributed to *New York Encounter*, and a special thanks to the always encouraging Jennye Garibaldi. To the cartographers in Australia, thanks for sorting me out and forgiving me my terrible POI sins.

THE PHOTOGRAPHER

Dan Herrick has been based in New York City for the past six years after having lived and studied in Latin America and Europe. He enjoys documenting the city's changes and its frenetic way of life. On occasion he is able to pull himself away from it all to travel abroad, or more often to travel to one of the many different worlds that exist within the city's boundaries.

Our readers Many thanks to the travelers who wrote to us with helpful hints, useful advice and interesting anecdotes: Leonieke Broekman, Fran Hayes, Johanna Rhodes.

Cover photograph Radio City Music Hall at night, New York City, Brent Winebrenner/LPI.
Internal photographs p81, p177, p207, p218 Ginger Adams Otis; p238 Bloomberg via Getty Images; p136 LOOK Die Bildagentur der Fotografen GmbH/Alamy; p26 Design Pics Inc. - RM Content/Alamy; p13 Panoramic Images/ Getty Images. All other photographs by Lonely Planet Images and Dan Herrick, except p33, p133 Michelle Bennett; p8 Bruce Bi; p50, p165 Richard Cummins; p4, p6 Mark Daffey; p34 Gavin Gough; p240 Kim Grant; p17 Richard l'Anson; p18 Ionas Kaltenbach; p186, p246 Jean-Pierre Lescourret; p250 Rachel Lewis; p28 Diana Mayfield; p153, p194 Allan Montaine; p11, p29, p229, p232, p237, p245, p251 Angus Oborn; p181 Brent Winebrenner; p12, p15, p21, p27, p30, p45, p155, p167, p185, p215 Corey Wise.

All images are copyright of the photographers unless otherwise indicated. Many of the images in this guide are available for licensing from **Lonely Planet Images:** www.lonelyplanetimages.com.

Central Park (p174) – sun worshippers, not livestock, congregate on Sheep Meadow

CONTENTS

THIS IS NEW YORK CITY

It's a mad, mad world in Manhattan, where taxis, pedicabs, commuters, pedestrians – even horse-drawn carriages – career around looking for space. The city is heady, frustrating, shocking, almost overwhelming in its intensity and, ultimately, incredibly exhilarating.

And yet it's not all chaos and grit. Inside New York's pocket-sized parks, like Riverside (p195) and Tompkins Sq (p95), bluesy buskers blow their horns, delighted toddlers run through sprinklers, chess players frown in fierce concentration, and dogs nip and bark inside their runs.

The bigger green spaces, such as Central Park (p174) and Prospect Park (p219), whisk you away from the grimy streets and set you down alongside flowing rivers, dark, primal ponds and gently tangoing couples, who gather on Saturday nights in summer to flirt with their feet in the shadows of birch trees.

Romance and ruin weave together in New York City, a group of five boroughs offering endless contrasts and captivating diversity. Anchored by back-to-back buildings and more than nine million people, the city is a series of interlocking enclaves, each with its own flavor and appeal. Brooklyn is the domain of writers, artists, young couples and families seeking to live in creative peace without the yoke of Manhattan's sky-high rents. Vibrant Queens is a maelstrom of ethnicities and nationalities that live together – for the most part – in quiet harmony. This sprawling borough, studded with housing projects, alternative museums and galleries, and countless neat, single-family homes, contains some of the tastiest Indian, Korean, Greek and Albanian food anywhere. The boogie-down Bronx is still New York City's least appreciated borough, but even Manhattanites know there's no better place than Arthur Ave for an authentic Italian dinner – not even Staten Island, full of third-generation Napolitanos, can compare.

In the middle of it all is glorious Manhattan, that scintillating sliver of land where anything – absolutely *anything* – can happen.

Top left Different races, same song – New York subway (p261) **Top right** Brooklyn Bridge and Lower Manhattan (p42) as night moves in and lights flicker on **Bottom** Mural in the pulsing heart of Harlem: 125th St (p202)

> HIGHLIGHTS

Watch New Yorkers pass by in a blur at Grand Central Terminal (p152)

> 1 NEW YORK HARBOR
RIDE THE WAVES TO THE STATUE OF LIBERTY

Half tourist attraction, half busy industrial byway, the wide, watery mouth of Lower Manhattan is full of things to see and do. Hugging the island's southernmost tip, New York's harbor offers stellar views of Brooklyn's creaky old waterfront to the east, Staten Island to the south, and a nice chunk of the Jersey coast to the west.

But the best views of all, of course, are of Lady Liberty (p46) herself: tall, lean and green, and rising up proudly out of the waters. Whether you admire her from afar or take one of the ferries constantly circling the harbor out to her rocky toehold, she is magnificent. Guarding the entrance to Lower Manhattan since 1886, Lady Liberty is positioned to gaze sternly across the waters at 'unenlightened Europe.' Known as the 'Mother of Exiles,' the statue serves as an admonishment to the rigid social structures of the old world. 'Keep your ancient lands, your storied pomp!' says Lady Liberty's famous poem. 'Give me your tired, your poor, your huddled masses yearning to breathe free.'

When those masses came – which they did in droves – they most likely ended up behind the statue at Ellis Island, a must-see New York experience. Its moving exhibits include early photos of gaunt, hollow-eyed émigrés clutching papers and their worldly goods.

Ferries to and from the islands depart from Battery Park (p44), which is worth a stroll in its own right. The park's thick green grass leads to an esplanade along the Hudson River, and it's studded with outdoor installations and other works of art.

For a less personal but still stellar look at the Old Green Lady, skip the official tour and jump on the Staten Island Ferry (p46), which departs from Whitehall Terminal, also in Battery Park. This free half-hour ride swings you right past the Statue of Liberty. Another ferry ride that gives you spectacular Manhattan-skyline views takes you to Governor's Island (p47), a small strip of land in New York Harbor that used to be an old coast-guard base. Soon it will be completely transformed into public parkland.

>2 CENTRAL PARK

GET LOST IN THE MIDDLE OF MANHATTAN

Hard to believe that verdant grasses, dappled forests, rioting wild-flowers and cool, meandering streams exist in such a cacophonous, car-heavy city, but – praise be – they do. 'The People's Park' was designed in the 1860s and '70s by Frederick Law Olmsted and Calvert Vaux, and it serves as the city's collective backyard.

Stretching from Midtown at 59th St to the beautifully restored Harlem Meer at 110th St, these rolling hills are thronged every morning with in-line skaters, cyclists, walkers, joggers and yoga enthusiasts. Couples, friends and sometimes even strangers meet at the center, Bethesda Tce, recognizable by the famous *Angel of the Waters* statue (p178) in its middle.

Walkers and joggers gravitate to the Jacqueline Kennedy Onassis Reservoir (p176), while the park's west side, near the 79th St Transverse Rd, is home to an ever-evolving, changing memorial to John Lennon, who liked to hang out in the ethereal stretch of park now known as Strawberry Fields (p178) and who was shot by a deranged fan while entering his apartment across the street in 1980. The list of must-sees and -dos goes on and on in Central Park; for more information, visit the **Dairy Visitor Center** (☎ 212-794-6564; www.centralpark.org).

>3 THE HIGH LINE

PARK YOURSELF ABOVE THE CITY

Rise above it all with a stroll on this grassy gem, a 1.5-mile stretch of old, elevated train track that's been reclaimed as a breezy, flower-filled public park running along the Meatpacking District's picturesque west side. The sturdy track is blissfully quiet, save for the buzzing of the many honeybees that flock to the sweet wildflowers that flourish along the edges.

The tracks vertically follow a road formerly known as 'Death Avenue' (today Tenth Ave). In the heyday of shipping, cargo was brought from the docks to Midtown rail yards along that road – and many a horse, driver and pedestrian who were too slow crossing the busy tracks suffered for it. The city finally elevated the train tracks in 1934, and trains blared along them until 1980. When industry abandoned the city center in 1980, the tracks fell quiet, and wild grasses, birds and urban creatures took over. The tracks were slated for destruction in 2002, until a group of inspired artists and philanthropists convinced city officials to make it a sustainable public park that could also display local artwork. Now it's such a hit that it will expand further north in the coming years.

>4 METROPOLITAN MUSEUM OF ART

MEET AN EGYPTIAN MUMMY AT THE TEMPLE OF DENDUR

One of the first things that will greet you as you walk into this Fifth Ave behemoth is the Sackler Wing, home to an ancient Egyptian temple from 15 BC. This 82ft sandstone wonder, saved in 1967 from submersion in the Aswan Dam, doesn't even come close to dwarfing the room – that's how big the Met is.

Its permanent collection holds three million pieces, and an average of five million art lovers tramp through every year.

You'll want plenty of time to explore. The European galleries above the marble staircase at the Fifth Ave entrance could easily consume a day, as could the larger-than-ever Greek and Roman galleries, and the newly expanded Egyptian gallery, with its perfectly preserved mummies. Don't miss the dark and lovely medieval galleries, full of glinting Byzantine enamels, or the Lehman Wing, full of glowing Renaissance works by Rembrandt, El Greco and others.

For more information, see p185.

>5 MUSEUM OF MODERN ART

DINE AMID PICASSOS AT THE MOMA

Tucked into a Midtown side street, the Museum of Modern Art (p164) is a gleaming gem. It's easy to spend a day here, starting at the top of its spiraled multilevel floors and strolling ever downward, stopping at any of its excellent coffee shops or restaurants for a break, before winding up the day with a contemplative exploration of its 1st-floor sculpture garden.

If you follow the museum's contours, you'll move downward from floor to floor, and chronologically through the major art movements of the 20th century. Floors five and four are MoMA's intro to modern art – Picassos, Matisses, Dalis, Mondrians, Pollocks, de Koonings and a few Marcel Duchamp originals.

The museum's world-class restaurant, the Modern, overlooks the 1st-floor sculpture garden with its crooked trees and eclectic installations. On the 2nd floor there's a rustic Italian eatery with an airy espresso bar.

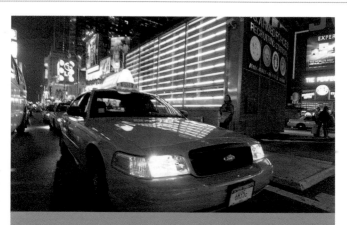

>6 BROADWAY & TIMES SQUARE
TAKE IN THE DAZZLING LIGHTS OF THE GREAT WHITE WAY

There's a reason it's known as the 'Crossroads of the World' – because everybody who comes to town has to take a peek at the crazy, zany intersection of 42nd St and Broadway.

All traces of its early 1900s incarnation as a tranquil horse-trading plaza are long gone, as are its days as a seedy sex-shop hangout. Now there are a thousand blinking lights and flashing neon advertisements, and Times Sq is defined by its blazing kilowatt power.

But it's not all big-name chain stores, novelty restaurants and gaudy billboards. Many of the marquee lights belong to the theaters running along Broadway. When electric signs first came into vogue back in the day (1906, to be precise), the colored bulbs burned out too quickly, so only white lights were used. The sprawling length of Broadway held so many new-fangled theaters it soon got the nickname 'The Great White Way.' Many are the legends who've pulled into town nameless, faceless and penniless, only to find fame and fortune amid the worn-out floorboards of historic old theaters like the Ambassador (p170), the Samuel J Friedman Theater (p173) and Longacre.

For more information on the area, see p162.

>7 FIFTH AVENUE & ROCKEFELLER CENTER

ZIP TO THE TOP OF THE ROCK

A ritzy, upscale enclave full of big media companies and fine wine bars, Rockefeller Center (p154) also doubles as a public art plaza. Its most famous mural, done by the Socialist-leaning Mexican painter Diego Rivera, is long gone (Rivera included Lenin in his commissioned mural, which didn't please his capitalist boss) but other works abound.

Prometheus overlooks the famous skating rink, there's an *Atlas Carrying the World* on Fifth Ave, and the aptly named News, an installation by Isamu Noguchi, sits not far from NBC studios. On the Sixth Ave side, red-velvet-seated Radio City Music Hall (p153) houses the high-kicking Rockettes.

Inside Rockefeller Center, you can zip up to its vertigo-inducing observation deck (pictured above; see p154) in a stomach-dropping elevator with blue neon lights for unobstructed views into Central Park. From Rockefeller Center, a stroll north on Fifth Ave will bring you past the soaring St Patrick's Cathedral (p154) into a glitzy shopping district: Fendi, Prada, Saks Fifth Avenue, Bergdorf's, Bulgari, Ferragamo, Tiffany's and more.

>8 SOHO, NOHO & NOLITA

SHOP TILL YOU DROP DOWNTOWN

These three neighborhoods (p76), all on the cusp of Lower Manhattan, function as an urban Bermuda Triangle for celebrities: they get sucked in and – given the shopping, restaurants and nightlife – they simply never leave.

Noho is the northernmost section, a tiny crossroads of shops and trendy eateries that stretches across Bond St and Great Jones St and then flows into the East Village. Nolita, an even smaller warren of crooked streets just south of Houston St and east of Broadway, is – if it's possible – even more hip than Noho. The name means North of Little Italy, and its four quaint main streets (Elizabeth, Mott, Mulberry and Prince) retain an enticing aura of Old Italy. Film director Martin Scorsese grew up on Elizabeth St and was an altar boy at the original St Patrick's Old Cathedral (p80) on the corner of Mott and Prince Sts. For an afternoon of shopping, cafe-hopping and then fine dining, Nolita can't be beat.

On the west side of Broadway, below Houston St (but north of Canal St), is Soho, the original hipster haven. It's slightly more corporatized than a decade ago, but is still infused with that unique New York glamour, courtesy of its big old loft buildings, quirky cobblestone streets and endless shops and galleries.

>9 CHELSEA & THE MEATPACKING DISTRICT

COMBINE YOUR GALLERY TOUR WITH A PUB CRAWL

Who says high art and a good beer don't mix? Certainly not the residents of Chelsea (p126). Their free-spirited neighborhood has now supplanted Greenwich Village as the locus of gay life, even as it continues to nurture the art world and most of the city's clubbing activities.

Much of Chelsea's extreme west side contains huge galleries and art studios. Its wide, industrial streets are sometimes lonesome and windswept, but it suits the neighborhood's avant-garde mood. Exhibition spaces such as White Columns (p117) are bringing new life to the scene.

Chelsea's not particularly up-to-the-moment when it comes to fab new eateries – although it's got more than its share of arty standouts like Klee Brasserie (p135). Where Chelsea does shine is in its nightlife: big, brash clubs that line up along 27th and 28th Sts, and upscale gay/straight bars clustered in the lower 20s.

Whatever Chelsea lacks in trendy restaurants can be found in its neighbor, the always-packed Meatpacking District (p116). This abattoir-turned-hipster-hangout was once a working butchery – and nobody wanted to live among the fecund, fetid smells. Now people can't stay away, and this popular pocket has stellar eateries and insane shopping, and is even catching up with Chelsea in nightclubs.

HIGHLIGHTS

>10 WEST VILLAGE

LAZE AWAY THE AFTERNOON ON OLD, CROOKED STREETS

It's hard to find traces of the former political and social fervor that at one time had this quaint, serene residential neighborhood buzzing with radical activities. Only a few old bars and relics of the seminal gay rights fight of the 1960s and '70s remain: Stonewall, the Duplex (p115) and a string of S&M shops on Christopher St. But otherwise its pioneering spirit is mostly gone. Where it once attracted literary lights like EE Cummings, Edna St Vincent Millay, Williams S Burroughs, James Baldwin and more, it now has A-list celebrities raising families, wealthy bankers, investors and a few grown-up rock stars. Nonetheless, the West Village's (p104) striking visual charm is intact – winding streets built on old cow paths, and hidden courtyards behind narrow, tree-lined alleys. It's still worth visiting, as much for its history as for its quirky cafes, specialty shops and people-watching.

>11 EAST VILLAGE & LOWER EAST SIDE

PARTY IN THE MIDST OF ROCK 'N' ROLL HISTORY

Separated by busy Houston St, these two closely intertwined neighborhoods are but a stone's throw apart: the East Village (p90) begins on Houston's north side, while its close cousin the Lower East Side (p62) sits on the southeast side. The resemblance is striking. Both of the formerly grungy and gritty enclaves are still full of crumbling tenements and graffiti-scarred buildings – but not for long.

Waves of gentrification continue to knock down the old squatter lofts and turn community-run cooperatives into luxury condos, particularly in the East Village. Tompkins Sq Park (p95) and St Marks Pl, two bastions of punk-rocker energy and counter-culture upheaval, are now attractive areas to hang out in and get a beer (or a tattoo).

Still, both neighborhoods retain a singular, electric energy, fueled mostly by the burgeoning nightlife along Second Ave in the East Village and Rivington St in the Lower East Side. There's a continuous influx of new bars, restaurants and nightclubs to draw you in. The constant change lends both areas the kind of creative buzz that lured in jazz great Charlie Parker, the Ramones, the Rolling Stones and a young Madonna.

>12 BROOKLYN

GO OFF THE BEATEN PATH IN BROOKLYN

Welcome to 'Breukelen,' a former Dutch settlement of neatly divided little towns. Those outlines can still be traced in the many small neighborhoods that today make up Brooklyn (p214), New York's most populous borough (2.5 million residents) outside of Manhattan.

For most people, Brooklyn is Coney Island (p219), that strange stretch of sea and sand on the coast that's also a famous outdoor amusement park and freak show (now slated for a major face-lift). But there's so much more: the gentle slopes of laid-back Prospect Park (p219), the often overlooked Brooklyn Museum of Art (p215) and its five floors of Egyptian, African and European art, including one whole wing of Rodin sculptures. Brooklyn Botanical Gardens, next door, is a 52-acre flowery oasis. In spring its Japanese Hill and Pond garden comes alive with cherry blossoms, and its Rose Garden blooms seem to scent the whole nabe.

Northwest Brooklyn includes some of the borough's most breathtaking brownstones, mostly in the fairly affluent enclaves of Brooklyn Heights, Carroll Gardens, Park Slope and Vinegar Hill. Up-and-coming Red Hook and Fort Greene are now attracting the creative 20-somethings priced out of the artistic haven of Williamsburg.

Borough Park is home to a large ultra-Orthodox Jewish community, and Bensonhurst is still largely Italian, while Sunset Park contains a flourishing community of Mexican and Chinese-American families.

Brighton Beach, right behind Coney Island, is where you go to practice your Russian. 'Little Odessa,' as the area is known, has become the haven of immigrants from former Soviet Union nations, and it's where you can get a good cup of hot tea, caviar and sturgeon, and pick up a souvenir samovar.

For those who wish to experience Brooklyn without straying too far from Manhattan, a trip to Dumbo (Down under Manhattan Bridge Overpass) fits the bill. An easy and panoramic walk across the slender span of steel known as the Brooklyn Bridge (onlookers on Brooklyn Bridge, pictured opposite) will bring you to this waterfront neighborhood, full of old warehouses and factories. The abandoned

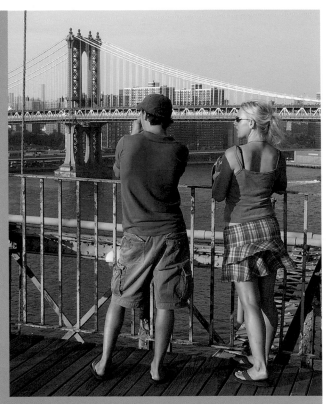

and decaying loft buildings were gradually reclaimed in the 1980s by artists priced out of fast-gentrifying Tribeca. Now Dumbo is the driving force for Brooklyn's artistic community; even those creative types who don't live here benefit from its residents' willingness to share gallery space and put on cutting-edge shows.

>13 LOWER MANHATTAN

WANDER NEW YORK'S COLONIAL BYWAYS

An eye-catching combination of old and new, Lower Manhattan (p42) contains some of the island's most grandiose skyscrapers, crammed on to tiny colonial streets. If you've always wanted to eat lunch in one of George Washington's old watering holes, this is the place for you.

Lower Manhattan overflows with both Revolutionary and modern landmarks. Not only did Washington eat at Fraunces Tavern (p44), he was sworn in at Federal Hall (pictured opposite; p44), he worshipped at St Paul's Chapel (p46) and Trinity Church (p47), and he buried many of his contemporaries in the church's cemetery. Another Lower Manhattan fixture, the New York Stock Exchange (p46), got its start on Wall St, named after the original Dutch fortifying wall, and remains headquartered there.

On the east side of Lower Manhattan you'll find South Street Seaport (p46), an old working port reached by cobblestone streets. Amid these colonial byways you'll find an influx of trendy eateries and bars, with a strong international feel. Japanese sushi, New Zealand seafood, traditional Irish pub fare and Aussie eats are all available in these few small blocks.

Busy Fulton St is a great place to shop for souvenirs, T-shirts and trinkets, and if you want a glimpse of New York City's bureaucratic heartbeat, City Hall is right across the street from legendary electronics/music/computer store J&R (p48).

GROUND ZERO

Lower Manhattan has largely rebounded from the terrible events of September 11, 2001. The gaping hole left by the fallen Twin Towers is now a massive construction site, slowly turning grime and grit into a memorial park that will, hopefully some day soon, be graced with a waterfall, memory pool and newly constructed office space. In the interim, one can pay homage to those lost from the observation decks surrounding the site, or on a tour led by a volunteer from the WTC Tribute visitors center (p45).

>14 HARLEM

DISCOVER THE HIDDEN DELIGHTS OF HARLEM

Everything is changing in New York City, and Harlem (p202), the mecca of urban African American life for over a century, is no exception.

Today's Harlem has high-rise condos, an influx of banks and new businesses, sky-rocketing rents and home prices. But its traditional base, working-class and middle-income earners, mostly African American but with a hefty mix of other ethnicities and nationalities, hasn't crumbled in the face of developers. The result is a neighborhood in flux: pockets of blight are next to sleek, $2-million glass condos, and a diverse but solid offering of restaurants, clubs and entertainment.

For many decades Harlem was overlooked as a tourist destination and its many local treasures went unnoticed by the world below 96th St. Thankfully, community leaders stepped up to preserve Harlem's artistic legacy, revitalizing and restoring cultural icons like the Apollo Theater (p204), the Lenox Lounge (p212), the Studio Museum (p208) and the Schomburg Center for Research in Black Culture (p206).

Famous soul food restaurants like Sylvia's (p210) and Amy Ruth's (p210) flourish next to newcomers like Chez Lucienne (p209) and Caffe Latte (p209), while African spots like Africa Kine (p209) and Shrine (p212) abound. Check out the main shopping strip on 125th St, a hodgepodge of national chains and offbeat mom-and-pop shops.

>A YEAR IN NEW YORK CITY

Celebration is a way of life in busy New York City, where the population's diversity means plenty of reasons for fun. The biggest annual events include New Year, Chinese New Year, the Puerto Rican Day Parade, Gay Pride Month, Fourth of July, the West Indian American Day Carnival, Halloween and the Thanksgiving Day Parade. In December, when Hanukkah, Christmas and Kwanzaa usually collide, the city is truly a movable feast.

Stilt-walkers at West Indian American Day Carnival in Brooklyn

JANUARY

Three Kings Parade

www.eastharlempreservation.org

On January 5, Spanish Harlem, up Fifth Ave to 116th St, is full of parading schoolchildren, donkeys and sheep.

Winter Restaurant Week

www.nycvisit.com

High-profile restaurants offer three-course lunches or dinners from $20 to $30.

Martin Luther King Jr Parade

Civil rights leader Martin Luther King is commemorated annually with a birthday gala parade down Fifth Ave from 86th to 61st Sts.

FEBRUARY

Olympus Fashion Week

www.olympusfashionweek.com

The couture world descends upon Manhattan in the second week of February to flounce, and gawk at the new looks. A second fashion week is held in the second week of September.

Westminster Kennel Show

www.westminsterkennelclub.org

Catch the much-mocked parade of show dogs at this dead-serious annual showcase for purebreds.

The city turns green for the St Patrick's Day Parade down Fifth Ave

Moments before take-off – LGBT Pride parade (p30)

MARCH

New York Underground Film Festival
www.nyuff.com
Edgy, sexy and just plain weird documentaries and narratives at the Anthology Film Archives.

St Patrick's Day Parade
www.saintpatricksdayparade.com/nyc
/newyorkcity.htm
On March 17 everything goes green along Fifth Ave, from 44th to 86th Sts, when the world-famous parade starts at 11am.

APRIL

Easter Parade
www.ny.com
From 10am to 4pm on Easter Sunday, cars are blocked off of Fifth Ave from 57th to 49th Sts. People show off their Easter costumes and fine, fluffy Easter hats.

Orchid Show
www.rockefellercenter.com
This massive display of orchids, well into its second decade, includes competitions in both the orchid-art and fragrance categories.

MAY

Bike New York
www.bikemonthnyc.org
May is Bike Month, with weekly bike-oriented tours, parties and other events for pedal-pushing New Yorkers.

Fleet Week
www.intrepidmuseum.com
Ships arrive from around the world for this annual end-of-the-month celebration.

JUNE

Puerto Rican Day Parade
www.nationalpuertoricandayparade.org
Thousands of revelers show up in the second week of June for this massive march along Fifth Ave from 44th to 86th Sts.

Ctrl-Alt-Del...computer virus on Halloween (p32)

Lesbian, Gay, Bisexual & Transgender Pride
www.heritageofpride.org
Gay Pride Month lasts throughout June and culminates in a major march down Fifth Ave on the last Sunday of the month.

Restaurant Week
www.nycvisit.com
Big-time discounts at top-notch eateries during the last week of June; three-course lunches and dinners for $20 to $35.

Mermaid Parade
www.coneyisland.com
Elaborately costumed folk display their mermaid finery along the Coney Island boardwalk on the last Saturday of the month.

JULY

July Fourth Fireworks
www.macys.com
Independence Day fireworks start at 9pm. For good viewing spots, try the Lower East Side waterfront park, Williamsburg, Brooklyn or high rooftops.

Nathan's Hot Dog Eating Contest
www.nathansfamous.com
A celebration of gluttony brings food inhalers to Coney Island each Fourth of July.

Philharmonic in the Park
www.newyorkphilharmonic.org
Enjoy free concerts in Central Park, Prospect Park, Queens, the Bronx or Staten Island.

AUGUST

Fringe Festival
www.fringenyc.org
This annual festival features the edgiest, most creative stage talent in New York.

Howl! Festival
www.howlfestival.com
A week-long celebration of arts in the East Village, including the Charlie Parker Jazz Festival and other readings and performances.

US Open Tennis Tournament
www.usopen.org
One of the four Grand Slam tournaments for professional tennis players; held in Queens.

Harlem Week

www.harlemweek.com

Throughout the month of August there are ongoing street celebrations – including music, theater performances and food fairs – all over Harlem.

SEPTEMBER

West Indian American Day Carnival

www.wiadca.com

Two million Caribbean Americans head to Eastern Parkway in Brooklyn for the annual Carnival Parade.

Olympus Fashion Week

www.olympusfashionweek.com

Round two for designers and fashionistas strutting their stuff on the catwalk.

OCTOBER

Dumbo Art under the Bridge Festival

www.dumboartscenter.org

Celebrates local artists; you can enjoy open studios, performances and street displays.

Blessing of the Animals

www.stjohndivine.org

In honor of the Feast Day of St Francis, pet owners flock to the grand Cathedral of St John the Divine with their creatures.

Open House New York

www.ohny.org

For one weekend a year, the doors to New York's secret places are thrown open.

Each year a primeval battle between human and hot dog takes place at Nathan's

ANNUAL FESTIVALS

Chinese Lunar New Year Festival (www.explorechinatown.com) An awesome display of fireworks and dancing dragon parades, usually in either late January or February depending on the lunar calendar.

Cherry Blossom Festival (www.bbg.org) Held during the first weekend in May, this festival celebrates the annual flowering of cherry trees in Brooklyn's Botanical Gardens.

Tribeca Film Festival (www.tribecafilmfestival.com) This film fest invigorates Lower Manhattan in the first week of May.

JVC Jazz Festival (www.festivalproductions.net/jvcjazz.htm) Forty jazz shows take place around the city during this mid-June fest.

River to River Festival (www.rivertorivernyc.org) Performers bring theater, music, dance and film to downtown parks all summer long (June to August).

San Gennaro Festival (www.sangennaro.org) Rowdy crowds descend on Little Italy for carnival games, sausage-and-pepper sandwiches, deep-fried calamari and more during the Feast of San Gennaro, usually mid-to-late September.

Halloween Parade

www.halloween-nyc.com

Freaks and geeks gather in the streets for a wild night of prancing about in costume.

NOVEMBER

New York City Marathon

www.ingnycmarathon.org

This annual 26-mile run through the five boroughs draws thousands of athletes from around the world.

Thanksgiving Day Parade

www.macys.com

Famous floats waft down Broadway, from 72nd St to Herald Sq. Balloons are inflated at the southwest corner of Central Park the night before.

DECEMBER

Rockefeller Center Christmas Tree Lighting

Join the hundreds encircling Rockefeller Center in Midtown and watch the world's tallest Christmas tree lit up to a chorus of 'ooohs' and 'aaahs.'

New Year's Eve

www.nycvisit.com

In addition to the world-famous countdown to midnight in Times Sq, the city has plenty of other celebratory events, namely the **Midnight Run in Central Park** (☎ 212-860-4455) and midnight fireworks in Central Park, Prospect Park and the South Street Seaport.

Fresh food heaven, Chelsea Market (p133)

ITINERARIES

Public transportation is your best friend in New York City. Sure, the subway system is a bit old, smells funny and sometimes goes a bit fitfully. But, overall, it zips up and down Manhattan with dependable regularity. For the scenic route, take the above-ground buses that trundle along Manhattan's famous avenues.

You'll need a MetroCard (p261) to get around, and you can buy them at newsstands or from vending machines inside subway stations.

Taxis are a good option if you're trekking to the far edges of the city, but during rush hour (anywhere from 7am to 9am and 4pm to 7pm), traffic is brutal. Fast-moving pedicabs will also compete for your business; there's nothing wrong with these rickshaws, but keep in mind that few of the operators are insured.

ONE DAY

Head to Lower Manhattan and walk around Battery Park (p44), Ground Zero (p45) and the South Street Seaport (p46). If you're really dying to see the Statue of Liberty, skip the lengthy lines on the official visit and grab the Staten Island Ferry (p46) for the drive-by view instead. Head to Chinatown for lunch, and spend the afternoon exploring Soho, Noho and Nolita. Dine amid the neon of Times Sq, and then try to catch a show. If you're out of the theater before 11pm, rush to the Empire State Building (p152) to catch the last elevator (at 11:15pm) to the observation deck.

TWO DAYS

Spend a leisurely morning on the Upper West Side, with a breakfast bagel at Barney Greengrass (p197), a stop to pick up some snacks at Zabar's (p197), and then a stroll around the mom-and-pop shops clustered near 79th St and Broadway. Make your way to the American Museum of Natural History (p194), but before you go in, step into Central Park (p174) and picnic on your snacks. Hit the museum for the afternoon, and then meander south, ending your day with dinner in either Chelsea or the Meatpacking District. Spend your next morning exploring Lower Manhattan, and aim to have lunch in Greenwich Village. Walk through

---

Top Immerse yourself in a classic New York read (p241) **Bottom** The Guggenheim (p186) — Interior view of The Solomon R. Guggenheim Museum New York © The Solomon R. Guggenheim Foundation, New York

Washington Sq Park (p105) and head into the East Village to shop, sightsee and have some drinks in the late afternoon. Head south across Houston St to have dinner on the Lower East Side.

THREE DAYS

With three days in the city, you can pace yourself a bit. Start off with a museum crawl down the Upper East Side. Hit El Museo del Barrio (p205) high up on Fifth Ave (and do peek across the street at Central Park's Conservatory Garden and Harlem Meer while you are there). If your stamina holds, stroll south for a tour of the Guggenheim (p186), the Neue Galerie (p185) and the Frick Collection (p184). Lunch at the Metropolitan Museum of Art (p185) and spend the afternoon embracing the behemoth collection inside. Day two calls for some action: a brisk morning walk around Central Park's Jacqueline Kennedy Onassis Reservoir (p176), followed by a tour of Rockefeller Center (p154), lunch in Little Korea (p172) and an afternoon gallery hopping in Chelsea (p126). Pick a show for the night and lose yourself in Times Sq's neon glow. For your last day, head to Lower Manhattan and wander the narrow streets, take a ferry ride to Staten Island for the requisite adoration of Lady Liberty, then fritter away your remaining hours exploring Chinatown, Soho, Noho and Nolita, and partying in the Lower East Side and East Village.

RAINY DAY

The Guggenheim (p186) is perfect for any inclement weather because the out-of-this-world atmosphere creates its own little reality bubble anyway. Spend the day enjoying the museum, then check out the Schomburg Center (p206) in Harlem. It's not far from the Cathedral of St John

FORWARD PLANNING

Three weeks before you go Pick a Broadway show and book tickets, and pick a backup as well in case you need to try your luck at the TKTS booth (www.tdf.org/tkts).

Two weeks before you go Visit www.opentable.com and make a reservation for Babbo (p110) or another restaurant you'd like to try.

Three days before you go Start checking out what will be going on while you're in town at www.freeinnyc.net and www.clubfreetime.com.

The day before you go Start testing your online reflexes and see if you can snag a seat at Momofuku (p98). Check out what sample sales will be on while you're in town.

the Divine (p205), where you can admire the still-unfinished spires before topping off the day with some soul food at Amy Ruth's or Sylvia's (p210).

NYC ON A SHOESTRING

The greatest things in life are free, as the saying goes, and that's true in New York, where it costs you nothing to enter Central Park or check out the city's iconic architecture. Catch the splendors of Grand Central Terminal (p152) and admire the jutting lines of Le Corbusier's UN building (p155) without spending a dime. Head to Midtown and lunch at the Hallo Berlin food cart at Fifth Ave and 54th St. Bargain hunters do well in Chinatown, and while it'll cost you a mint to eat in Little Italy, strolling there is free. Head uptown to Morningside Heights to check out the Cathedral of St John the Divine (p205), then dine with the students at Community Food and Juice (p210).

OPEN ALL DAY

Many museums are closed on Monday, making that the perfect day to really explore Central Park (p174). Start at the northern tip and head south, through the Ramble and the Mall, taking a peek at the Central Park Wildlife Center and Strawberry Fields. If you emerge on the park's west side, take the subway to Chelsea. Not all the galleries will be open – but the stores will be. Do a little window-shopping and inhale the fresh-cookie smell of the Chelsea Market (p133).

Explore the Lower East Side, stopping for some gourmet bar food at Schiller's Liquor Bar (p72). Then hit the bargain shops along Orchard St before heading north into the East Village. End the night with a pub crawl along Second Ave.

>NEIGHBORHOODS

Art comes in all shapes, forms and locations in New York City

NEIGHBORHOODS

Manhattan rolls south from Harlem in a wave of arbitrarily drawn but identifiable neighborhoods, each with its own sense of community and pace. Real-estate agents like to coin trendy monikers for on-the-cusp enclaves (SoHa for South Harlem, for example), but don't believe the hype. New York has always been defined by its traditional neighborhoods.

Harlem's wide boulevards, lined with brownstones and beaux-arts buildings, encompass two diverse sections between 96th and 150th Sts. Columbia University students, young professionals and clusters of old-time hippies hang out between 100th St and 125th St on the west side. On the east side of Fifth Ave you find El Barrio, aka Spanish Harlem, a formerly Italian nabe that's now decisively Latino.

In the city's center sits that glorious green no-man's land, Central Park. From 96th St south, the neighborhood on the west of Central Park is the Upper West Side; to the east is the Upper East Side. It's as simple as that.

Busy Midtown takes over at 59th St, stretching down to 42nd St. The same rule applies, this time divided by Fifth Ave: everything to the west is Midtown West; everything to the east is Midtown East. Below 42nd St is a mish-mash of Manhattan's best-known nabes, starting with arty Chelsea, full of gay-friendly nightclubs, which overlaps with the trendy Meatpacking District, which in turn blends into bohemian Greenwich Village, all on the west side of Fifth Ave. On the east side is Union Sq, the center of activist life in New York, and a dizzying array of bars, gastropubs and bistros that make up the East Village, Lower East Side and Nolita.

The city converges in Lower Manhattan, where the 'concrete canyons' of Wall St are filled with hulking skyscrapers. Lower Manhattan's Brooklyn Bridge crosses the East River into artistic Dumbo and tony Brooklyn Heights. Behind them, the rest of the borough stretches southeast, all the way to Coney Island and the Atlantic Coast.

>LOWER MANHATTAN

Full of byways and sky-high structures, Lower Manhattan comes splendidly to life every weekday morning as thousands of workers pour through the narrow streets, hurrying to their jobs in banking and high finance.

Coming to a rounded tip at its southern end, Lower Manhattan is surrounded by water: the East River to the east, New York Harbor at its center and the mighty Hudson to the west. Boats to Lady Liberty, Ellis Island, Governor's Island and Staten Island depart from Battery Park, which is full of memorials and public art and great views of New Jersey. Colonial New York is south of Wall St – named after the barrier put in place by the Dutch over 200 years ago – and around South Street Seaport, a briny and somewhat touristy old docking area.

The World Trade Center site is still a barren hole, marred by construction efforts that try but never quite seem able to make progress on a planned memorial park. North of that is trendy Tribeca, full of gorgeous shops and gourmet eateries.

LOWER MANHATTAN

◉ SEE
Battery Park **1** B6
Bowling Green **2** B5
Federal Hall **3** C4
Ferry to Statue of
  Liberty & Ellis Island ...**4** B6
Fraunces Tavern
  Museum **5** C5
Ground Zero **6** B3
Museum of Jewish
  Heritage **7** A5
National Museum of
  the American Indian ...**8** B5
New York Stock
  Exchange **9** B4
Skyscraper Museum ...**10** A5
South Street Seaport ...**11** D4
South Street Seaport
  Museum **12** D4

St Paul's Chapel **13** B3
Staten Island Ferry
  Terminal **14** C6
Trinity Church **15** B4
WTC Tribute Visitors
  Center **16** B4

🛍 SHOP
A Uno **17** B2
Century 21 ....**18** B4
Issey Miyake **19** A1
J&R **20** B3
Urban Archaeology **21** A1

🍽 EAT
Blaue Gans **22** B2
Financier Patisserie **23** A4
Financier Patisserie **24** C5

Financier Patisserie **25** C4
Nelson Blue **26** D3
Stella Maris **27** D3
Zaitzeff **28** C4

🍸 DRINK
Another Room **29** B1
Brandy Library **30** A1
Macao **31** B1
Ulysses **32** C5

★ PLAY
Michael Schimmel
  Center for the Arts ...**33** C3
TKTS Booth **34** D4
Tribeca Performing
  Arts Center **35** A2

SEE

BATTERY PARK
☎ 311; www.nycgovparks.org; Broadway at Battery Pl; ☼ sunrise-1am; ◉ 4, 5 to Bowling Green, 1 to South Ferry; ♿

With its 13 works of public art, the Holocaust Memorial, the NYC Police Memorial, the Irish Hunger Memorial, the rose-filled Hope Garden and sweeping views of Lady Liberty, this delightful bit of green is practically an outdoor museum. Check out the **Museum of Jewish Heritage** (☎ 646-437-4200; www.mjhnyc.org; 36 Battery Pl; adult/child/student/senior $10/free/5/7, admission free 4-8pm Wed; ☼ 10am-5:45pm Sun-Tue & Thu, to 8pm Wed, to 5pm Fri; ◉ 4, 5 to Bowling Green) and the **Skyscraper Museum** (☎ 212-968-1961; www.skyscraper.org; 39 Battery Pl; adult $5, senior & student $2.50; ☼ noon-6pm Wed-Sun; ◉ 4, 5 to Bowling Green), an ode to the art of vertical building.

BOWLING GREEN
cnr Broadway & State St; ◉ 4, 5 to Bowling Green

A handkerchief-sized piece of grass with an important past, Bowling Green is believed to be the spot where Dutch settler Peter Minuit paid $24 to the Lenape for the island of Manhattan. Now it's home to *Charging Bull,* Arturo di Modica's famous bronze statue that symbolizes America's economic vitality.

FEDERAL HALL
☎ 212-825-6888; www.nps.gov/feha; 26 Wall St; admission free; ☼ 10am-4pm Mon-Fri; ◉ 2, 3, 4, 5 to Wall St, N, R to Rector St

The big daddy of all founding fathers – George Washington – was inaugurated at this Greek Revival–style building, and the museum inside is dedicated to postcolonial New York and its struggle to define freedom of the press, as well as many other 'inalienable' rights.

FRAUNCES TAVERN MUSEUM
☎ 212-425-1778; www.frauncestavernmuseum.org; 54 Pearl St; adult $10, senior, student & child $5; ☼ noon-5pm Mon-Sat; ◉ 4, 5 to Bowling Green, 2, 3, 4, 5 to Wall St, R, W to Whitehall St, J, M, Z to Broad St

This unique museum-restaurant combo, a complex of four early-18th-century structures, is an homage to the nation-shaping events of 1783 – when the British left New York and General George Washington gave a farewell speech to his officers. It was the most popular watering hole of its day, and is still a working pub/restaurant that serves up hearty farmer fare like shepherd's pie and roast-beef platters. The museum section hosts rotating exhibits, walking tours and lunchtime lectures.

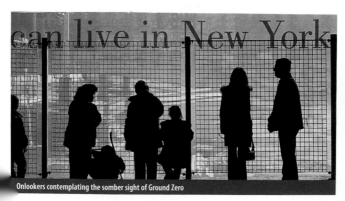 GROUND ZERO

Church St btwn Vesey & Liberty Sts;
E, 2, 3 to World Trade Center, N, R to Rector St

The site is as blighted as ever, but signs of progress are finally showing up around the perimeter of Ground Zero. The **WTC Tribute visitors center** (☎ 866-737-1184; www.tributewtc.org; 120 Liberty St; admission $10; 10am-6pm Mon & Wed-Sat, noon-6pm Tue, noon-5pm Sun; E, 2, 3 to World Trade Center, N, R to Rector St), a nonprofit run by the WTC Families' Association, features a gallery of moving images and artifacts, and leads tours of the site. All the tours are led by New Yorkers who experienced the Twin Towers' destruction on September 11, or lost a loved one to the disaster.

Around the corner, on the west side of the Engine 10 Ladder 10 Firehouse is a massive bronze plaque that tells the story of what happened on September 11 from the firefighters' point of view. It's dedicated to all the lost firefighters, and Glenn Winuk, a partner in a nearby law firm and a volunteer medic who dashed into the burning buildings to help fleeing victims and perished himself.

NATIONAL MUSEUM OF THE AMERICAN INDIAN

☎ 212-514-3700; www.nmai.si.edu;
1 Bowling Green; admission free;
10am-5pm Fri-Wed, to 8pm Thu;
4, 5 to Bowling Green

Housed in an ornate building right behind Bowling Green, this Smithsonian-run museum has crafts, art and everyday objects from American Indian tribes, augmented

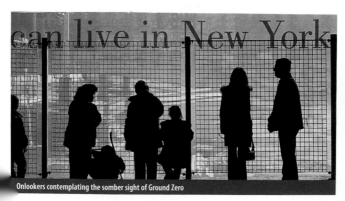

Onlookers contemplating the somber sight of Ground Zero

by interactive displays offering insights into Indian beliefs and culture. The building was once the US Customs House where Herman Melville wrote parts of *Moby Dick*.

◉ NEW YORK STOCK EXCHANGE

☎ 212-656-5168; www.nyse.com; 8 Broad St; ◉ 2, 3, 4, 5 to Wall St, N, R to Rector St

There's no getting inside the adrenaline-filled NYSE, but you can enjoy the gorgeous Roman-esque facade and the hordes of blue-jacketed traders who step outside to puff furiously on cigarettes and gobble a hot dog during their two-minute lunch break. During the holiday season Exchange Place gets seriously decked out – it rivals Rockefeller Center with the size of its tree.

◉ SOUTH STREET SEAPORT

☎ 212-732-7678; www.southstreetsea port.com; Pier 17 btwn Fulton & South Sts; ◉ 10am-9pm Mon-Sat, 11am-8pm Sun; ◉ J, Z, 3, 4, 5 to Fulton St; ♿

Slated for an overhaul that will turn this kitschy tourist trap into a sleek waterfront hangout, South St is for now still an old collec-tion of waterlogged boats, naval memorabilia, and the **South Street Seaport Museum** (☎ 212-748-8600; www. seany.org; 12 Fulton St; adult $15, senior, student & child $12; ◉ 10am-5pm Thu-Sun Jan-Mar, 10am-6pm Tue-Sun Apr-Dec) for

history buffs who like to know everything about historic ships.

◉ ST PAUL'S CHAPEL

☎ 212-233-4164; www.trinitywallstreet .org; Broadway at Vesey St; ◉ 2, 3 to Park Pl

St Paul's Chapel was built as a companion to the larger, more elaborate Trinity Church. Its homey style wasn't too humble for George Washington, who had – and still has – a pew inside. St Paul's was the center of rescue and recovery operations post–September 11 and has a perma-nent exhibit about that effort.

◉ STATEN ISLAND FERRY

☎ 718-815-2628; www.nyc.gov/html /dot/html/ferrybus/statfery.shtml; Whitehall Terminal at Whitehall & South Sts; admission free; ◉ 24hr; ◉ 1 to South Ferry; ♿

This is the life – a nice breeze, plenty of room, and a good long look at Lower Manhattan, the Statue of Liberty and Ellis Island – and it costs nothing. The Staten Island Ferry has got to be the best deal in town.

◉ STATUE OF LIBERTY & ELLIS ISLAND

☎ 877-523-9849; www.statuecruises. com; Battery Park City at Castle Clinton; admission to crown adult $12, child un-der 12 $5, senior $10; ◉ 8:30am-6:30pm May 29-Oct 11, 9am-5pm Oct 12-May 28,

GOVERNOR'S ISLAND

For decades, New Yorkers knew the 172-acre swath of **Governor's Island** (☎ 212-514-8285; www.nps.gov/gois; admission free; ⏱ 10am-5pm Fri, to 7pm Sat & Sun, May 31-Oct 12; 🚇 4, 5 to Bowling Green) only as an untouchable, mysterious patch of green out in the harbor. Now that the island has become part of the National Park Service, it's transformed into an elaborate public parkland. A ferry service (from Manhattan and also Brooklyn) brings you to the green gem, with three-tiered, sandstone Castle Williams and unsurpassed city views. The island's under renovation in places, but biking and picnicking along the promenade is a stellar experience.

closed Dec 25, ask about night cruises in summer; 🚇 4, 5 to Bowling Green, 1 to South Ferry; ♿

She's great, grand and somewhat of a challenge to visit. Lady Liberty, that beacon of freedom, ironically keeps her visitors under tight scrutiny (security checks at boarding points can be long). The good news is that visitors are now able to climb the 300+ stairs – narrow and twisty – into her green crown and stare out across the harbor. Those who want to make the climb have to buy tickets with crown access. Space is tight, and there's a cap on how many crown tickets are sold daily, so advance reservations are a must. Ferries load at Battery Park City in New York and also at Liberty State Park in New Jersey.

Adjacent Ellis Island, the second ferry stop, is equally worth visiting for its fascinating glimpse of harrowing immigrant life back in the day. If you depart after 2pm, you can only visit either Lady Liberty or Ellis Island, not both.

🔵 TRINITY CHURCH
☎ 212-602-0800; www.trinitywallstreet.org; Broadway at Wall St; ⏱ 8am-6pm Mon-Fri, 8am-4pm Sat, 7am-4pm Sun; 🚇 2, 3, 4, 5 to Wall St, N, R to Rector St
A hugely influential church in the annals of New York history, Trinity was built in 1697 by King William III. Its clergy were required to be Loyalists, even though many of its members were dedicated to American independence by the mid-1700s. Its serene and tiny cemetery has headstones bearing some last names that would be very familiar to any student of the American Revolution.

🛍 SHOP

🔲 A UNO Fashion
☎ 212-227-6233; www.aunotribeca.com; 123 W Broadway near Duane St; ⏱ 11am-7pm; 🚇 1, 2, 3 to Chambers St
Sleek European brands for the 30-plus crowd who like to look sophisticated and fashionable without sacrificing comfort.

🖸 CENTURY 21 *Fashion*
☎ 212-227-9092; www.c21stores.com; 22 Cortlandt St at Church St; 🕙 7am-9pm Mon-Wed, 7am-9:30pm Thu & Fri, 10am-9pm Sat, 11am-8pm Sun; 🚇 A, C, 4, 5 to Fulton St/Broadway-Nassau St
Designer duds at gasp-inducing prices keep the crowds pouring into Century 21. It gets crowded and competitive, so keep your elbows out, and if you see something you like, get hold of it fast. Not everything is a knockout or a bargain, but persistence pays off.

🖸 ISSEY MIYAKE *Fashion*
☎ 212-226-0100; www.tribecaisseymiyake.com; 119 Hudson St; 🕙 11am-7pm Mon-Sat, noon-6pm Sun; 🚇 1 to Franklin St
The downtown crowd goes wild for Miyake's pretty and delicate dresses, blouses, skirts and slenderizing slacks.

🖸 J&R Music *Electronics*
☎ 800-806-1115; www.jr.com; 15 Park Row; 🕙 9am-7:30pm Mon-Sat, 10:30am-6:30pm Sun; 🚇 4, 5, 6 to Brooklyn Bridge-City Hall
Three multistory stores line up between Ann and Beekman Sts and sell anything and everything that's related to computers, phones, stereos, radios, iPods, recording equipment and other electronic goods. There's also a store packed with CDs and video games.

🖸 URBAN ARCHAEOLOGY *Homewares*
☎ 212-431-4646; www.urbanarchaeology.com; 143 Franklin St;

Run the bargain-shopper gauntlet at Century 21

🕙 9am-6pm Mon-Fri; 🚇 1 to Franklin St

A pioneer in recycled design, owner Gil Shapiro continues his tradition of remixing, reconstructing and reclaiming old parts from abandoned buildings and construction sites. What he salvages and restores (or repurposes) is now sought after in the hippest Manhattan apartments; check out his Tribeca showroom/ studio for his latest designs.

EAT

🍴 BLAUE GANS

German-Austrian $$

☎ 212-571-8880; www.wallse.com; 139 Duane St; 🕙 lunch & dinner; 🚇 A, C, 1, 2, 3 to Chambers St; ♿ 🚼

Step inside chef Kurt Gutenbrunner's homage to minimalist Austrian cuisine and dive into some delectable *kavallerspitz* (boiled beef with horseradish), various wursts and, of course, yummy fried schnitzels. Kids get their own menu, and non-Austrian foodies can try delicate fish dishes, spicy soups, salads and pastas.

🍴 FINANCIER PATISSERIE

Bakery & Sandwiches, Desserts $

☎ 212-334-5600; 62 Stone St at Mill Lane; 🕙 7am-8pm Mon-Fri, 8:30am-6:30pm Sat; 🚇 2, 3, 4, 5 to Wall St, J, M, Z to Broad St; ♿ 🚼

There are now three Patisserie outposts in Lower Manhattan (the sec-

ond is in the World Financial Center and the third is at 35 Cedar St) because nobody can get enough of the flaky, buttery croissants, almond, apricot and pear tarts, aromatic coffee, homemade soups, creamy quiches and fresh salads on the regular menu. Dig in.

🍴 NELSON BLUE

New Zealand Cuisine $$

☎ 212-346-9090; www.nelsonblue .com; 233-235 Front St; 🕙 lunch & dinner; 🚇 A, C, J, M, Z, 2, 3, 4, 5 to Fulton St/Broadway-Nassau St; ♿ 🚼

Good for a drink as well as a lamb curry pie, Nelson Blue claims to be the only Kiwi pub in town. It's certainly the only one in Lower Manhattan. The beer and wine list is heavy on New Zealand brews, which are perfect accompaniment for the pie, or New Zealand crab cakes or mussels, all sorts of skewers, burgers and grilled fish platters.

🍴 STELLA MARIS

Irish Pub, Seafood $$

☎ 212-233-2417; www.stellanyc.com; 213 Front St; 🕙 breakfast, lunch & dinner; 🚇 J, M, Z, 1, 2, 4, 5 to Fulton St/Broadway-Nassau St

An Irish-owned spot with a polished and modern vibe on a cobblestoned, old-world corner of the city. Tuck into warm asparagus salad topped with a poached egg, done-right steak *frites*, charcuterie plates, grilled Scottish salmon or

NEIGHBORHOODS

LOWER MANHATTAN

an array of fresh shellfish from the black-onyx raw bar.

🍴 ZAITZEFF *Organic Diner* $
☎ 212-571-7272; www.zaitzeffnyc.com; 72 Nassau St; ⏲ 8am-10pm Mon-Fri, 10am-6pm Sat & Sun; ⊕ A, C, J, M, Z, 2, 3, 4, 5 to Fulton St/Broadway-Nassau St; 👍 Ⓥ 👶

Classic New York diner food served with everything but the grease. The burgers, sandwiches and hot dogs are organic, as are the buns, and there are plenty of veggie dishes too.

🍸 DRINK
🍸 ANOTHER ROOM *Bar*
☎ 212-226-1418; www.anotheroom tribeca.com; 249 W Broadway; ⏲ 5pm-3am; ⊕ 1, 2 to Franklin St

Mellow and artsy and filled with long-time Tribeca residents, Another Room manages to be welcoming despite its narrow space and industrial decor. Wine and beer only; no mixed drinks.

🍸 BRANDY LIBRARY *Bar*
☎ 212-226-5545; www.brandylibrary .com; 25 N Moore St at Varick St; ⏲ 5pm-1am Sun-Wed, 4pm-2am Thu, 4pm-4am Fri & Sat; ⊕ 1 to Franklin St

When sipping means serious business, it's easy to settle into this library, with soothing reading lamps and club chairs facing backlit, floor-to-ceiling, bottle-filled shelves. Go for top-shelf cognac, malt scotch or 90-year-old brandies (prices range from $9 to $280). Call ahead about tastings and other events.

Alfresco dining in Lower Manhattan

☷ MACAO *Bar*
☎ 212-431-8750; www.macaonyc.com; 311 Church St near Lispenard St; ⌚ 5pm-3:30am; ⓜ N, R, W, Q, 6 to Canal St

Shhh, here's a secret: skip the lines for Macao restaurant and duck into the dark, red-walled lounge downstairs (look for the red lantern at the door). A fusion of Portuguese and Asian cuisine and liquor, Macao's a hot spot for late-night drinking and snacking, especially if you like inventive, sizzle-on-your-tongue cocktails.

☷ ULYSSES *Pub*
☎ 212-482-0400; 95 Pearl St; ⌚ 11am-4pm; ⓜ 2, 3 to Wall St

An Irish bar with big easy chairs and comfy couches, Ulysses is part laid-back lounge and part neighborhood watering hole. The crowd's diverse and fun, the choice of drinks immense, and the owners run a shuttle between this and their two other bars, Puck Fair and Swift.

☆ PLAY

☆ MICHAEL SCHIMMEL CENTER FOR THE ARTS
Arts
☎ 212-346-1715; www.pace.edu; 3 Spruce St near Gold St & Park Row; tickets vary by performance $10-45; ⓜ 4, 5, 6 to Brooklyn Bridge-City Hall

Found inside Pace University, this space hosts the TV show *Inside the Actors Studio*. It's also where you can see world-class ballet, live music and Broadway stars in more offbeat and esoteric plays – and at (comparatively) bargain prices.

☆ RIVER TO RIVER FESTIVAL
Festival
www.rivertorivernyc.com; various locations around Lower Manhattan; admission free; ⓜ any train to Lower Manhattan; ♿

All summer long this nonprofit organization puts on film screenings, live music performances, dance nights, children's events and many other culturally enriching activities all across Lower Manhattan. Each summer's schedule is posted on the website. Favorite local choices include Latin nights at South Street Seaport.

☆ TRIBECA PERFORMING ARTS CENTER *Theater*
☎ 212-220-1460; www.tribecapac.org; 199 Chambers St; ⌚ hours vary; ⓜ A, C, 1, 2, 3 to Chambers St

A grassroots artists' collective, Tribeca PAC likes to put on performances from local residents on diverse topics related to city life. Works are multidisciplinary and unexpected, like *Lost Jazz Shrines,* which celebrates New York jazz clubs no longer in existence.

>CHINATOWN & LITTLE ITALY

One of Manhattan's busiest, most chaotic sections, vibrant Chinatown has all but eclipsed tiny Little Italy, which spiritually is still the soul of New York's Italian heritage but physically has been reduced to just a few quaint, picturesque blocks along Mott and Mulberry Sts.

The 15,000 Chinese immigrants who call this enclave home have turned it into a vibrant shopping market – all manner of snakes, snails, frogs and fish slither and flop in the open-air markets, and glistening, golden-skinned roast ducks hang in restaurant windows. Knock-off designer bags and watches – faux versions of Louis Vuitton, Chanel and Rolex – are hawked up and down Canal St.

With a growing Vietnamese presence and waves of Chinese immigrants from Fuzhou, Guangdong and Toisan, there's a constant overlapping of festivals, holidays and traditions. Get oriented at the official **Explore Chinatown information kiosk** (☎ 212-484-1216; www.explorechinatown .com; Canal St btwn Baxter & Walker Sts; 🕙 10am-6pm Mon-Fri & Sun, to 7pm Sat), where helpful, multilingual folk can guide you to specific eateries, shops, sights and events.

CHINATOWN & LITTLE ITALY

🔵 SEE

📷 SHOP

🍴 EAT

🍸 DRINK

⭐ PLAY

Please see over for map

⊙ SEE

⊙ BUDDHIST TEMPLES

There are Buddhist temples all over Chinatown. The **Eastern States Buddhist Temple** (64 Mott St btwn Bayard & Canal Sts; ☯ 9am-6pm; ⊙ J, M, Z, 6 to Canal St) holds hundreds of statues in all different sizes. It's a landmarked site, as is the **Mahayana Buddhist Temple** (133 Canal St & Manhattan Bridge Plaza; ☯ 8am-6pm; ⊙ B, D to Grand St, J, M, Z, 6 to Canal St), which holds one large 16ft Buddha. You'll know you've arrived when you see two golden lions guarding a door.

⊙ CHATHAM SQUARE

btwn Doyers & Catherine Sts; ⊙ J, M, Z, 6 to Canal St

You've hit Chatham Sq when you see a large arch on two columns, with fresh flowers on each one. That's the Kim Lau Memorial Arch, built in 1962 to commemorate fighter pilot Benjamin Ralph Kim Lau and other Chinese Americans who were killed in WWII. The other statue in Chatham Sq is an homage to Lin Ze Xu, a 19th-century Ching-dynasty anti-drugs crusader who fought against the opium trade. Looking to the east, to Division St, you'll see a statue of Confucius; he's standing next to what's believed to be the tallest building in Chinatown. At St James Pl, just behind Chatham Sq, is the First Shearith

Israel Cemetery, which dates to 1683 and is believed to be the oldest Jewish cemetery in the city.

⊙ CHURCH OF THE TRANSFIGURATION

☎ 212-962-5157; www.transfiguration nyc.org; 29 Mott St; admission $4; ☯ noon-6pm Tue-Sun; ⊙ J, M, N, Q, R, W, Z, 6 to Canal St

It's been serving New York's immigrant communities since 1801, and the Church of the Transfiguration doesn't stop adapting. First it was the Irish, then Italians, and now Chinese. The same priest delivers sermons in Cantonese, English and sometimes even Latin. This small landmark is not far from Pell St and Doyers St, two winding paths worth exploring.

⊙ COLUMBUS PARK

Mulberry & Park Sts; ⊙ J, M, Z, 6 to Canal St

You'd never guess from the gentle sounds of neighborhood residents playing mah-jongg and dominoes, but this park was once part of the notorious Five Points neighborhood that was the inspiration for Martin Scorsese's *Gangs of New York*. Although the tiny triangle is now a peaceful playground, the surrounding tenements are the same ones that were built in 1890.

NEIGHBORHOODS

CHINATOWN & LITTLE ITALY

⊘ EDWARD MOONEY HOUSE
cnr 18 Bowery & Pell St; ⌚ **9am-5pm Mon-Fri, to 3pm Sat;** ⊖ **J, M, Z, 6 to Canal St**

The oldest townhouse in Manhattan stands at the corner of Bowery and Pell St, courtesy of a Mr Edward Mooney, who in 1785 took the wealth he made as a butcher and invested it in real estate. His post–Revolutionary War townhouse became a tavern in the 1800s, then a store, hotel, pool hall, restaurant, private club and now a bank. The architecture is a combination of Georgian and Federalist styles.

⊘ MULBERRY STREET
⊖ **C, E to Spring St**

Even though the original Italian essence is long gone, Mulberry St still bursts with true ethnic pride. Mobster Joey Gallo was shot to death at the former location of Umberto's Clam House (now found at 386 Broome St) in the '70s, John Gotti was wiretapped by the Feds in the long-gone Ravenite Social Club, and Ol' Blue Eyes himself, Frank Sinatra, caroused his way up and down this street back in the day. Visit the **Museum of Italian American Heritage** (www .italianamericanmuseum.org; 155 Mulberry St; admission free; ⌚ 11am-6pm Wed, Thu, Sat & Sun, to 8pm Fri) on the corner of Grand St for a real education on the 'hood. Hours change frequently; check the website for the latest before you go.

⊘ MUSEUM OF CHINESE IN AMERICA
☎ **212-619-4785; www.mocanyc.org; 211-215 Centre St near Grand St; admission $7;** ⌚ **11am-5pm Mon & Fri, 11am-9pm Thu, 10am-5pm Sat & Sun;** ⊖ **J, M, N, Q, R, W, Z, 6 to Canal St**

This relocated museum – now housed in a 12,350-sq-ft space designed by architect Maya Lin (who did the famed Vietnam Memorial in Washington DC) – is chock-full of facts about Chinese American life. Browse through interactive multimedia exhibits, maps, timelines, photos, letters, films and artifacts, and catch rotating exhibits. Its anchor exhibit is the Chinese-American Experience, which touches on subjects such as immigration, activism and globalization.

🛍 SHOP

⊘ CANAL STREET *Bric-a-Brac*
⊖ **M, N, Q, R, W, Z, 6 to Canal St**

Bustling, busy and perpetually congested, Canal St is packed with everything from treasure to junk; sifting through takes a keen eye and loads of patience. Or, you can simply walk around, taking in the strange creatures flopping in the food markets, the homeopathic drugstores with Chinese remedies, and the sound of a thousand tongues speaking at once.

Countless shoppers, numerous vendors, many goods – but only one Canal St

PEARL PAINT COMPANY
Arts & Crafts

☎ 212-431-7932; www.pearlpaint.com; 308 Canal St; 🕙 9am-7pm Mon-Fri, 10am-7pm Sat, 10am-6pm Sun; 🚇 J, M, N, Q, R, W, Z, 6 to Canal St

An institution in art circles, Pearl Paint sticks out a mile on Canal St. Taking up four floors of a sprawling warehouse, it's got an obscene amount of space and it's all filled with anything and everything to do with painting, drawing, arts and crafts, gold leaf, glitter, glue – the list is endless.

PEARL RIVER MART
Bric-a-Brac

☎ 212-431-4770; www.pearlriver.com; 477 Broadway; 🕙 10am-7pm; 🚇 J, M, N, Q, R, W, Z, 6 to Canal St

An Asian emporium that stocks all sorts of knick-knacks, Pearl River Mart's swanky storefront showcases bright kimonos, bejeweled slippers, Japanese teapots, paper lanterns, jars of mysterious spices, herbs, teas (and a Zen-like tea room) and more.

🍴 EAT

🍴 BIG WONG *Asian* $

☎ 212-964-0540; 67 Mott St btwn Walker & Bayard Sts; 🕙 breakfast, lunch & dinner; 🚇 J, M, N, Q, R, W, Z, 6 to Canal St; 🚻 🚾 🚻

A fast-moving favorite that's famous for its roast pork and BBQ-style chicken, duck and ribs, Big Wong also does a mean rice crepe for breakfast. You'll likely

NEIGHBORHOODS

CHINATOWN & LITTLE ITALY

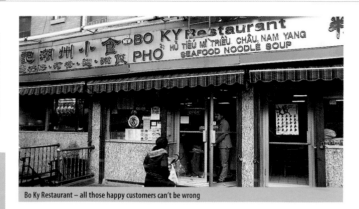
Bo Ky Restaurant – all those happy customers can't be wrong

have to share a table, and the food (and your check) comes lightning quick, but it's a fun, communal (and affordable) experience.

🍴 BO KY RESTAURANT
Pan-Asian $

☎ 212-406-2292; 80 Bayard St btwn Mott & Mulberry Sts; ⏱ breakfast, lunch & dinner; ⊕ J, M, N, Q, R, W, Z, 6 to Canal St; Ⓥ

Cheap, quick and delicious, Bo Ky's meat-studded soups, fish-infused flat noodles and curried rice dishes keep customers rotating in and out the door, usually in twos and threes. Join the crowds and dig in.

🍴 FOCOLARE *Italian* $$$

☎ 212-993-5858; 115 Mulberry St btwn Canal & Hester Sts; ⏱ lunch & dinner;

⊕ J, M, Q, R, W, Z to Canal St

If you're determined to experience a Little Italy dinner while in the city, this friendly restaurant is a fine choice. With a cozy interior warmed by a fireplace in winter and adorned with photos of Frank Sinatra and company, the kitchen turns out classics in fine style: homemade pasta, cooked al dente, is an excellent base for various red and cream-based sauces; crisp rice balls ooze with cheese; fried calamari zings with flavor.

🍴 ORIGINAL CHINATOWN ICE CREAM FACTORY *Ice Cream* $

☎ 212-608-4170; www.chinatown icecreamfactory.com; 65 Bayard St; ⏱ 11am-10pm; ⊕ J, M, N, Q, R, W, Z, 6 to Canal St; Ⓥ ♿

Ask the servers here and they'll tell you that ice cream was invented in China during the Tang dynasty, and based on the flavors the Factory can produce, you might just believe them. Sorbets and more in flavors such as avocado, durian, sesame and peppermint, plus the standards like vanilla and chocolate.

🍴 PEKING DUCK HOUSE
Chinese $$

☎ 212-227-1810; 28 Mott St; ☽ lunch & dinner; ⊕ J, M, N, Q, R, W, Z, 6 to Canal St; ♿ Ⓥ ⚹

You already know what the specialty of the house is – big, brown, crispy glazed duck, served with

sides of pancakes and *hoisin* sauce for tearing, rolling and dipping. There are plenty of other dishes to choose from, all bearing imprints of Peking, Shanghai and Szechuan flavors, mixed expertly together. Peking Duck is slightly fancier than other Chinatown spots, but not at all stuffy; it's a popular choice for local families celebrating a big event.

🍴 SHANGHAI KITCHEN
Chinese $

☎ 212-513-1788; 67 Bayard St; ☽ lunch & dinner; ⊕ J, M, N, Q, R, W, Z, 6 to Canal St; ⚹ Ⓥ

Delectable pork steamed buns, juicy spring rolls and hearty

Decisions, decisions – shopping on Mott St

CHINATOWN & LITTLE ITALY

SWEET TREATS

Chinese bakeries are ubiquitous in Chinatown, as hardworking patrons stop by for a quick, filling treat. Many of the delicacies aren't found in the American pastry lexicon, but are delicious nonetheless. Cash-only **Tai Pan Bakery** (☎ 212-732-2222; 194 Canal St near Mott St; ⏱ 7:30am-8:30pm; ⊖ J, M, N, Q, R, W, Z, 6 to Canal St) carries most of these.

> Cock tail buns *(gai mei bao)*: shaped vaguely like a rooster's tail, and stuffed with sweet coconut filling.
> Coconut tarts *(ye tot)*: bright yellow tarts flavored with coconut and usually sporting a cherry or berry on top.
> Custard egg tart *(dan tot)*: every Chinatown bakery has these egg custards baked into a dry, flaky crust.
> Hot dog buns *(cheung zai bao)*: only found in NYC's Chinatown, these treats feature a hot dog in a sweet, fluffy bun and covered in a honey glaze.
> Pineapple buns *(bo lo bao)*: they look like pineapples on the outside, but the filling is usually custard or coconut.
> Red bean paste buns *(hong dau sa bao)*: a popular dessert made of sweet bread and red beans crushed into a semi-sweet paste.
> Roast pork buns *(char siu chan bao)*: sometimes steamed, other times baked, these sweet bread buns contain Chinese-style BBQ pork.

noodles, soups and other Chinese dishes (some with tofu and veggies). It's cash only, quite a bargain, and you'll have to smile and point a lot because English is not spoken.

DRINK
APOTHEKE BAR
Late-night Bar

☎ 212-406-0400; www.apothekenyc .com; 9 Doyers St; ⏱ 6pm-2am Mon-Sat, 8pm-2am Sun; ⊖ J, M, Z to Canal St
It takes a little effort to track down this former opium den–turned–apothecary-bar located on Doyers St (known as the Bloody Triangle back when this was gang territory). Look for a Golden Flower sign – that's the clue you've arrived. The sleek red interior, with marble bar and apothecary-type mortars, pestles and cylinders, gives the Apotheke Bar a cool vibe, enhanced when the owner passes around his homemade absinthe. The cocktails are intense and flavorful: try the Five Points (hibiscus, Italian bitters, grape juice and sugar-cane-infused rum) or the Saffron Sazerac (with saffron-infused bourbon).

NEIGHBORHOODS

CHINATOWN & LITTLE ITALY

Y BACARO *Wine Bar*
☎ 212-941-5060; www.bacaronyc.com;
136 Division St btwn Orchard & Ludlow
Sts; ☼ dinner; ◎ M to East Broadway
Behold Venice in Chinatown
(minus the rising canal waters).
Based on a blue-collar Venetian
pub, Bacaro serves up filling
snacks called *cicchetti*, which you
can wash down with robust wine
from northern Italy. The downstairs is a spacious and cavernous
dining area, while the rustic bar
space on the 1st floor – made
from reclaimed barn wood – is
where the drinking gets done.
Popular *cicchetti* include fried
rice balls, asparagus with baked
egg, crostini, bruschetta, meat

and cheese platters, and *insalata
polpi* (octopus salad).

PLAY
☆ EXPERIENCE CHINATOWN
Tour
☎ 212-619-4785; www.moca-nyc.org;
tours adult $15, senior & child $12;
☼ weekly May-Dec
To truly penetrate the layers that
make up bustling Chinatown,
you'll need a guide. And trusting
one from the Chinatown-based
Museum of Chinese in America
(p56) is definitely a good move. The
tours are led by museum docents
with family roots in the community, and they give you a sense of
Chinatown's past and present.

>LOWER EAST SIDE

Signs of a louche, lush past abound in the Lower East Side (LES). Its slightly seedy streets are now dotted with trendy restaurants and cafes, but it's difficult to erase centuries of grit and grime. The LES was once a ghetto slum, full of Jewish and Eastern European immigrants who lived cramped, dank lives in crowded tenements and worked in nearby factories. They also built beautiful synagogues and neighborhood markets, and enjoyed a vibrant street life full of theater, music and art. Later came waves of Latinos, who wove their own traditions into the fluid neighborhood.

Now that condos and hotels have replaced many of the tenements, and expensive restoration projects have returned many cultural gems to their original beauty, the LES is hipster central, offering some of the best nightlife and dining in the city. Its flashy mix of modern and old – the stalwart Lower East Side Tenement Museum, for example, contrasts nicely with the innovative New Museum of Contemporary Art – gives this nabe a unique allure.

LOWER EAST SIDE

👁 SEE
ABC No Rio **1** D3
Angel Orensanz
  Foundation **2** D2
Artists Alliance **3** D3
Clemente Solo Velez ....(see 3)
Eldridge Street
  Synagogue **4** C6
Essex Street Market **5** D3
Gallery
  Onetwentyeight **6** D3
Kehila Kedosha Janina
  Synagogue and
  Museum **7** C4
Lower East Side Jewish
  Conservancy **8** E5
Lower East Side Tenement
  Museum **9** C4
New Museum of
  Contemporary Art **10** A3
Orchard Street
  Bargain District **11** C3
Participant Inc **12** D2

St Augustine's Episcopal
  Church **13** F5

🛍 SHOP
Alife Rivington **14** D3
Bluestockings **15** C3
Economy Candy **16** C3
Foley + Corinna **17** C2
Honey in the Rough **18** D3
Reed Space **19** C3
September Wines &
  Spirits **20** C2
Still Life **21** C4

🍽 EAT
Antibes Bistro **22** D3
Bondi Road **23** D3
Georgia's East Side
  BBQ **24** C2
Kuma Inn **25** C3
Little Giant **26** C4

Schiller's Liquor Bar **27** D3
Yonah Schimmel
  Knishery **28** B2

🍸 DRINK
151 ....**29** D3
Happy Ending **30** B4
Magician **31** D3
Nurse Betties **32** D3
Whiskey Ward **33** C3

⭐ PLAY
Abrons Art Center **34** E4
Arlene's Grocery **35** C3
BEast **36** D6
Bowery Ballroom **37** B4
Living Room **38** C3
Mercury Lounge **39** C2
Pianos **40** C3
The Box **41** B3

Please see over for map

SEE

ELDRIDGE STREET SYNAGOGUE

☎ 212-219-0888; www.eldridgestreet .org; 12 Eldridge St btwn Canal & Division Sts; 🕙 10am-5pm Sun-Thu; 🚇 F to East Broadway

This landmarked house of worship, built in 1887, was once the center of Jewish life, before falling into squalor in the 1920s. Left to rot, it's only recently been reclaimed, and now shines with original splendor. Its onsite museum gives tours every half hour ($10; 10am to 5pm), with the last one departing at 4pm.

ESSEX STREET MARKET

☎ 212-312-3603; www.essexstreet market.com; 120 Essex St btwn Delancey & Rivington Sts; 🕙 8am-7pm Mon-Sat; 🚇 F, J, M, V, Z to Delancey St-Essex St

Fantastic food shopping and people-watching make it a pleasure to meander through this 80-year-old market, which still has old-fashioned pickle stalls right next to gourmet cheese shops. Just like the neighborhood, Essex St Market is a mix of Jewish and Latino vendors.

GALLERY ONETWENTYEIGHT

☎ 212-674-0244; www.onetwentyeight .com; 128 Rivington St; 🕙 call for appt; 🚇 F to Lower East Side-Second Ave

Like its opening hours, the art at this gallery is eclectic and hit or miss. You never know what you'll find – or when – and that's what keeps people coming back for more. Check out the website to see what's on display and call in advance to make sure someone will be there when you stop by.

HIDDEN LOWER EAST SIDE

There's a lot of history to discover in the Lower East Side. If you want to take a few hours to really get to know the nabe, try a tour with the **Lower East Side Jewish Conservancy** (☎ 212-374-4100; http://nycjewishtours.org; 235 East Broadway; tours $18-30; 🕙 office 10am-5pm Mon-Thu, to 2pm Fri; 🚇 F, J, M, Z to Delancey St-Essex St). Tours are by appointment. A public tour also takes place every month, and there's an annual nosh-tour extravaganza on Christmas day. The professional guides will take you in and out of every major historic site within walking distance, with frequent stops for a nosh on the way. As you stroll the streets, keep an eye out for **St Augustine's Episcopal Church** (☎ 212-673-5300; 290 Henry St), near the Abrons Art Center. Originally the All Saints Free Church, this landmark Greek Revival was finished in 1828. Recalling a bit of the city's past that doesn't often get acknowledged, the church is currently renovating its two original 'Slave Galleries,' where slaves who helped build parts of the city had to sit during services.

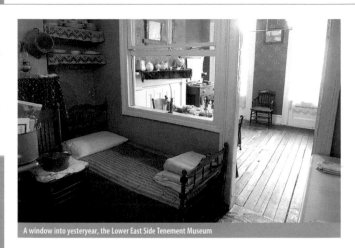

A window into yesteryear, the Lower East Side Tenement Museum

KEHILA KEDOSHA JANINA SYNAGOGUE AND MUSEUM

☎ 212-431-1619; www.kkjsm.org; 280 Broome St at Allen St; 🕙 11am-4pm Sun, worship service 9am Sat; 🚇 F, J, M, Z to Delancey St-Essex St

This small synagogue is home to an obscure branch of Judaism, whose people, known as Romaniotes, come from ancestors who were slaves sent to Rome but rerouted to Greece. Their only synagogue in the Western Hemisphere is here, and includes a small museum that bears artifacts like hand-painted birth certificates, an art gallery, a Holocaust memorial for Greek Jews and costumes from Janina, the Romaniote capital of Greece.

LOWER EAST SIDE TENEMENT MUSEUM

☎ 212-982-8420; www.tenement.org; 108 Orchard St near Delancey St; adult $20, student, child & senior $15, discounts available for combo-tour tickets; 🕙 visitor center 10:30am-5pm, museum tours every 40min from 1pm & 1:20pm until 4:30pm & 4:45pm Tue-Fri (reservations suggested); 🚇 B, D to Grand St, F, J, M, Z to Delancey St-Essex St; ♿

Get a firsthand look at the crowded conditions endured by Jewish and Eastern European immigrants at the turn of the century. The tours through restored and refurbished apartments raise poignant feelings about early settlers' enthusiasm for a future in the USA. You'll get to know the German-Jewish Gumpertz family, who lived in the LES in the 1870s, and the Sicilian-Catholic Baldizzi family from the 1930s, plus many others.

⬛ NEW MUSEUM OF CONTEMPORARY ART

☎ 212-219-1222; www.newmuseum .org; 235 Bowery near Prince St; adult/ senior/student $12/8/6; ☽ noon-6pm Wed & Sat, to 9pm Thu & Fri; ◉ 6 to Spring St, N, R to Prince St

New York's newest museum is an off-kilter stack of seven white, ethereal boxes, creating a seven-story structure designed by Tokyo-based architects Kazuyo Sejima and Ryue Nishizawa. The city's sole museum dedicated to contemporary art features edgy works in new forms, like seemingly random, discarded materials fused together and displayed in the middle of a vast room. Founded in 1977 by Marcia Tucker and moved to five different locations over the years, the museum's mission statement is simple: 'New art, new ideas.' The museum also houses a small and

ART INVASION

Creativity is no stranger to the Lower East Side. Long before uptown galleries starting arriving, the LES was home to artists, musicians, writers and painters who often shared space and resources in order to do their work. Many of those collectives are still around today, and are open to the public for browsing.

ABC No Rio (☎ 212-254-3697; www.abcnorio.org; 156 Rivington St; admission price varies; ☽ hours vary; ◉ F, J, M, Z to Delancey St-Essex St) Founded in 1980, this internationally known art and activism center features weekly hard-core/punk and experimental music shows, as well as regular fine-arts exhibits, poetry readings and more.

Angel Orensanz Foundation (☎ 212-529-7194; www.orensanz.org; 172 Norfolk St; admission price varies; ☽ hours vary; ◉ F to Delancey St-Essex St) Inside one of the oldest synagogues in the city, this artist-run foundation hosts art and photography exhibits and various live music events.

Artists Alliance (☎ 212-420-9202; www.ai-nyc.org; 107 Suffolk St; admission price varies; ☽ hours vary; ◉ F, J, M, Z to Delancey St-Essex St) A nonprofit artists' collective with more than 40 members, Artists Alliance has a rotating list of exhibits and contributors on its website.

Clemente Soto Velez (☎ 212-260-4080; www.el.net/csv; 107 Suffolk St; admission price varies; ☽ hours vary; ◉ F, J, M, Z to Delancey St-Essex St) Inside the AAI building, this collective focuses on the work of Puerto Rican poet Velez, but also brings in theater, music, art and film from artists across the world.

healthy cafe, and has the added treat of a city viewing platform, which provides a unique perspective on the constantly changing architectural landscape.

◉ ORCHARD STREET BARGAIN DISTRICT

Orchard, Ludlow & Essex Sts btwn Houston & Delancey Sts; ⌚ **Sun-Fri;** ◉ **F, J, M, Z to Delancey St-Essex St**

Back in the day, this large intersection was a free-for-all, as Eastern European and Jewish merchants sold anything that could command a buck from their pushcarts. The 300-plus shops you see now aren't as picturesque, but it's a good place to pick up some cheap shirts, tees and jeans. If you like to haggle, take a shot at bargaining over the price.

◉ PARTICIPANT INC

☎ **212-254-4334; 253 East Houston St;** ⌚ **noon-7pm Wed-Sun;** ◉ **F to Lower East Side-Second Ave**

Part gallery, part performance-art space, Participant Inc uses its 2nd floor for all sorts of innovative fun. Opened in 2002 by founder Lia Gangitano, it's stayed afloat even as many other galleries disappear. It has a rotating roster of international artists, and also makes a point of showcasing LES-based work.

⬛ SHOP

⬛ ALIFE RIVINGTON CLUB

Fashion & Accessories, Footwear

☎ **212-375-8128; www.rivingtonclub .com; 158 Rivington St near Clinton St;** ⌚ **11am-7pm Mon-Sat, noon-6pm Sun;** ◉ **J, M, Z to Delancey St-Essex St**

Unmarked doors and discreet buzzers put the 'club' in Alife Rivington's name. This temple to sneaker and T-shirt consumption has all the latest and hippest styles, in all the coolest colors, of course.

⬛ BLUESTOCKINGS *Books*

☎ **212-777-6028; www.bluestockings .com; 172 Allen St;** ⌚ **11am-10pm;** ◉ **F, V to Lower East Side-Second Ave**

It's run-down and ramshackle, but full of history and fueled by the alternative attitude that once permeated the Lower East Side. A holdover from the freewheeling '70s, Bluestockings offers books on a range of radical topics, including gender studies, black liberation theory and plenty more.

⬛ ECONOMY CANDY

Food & Drink

☎ **212-254-1531; www.economycandy .com; 108 Rivington St at Essex St;** ⌚ **9am-6pm Sun-Fri, 10am-5pm Sat;** ◉ **F, J, M, Z to Delancey St-Essex St**

Known as the 'Nosher's Paradise of the Lower East Side,' this second-generation family store has a jaw-dropping selection of old- and new-style nibbles. Jelly beans, halvah, Pez, Swedish Fish and so much more grace the shelves of this corner candy shop.

☐ FOLEY + CORINNA
Fashion & Accessories
☎ 212-529-2338; 114 Stanton St btwn Essex & Ludlow Sts; ☪ noon-7pm Sun & Mon, to 8pm Tue-Sat; ⊕ F, V to Lower East Side-Second Ave

This vintage store with a few of its own unique designs is pure girly romance. Delicate dresses, and tees, tanks and blouses matched with flirty skirts are the signature style, along with Corinna's unique shoe and jewelry designs.

☐ HONEY IN THE ROUGH
Fashion & Accessories
☎ 212-228-6415; http://honeyinthe rough.com; 161 Rivington St near Clinton St; ☪ noon-8pm Mon-Sat, to 6pm Sun; ⊕ F, J, M, Z to Delancey St-Essex St

Stocking colorful variations on the always-popular little black dress, Honey in the Rough is all about the party frock – vivid, youthful and still sophisticated. You won't miss your basic black once you try on one of these.

Sneak into Alife Rivington Club for the latest styles

Enlarge your mind at radical, ramshackle and historical Bluestockings (p68)

REED SPACE
Fashion & Accessories, Footwear
☎ 212-253-0588; http://thereedspace
.com; 151 Orchard St; ⏰ 1-7pm Mon-Fri,
noon-7pm Sat & Sun; ⊕ F to Delancey
St-Essex St
Sneakers, accessories, youthful
tees, pants and jackets for both
sexes line the bright and varied
shelves at Reed Space. Designer
Jeff Ng has found a blueprint for
the urban casual lifestyle.

SEPTEMBER WINES &
SPIRITS *Food & Drink*
☎ 212-388-0770; http://september
wines.com; 100 Stanton St at Ludlow St;
⏰ 11am-10pm Mon-Thu, 11am-11pm

Fri, noon-11pm Sat, 1-8pm Sun; ⊕ F, J,
M, Z to Delancey St-Essex St
A boutique wine shop that has
lots of unique bottles on display,
including a section on women
vintners, hard-to-find wines,
specialty drinks and big-budget
classics.

STILL LIFE
Fashion & Accessories
☎ 212-575-9704; www.stilllifenyc.com;
77 Orchard St near Delancey St; ⏰ noon-
7pm; ⊕ B, F, J, M, V, Z to Delancey
St-Essex St
The cool tones of Mobb Deep and
Quiet Village will likely greet you
inside Still Life, a haven for hat
lovers. Check out styles like the

Mingus and the Langston – it takes hats to a whole new level of hip.

🍴 EAT

🍴 ANTIBES BISTRO
French Bistro $$
☎ 212-533-6088; www.antibesbistro. com; 112 Suffolk St btwn Delancey & Rivington Sts; 🕑 lunch & dinner; 🚇 F, J, M, Z to Delancey St-Essex St
Quiet jazz and outdoor dining in summer, candlelight, cool-looking wrought-iron lamps and cozy red-brick walls – what's not to like? Antibes has a sunny Mediterranean vibe and an appealing American flexibility: you can order a late breakfast at lunch, or Guinness-soaked short-ribs for dinner if classics like seared tuna, grilled bass, whole snapper and haricots verts don't appeal. Save room for the banana and chocolate mousse dessert.

🍴 BONDI ROAD *Australian* $
☎ 212-253-5311; 153 Rivington St near Suffolk St; 🕑 dinner Mon-Fri, lunch & dinner Sat & Sun; 🚇 J, M, Z to Delancey St-Essex St; 🅥 🛗
What it lacks in width it makes up for in height. Still, Bondi Road is a tight squeeze on weekend nights. Slide onto one of the big barstools at the tables, check out the huge montages of Bondi Beach running down each wall, then take a stab at filling out your menu with the little

stub pencils handed out. You pick a fish (mackerel or cod, for example), a cooking method (like grilled, fried or sautéed) and a side dish (french fries, usually). Then drink as much Aussie beer as you can with the rowdy crowd till your food comes.

🍴 GEORGIA'S EAST SIDE BBQ
BBQ $
☎ 212-253-6280; www.georgiaseastside bbq.com; 192 Orchard St btwn Houston & Stanton Sts; 🕑 lunch & dinner; 🚇 F, V, M to Lower East Side-Second Ave; 🛗
Bring a big appetite to this little joint. The ribs are slow-cooked in beer then sizzled on the grill, the fried chicken is crisp outside and tender inside, the pulled pork melts in your mouth it's that succulent, and there's no way you can eat all that thick, sweet cornbread and decadent mac 'n' cheese. Cash only, and the bathroom's in the bar across the street (it's that tiny, really).

🍴 KUMA INN *Pan-Asian* $$
☎ 212-353-8866; 113 Ludlow St btwn Delancey & Rivington Sts; 🕑 dinner Tue-Sun; 🚇 F, J, M, Z to Delancey St-Essex St
Reservations are a must at this strikingly popular spot in a secretive 2nd-floor location that's a headache to find (look for a small red door next to a Chinese deli with 113 painted on the concrete side). The Filipino- and Thai-inspired tapas run the gamut, from

vegetarian summer rolls (with the unique addition of chayote) and edamame (soybean) drizzled with basil-lime oil to an oyster omelette and grilled salmon with mung beans and pickled onions. Pair anything with some chilled sake or mango nectar.

🍴 LITTLE GIANT
Seasonal American $$

☎ 212-226-5047; www.littlegiantnyc .com; 85 Orchard St; ⏰ lunch & dinner; 🚇 F to Delancey St-Essex St; ♿ Ⓥ
Fresh ingredients from organic farmers in upstate New York pepper Little Giant's revolving menu, which can carry dishes like chicken-liver mousse, maple-roasted brussel sprouts, sticky toffee pudding and a 'swine of the week' dish featuring pork. The 80-bottle wine list proudly offers only local vintners.

🍴 SCHILLER'S LIQUOR BAR
Bistro Cuisine $$

☎ 212-260-4555; www.schillersny.com; 131 Rivington St at Norfolk St; ⏰ 11am-midnight Mon-Thu, to 2am Fri-Sun; 🚇 F, J, M, Z to Delancey St-Essex St; ♿ 🚻
The combination of eclectic bistro fare and warm, brassy decor is a large part of Schiller's allure – the other element is the Rivington St location, a great place to sit with a cold beer on a hot day. The wine carafes are generous, por-

tions ample, and the food – steak *frites,* Cuban sandwiches, baked chicken and glazed cod – reliably good.

🍴 YONAH SCHIMMEL KNISHERY *Knishes* $

☎ 212-477-2858; 137 E Houston St btwn Eldridge & Forsyth Sts; ⏰ 9:30am-7pm; 🚇 F, V to Lower East Side-Second Ave; Ⓥ 🚻
Here's how to make a living the old-school way: buy a pushcart c 1890, sell your wife's knishes on Coney Island, save up for a mini storefront on the LES, and turn it into a century-old family business that still follows the original recipe and uses a century-old dumb-waiter to haul potato, cheese, cabbage and kasha knishes up from your wood-burning stove in the cellar. One bite of a Yonah Schimmel knish and you'll be hooked.

🍸 DRINK
🍸 151 *Bar*

☎ 212-228-4139; 151 Rivington St near Suffolk St; ⏰ 6pm-4am; 🚇 F, J, M, Z to Delancey St-Essex St
Down an unmarked set of stairs and behind a graffiti-covered door you'll find a local joint that gets pretty packed. Come early for the extended happy hour from 6pm to 10pm. Sunday nights you'll find a sweaty dance party dedicated

to those who have to work in the morning. Music progresses from pop (Lady Gaga) to hip-hop (Jay-Z) to hardcore rock tunes (Guns N' Roses); that seems to suit the edgier after-midnight crowd.

▼ HAPPY ENDING *DJ Bar*
☎ 212-334-9676; www.happyending lounge.com; 302 Broome St; 🕙 10pm-4am Tue, 7pm-4am Wed-Sat; ⊕ B, D to Grand St, J, M, Z to Bowery
Ignore the hideous pink, purple and spangled decor at Happy Ending – it used to be a 'massage parlor,' and the new owners clearly didn't feel the need to refurbish. Focus instead on the groove, hip-hop, funk and electronica. Tuesday nights are 'We Bite' and 'Shit Hammered' events; Wednesday nights feature literary readings (before the dancing starts); there are gay, goth and punk nights, and the 'Human Jukebox' DJ on Saturdays. Note that the entrance awning says 'Xie He Health Club' – the owners didn't feel the need to change that, either.

▼ MAGICIAN *Bar*
☎ 212-673-7851; 118 Rivington St btwn Essex & Norfolk Sts; 🕙 5pm-4am; ⊕ F, J, M, Z to Delancey St-Essex St
Pick out an old classic on the jukebox, take your pick of micro-brewed beers or specialty cocktails (mixed with a generous hand) and enjoy the spacious, never-crowded

bar at Magician, a low-key neighborhood joint that hasn't been discovered by the 'in' crowd.

▼ NURSE BETTIE *Bar*
☎ 917-434-9072; www.nursebettiesles. com; 106 Norfolk St btwn Delancey & Rivington Sts; 🕙 6pm-2am Sun-Tue, to 4am Wed-Sat; ⊕ F, J, M, Z to Delancey St-Essex St
Something a bit new is going on with this pint-sized charmer: plenty of roaming space between slick '00s-modern lounges and '50s-style ice-cream-shop stools and painted pin-ups on the brick walls. Cocktails get freaky: fruity vodka and brandies, plus bubble-gum martinis. You can bring food in, and many won-over locals do.

▼ WHISKEY WARD *Bar*
☎ 212-477-2998; www.thewhiskey ward.com; 121 Essex St; 🕙 5pm-4am; ⊕ F, J, M, Z to Delancey St-Essex St; ♿
Once upon a time, city officials divided Manhattan into wards, and the Lower East Side was the 'Whiskey Ward,' courtesy of its many drinking establishments. Modern owners of the Whiskey Ward apparently appreciate history as much as they adore single malts, rye whiskey, blended Scotch, Irish whiskey and bourbon. Patrons enjoy the single-mindedness of this brick-walled bar.

⭐ PLAY

⭐ ABRONS ART CENTER
Theater, Arts

☎ 212-598-0400; www.henrystreet.org; 466 Grand St; 🕙 hours vary; Ⓜ F, J, M, Z to Delancey St-Essex St; ♿

This venerable cultural hub has three theaters, the largest being the Harry de Jur Playhouse (a national landmark), with its own lobby, fixed seats on a rise, a large, deep stage and good visibility. A mainstay of the downtown Fringe Festival, Abrons Art Center is also your best bet to catch experimental and community productions – including avant-garde jazz brought to you by the former Tonic nightclub, which was driven out of the LES by rising rents. Not afraid of difficult subjects, Abrons sponsors plays and dance and photography exhibits that don't get much play elsewhere.

⭐ ARLENE'S GROCERY
Live Music, Karaoke

☎ 212-358-1633; www.arlenesgrocery .net; 95 Stanton St; cover charge for bands Tue-Sun $8-10; 🕙 6pm-4am; Ⓜ F, V to Lower East Side-Second Ave

Formerly a bodega and butcher shop, Arlene's Grocery now serves up heaping portions of live talent with shows every night. Drinks are cheap and the crowd is good-looking – make an impression on Monday night with Rock 'n' Roll Karaoke. It's free, and you're backed by a live band. Probably your best shot at getting a groupie.

⭐ BOWERY BALLROOM
Live Music

☎ 212-533-2111; www.boweryball room.com; 6 Delancey St; ticket price varies; 🕙 performance times vary; Ⓜ F to Delancey St-Essex St, J, M to Bowery

The clue to the Bowery's success, besides its cool location and look, is that it's the kind of place you want to hang in before and after the show, as well as during. Drinks are long and strong, acoustics are grand, and the list of talent is phenomenal. Dirty Pretty Things and Ziggy Marley play regularly, and the Losers Lounge nights (the Cure vs the Smiths) sell out instantly.

⭐ LIVING ROOM
DJ Bar, Live Music

☎ 212-533-7237; www.livingroomny .com; 154 Ludlow St; no cover charge, 1-drink minimum; 🕙 6:30pm-2am Sun-Thu, to 4am Fri & Sat; Ⓜ F, V to Lower East Side-Second Ave, J, M, Z to Delancey St-Essex St

There's never a cover charge at this intimate space, which has hosted Jealous Girlfriends and the Kidrockers. Most acts are acoustic, but the occasional amplifier will slip in. If the live music doesn't thrill you, the upstairs lounge – known as Googie's – features a DJ.

⭐ MERCURY LOUNGE
Live Music

☎ 212-260-4700; www.mercurylounge nyc.com; 217 E Houston St; cover charge $8-15; ⌚ 4pm-4am; Ⓢ F, V to Lower East Side-Second Ave

Featuring local, indie and up-and-coming talent, Mercury Lounge is a good place to catch bands just before they hit it big. The owners have an ear for talent, so don't be surprised to hear high-quality sounds – in all genres but heavy on rock – coming from the unassuming space.

⭐ PIANOS
Live Music

☎ 212-505-3733; www.pianosnyc.com; 158 Ludlow St at Stanton St; cover charge $8-17; ⌚ noon-4am; Ⓢ F, V to Lower East Side-Second Ave

Nobody's bothered to change the sign at the door, a leftover from the location's previous incarnation as a piano shop. Now it's a musical mix of genres and styles, leaning more toward pop, punk and new wave, but throwing in some hip-hop and indie bands for good measure. Sometimes you get a double feature – one act upstairs and another below. Happy hour is a good time to visit.

>SOHO, NOHO & NOLITA

It's amazing that so much hipster coolness can be packed into three such comparatively small corners of Manhattan. Long before it became celebrity central, Soho (the area south of Houston St) was an industrial hole that gradually filled up with artists who loved the old factory lofts. Now it's awash with luxury shops and million-dollar condos, and two other former triangles of depression have followed suit: Nolita, which is north of Little Italy, and Noho, just north of Houston St.

Of the three, Soho is still the most visually stunning, with massive, soaring cast-iron-facade buildings and a picturesque skyline. Nolita now has a similar concentration of pretty shops and eclectic designers but it moves at a slightly slower pace. Where Soho has its galleries and big stores, Nolita has its boutiques and rustic eateries.

On the north side of Houston St, below Astor Pl, is the triangle of Lafayette and Bond Sts. You couldn't pack more treats into a two-block radius. There are so many standout stores it looms large for shoppers in Manhattan.

SOHO, NOHO & NOLITA

Please see over for map

👁 SEE

◉ ARTISTS SPACE

☎ 212-226-3970; www.artistsspace
.org; 3rd fl, 38 Greene St; admission free;
🕙 11am-6pm Tue-Sun; Ⓜ A, C, E, J, M,
N, R, 1, 6 to Canal St

One of the first alternative spaces in New York, Artists Space was founded in 1972 to support contemporary artists working in the visual arts, including video, electronic media, performance, architecture and design. It offers an exhibition space for new art and artists, and tries to foster an appreciation for the role artists play in communities.

◉ CHILDREN'S MUSEUM OF THE ARTS

☎ 212-274-0986; www.cmany.org; 182 Lafayette St btwn Broome & Grand Sts; admission $10, suggested donation 4-6pm Thu; 🕙 noon-5pm Wed & Fri-Sun, to 6pm Thu; Ⓜ 6 to Spring St, N, R to Prince St; ♿

Trained artists run this interactive museum, which is more like a playhouse for kids than a stuffy institution. Kids are free to touch, run, pepper docents with questions and have a good time. Warning: children will leave knowing how to make Flubber at home.

◉ DRAWING CENTER

☎ 212-219-2166; www.drawingcenter
.org; 35 Wooster St; admission free;
🕙 noon-6pm Wed & Fri-Sun, to 8pm
Thu; Ⓜ A, C, E, 1 to Canal St

It's been around for ages, and the Drawing Center remains one of the city's premier nonprofits. It's dedicated exclusively to drawings, with examples from

For almost four decades, Artists Space has been showcasing emerging artists

Michelangelo, James Ensor and Marcel Duchamp, as well as Richard Serra, Ellsworth Kelly and Richard Tuttle.

⊙ HAUGHWOUT BUILDING
488 Broadway; ⊕ 6 to Spring St
Look past the glaring red Staples facade and try to imagine this building c 1880. The Haughwout (pronounced 'how-out') was the first to put in an unheard-of new contraption – the steam elevator, developed by Elisha Otis.

⊙ MUSEUM OF COMIC & CARTOON ART
☎ 212-254-3511; www.moccany.org; 594 Broadway; admission $5; ⊙ noon-5pm Fri-Mon, by appt Tue-Thu; ⊕ R, W to Prince St
Cartoon aficionados can't get enough of this museum and its wealth of graphic novels, comic lore and long-lost posters. Special exhibits include both well-known cartoonists and up-and-coming artists, with frequent opening parties and various festivals. Check the website for online exhibits and upcoming lecture series.

⊙ PUCK BUILDING
☎ 212-274-8900; www.thepuckbuilding.com; 295 Lafayette St; ⊕ 6 to Bleecker St
The southeast corner of Lafayette and Houston Sts is dominated by

Albert Wagner's round-arched bit of architectural genius. Wagner designed the building in 1885 as the printing facility for the German-language magazine *Puck* (now defunct, obviously). The building's dotted with little gold statues – Wagner's version of Puck the fairy – and he's a jolly, round-bellied, top-hatted fellow.

⊙ SINGER BUILDING
561-563 Broadway; ⊕ R, W to Prince St
An example of why this area was once known as the Cast Iron District, the Singer building's got all the signature touches of a post–Civil War factory building. Designers will recognize Singer as the manufacturer of sewing machines; this building was the company's main warehouse.

⊙ ST PATRICK'S OLD CATHEDRAL
260-264 Prince St at Mott St; ⊙ rectory 8am-5pm Mon-Fri; ⊕ R, W to Prince St
Before St Patrick's on Fifth Ave stole its thunder, this graceful 1809 Gothic Revival church was the seat of the Catholic archdiocese in New York. Built by new immigrants mainly from Ireland, it continues to service its diverse community by giving liturgies in English, Spanish and Chinese. There are Masses just about every hour on weekends and at least one every weekday. The brick-walled courtyard hides

Levi Okunov
Designer & fashion-show producer

So, what do you do all day? If it's around Fashion Week then I'll be working to get shows ready for designers – that means handling everything from music selection to lighting to even cutting and sewing some of the clothes. Otherwise, I'm here in my Tribeca factory, working on my own designs. **How did you learn to sew?** I grew up in a Hasidic Jewish community in Brooklyn, and it was just kind of all around me. My grandmother taught me how to use a sewing machine. I use the same kind today in my factory. **Where do you like to shop?** I enjoy walking around the East Village, it has a real Berlin feel. I like the rawness of what's being done by a lot of young designers who work there. **Your factory's right on the cusp of Chinatown and Little Italy. Where do you like to hang out?** There's a cool bar around here, Apotheke (p60), that I like. It's like an old opium den. I'll also go to The Box (p172) for a night out. And I like Ferrara's coffee and all the Chinese bakeries too.

an ancient cemetery, and the mausoleums of many a famous New York family.

🛍 SHOP

🏠 ANNA SUI
Fashion & Accessories

☎ 212-941-8406; www.annasui.com; 113 Greene St; 🕙 11:30am-7pm Mon-Sat, noon-6pm Sun; 🚇 R, W to Prince St
Boutique designer Anna Sui has a devoted following of *soigné* New Yorkers who trek to her downtown shop for the frilly, flirty dresses that skim the body in all the right places.

🏠 APPLE STORE SOHO
Computers & Accessories

☎ 212-226-3126; www.apple.com /retail/soho; 103 Prince St; 🕙 10am-8pm Mon-Sat, 11am-7pm Sun; 🚇 N, R, W to Prince St
The flagship Apple Store is always packed with curious tech heads and trend seekers who must have the latest in Mac accessories. Its gleaming, translucent decor still looks trendy. There is free email service at the store, and seminars on computer tips are given for free.

🏠 ATRIUM
Fashion & Accessories, Footwear

☎ 212-473-3980; 644 Broadway at Bleecker St; 🕙 10am-9pm Mon-Sat, 11am-8pm Sun; 🚇 B, D, F, V to Broadway-Lafayette St

Atrium has an excellent selection of funky designer wear, including shoes and accessories, for both men and women from Diesel, G-Star, Miss Sixty and other popular labels. Best, though, is the grand range of high-end denim, from folks including Joe's, Seven, Blue Cult and True Religion.

🏠 BLOOMINGDALE SOHO
Fashion & Accessories

☎ 212-729-5900; 504 Broadway; 🕙 10am-9pm Mon-Fri, 10am-8pm Sat, 11am-7pm Sun; 🚇 R, W to Prince St
A little more avant-garde than the 'real' Bloomies uptown, this Soho offshoot skews to the young, covering everything from beachwear to club duds.

🏠 BLUE BAG *Designer Bags*
☎ 212-966-8566; 266 Elizabeth St near Houston St; 🕙 11am-7pm Mon-Sat, noon-6pm Sun; 🚇 N, R, W to Prince St
Pick up the latest in handbag couture at this homey little shop that's often visited by the likes of J.Lo and Jessica Simpson, who love these leather creations. Bags are handcrafted, beautifully designed, and mostly priced at under $500.

🏠 BOND 07
Eyewear, Fashion & Accessories

☎ 212-677-8487; 7 Bond St; 🕙 11am-7pm Mon-Sat, noon-7pm Sun; 🚇 6 to Bleecker St

Selima Salaun's graceful glasses are the big draw, although Bond 07 also doubles as a chic boutique. Many a celebrity hides their orbs behind her perfectly tinted, boho chic styles. With more than 100 in stock, she can fit a pair to any face.

🏠 BOND 09 *Perfume*
☎ 212-228-1940; 9 Bond St; 🕑 11am-7pm Mon-Sat; 🚇 6 to Bleecker St
If you visit New York, you gotta smell like New York – that's the rule at Bond 09. It makes custom perfumes named after local nabes, like Eau de Noho, Chinatown and Chelsea Flowers. Don't worry – the fragrances actually smell good.

🏠 CHELSEA GIRL
Fashion & Accessories
☎ 212-343-1658; www.chelsea-girl.com; 63 Thompson St btwn Spring & Broome Sts; 🕑 noon-7pm; 🚇 C, E to Spring St
Get in there and dig – you never know what you'll find in this small, eclectic shop. Sometimes vintage Pucci prints and Dior dresses are sitting casually on a back rack.

🏠 DAFFY'S
Fashion & Accessories, Homewares
☎ 212-334-7444; www.daffys.com; 462 Broadway at Grand St; 🕑 10am-8pm Mon-Sat, noon-7pm Sun; 🚇 A, C, E to Canal St
Two floors of designer duds and accessories for men, women and

The latest Mac-cessories at Apple Store Soho

children (as well as a random handful of housewares), with prices that can be shockingly low. And the tags – like those at most discount shops – show you the item's suggested retail price, which, at an average of 50% off, just gives you even more incentive to buy.

🏠 HOUSING WORKS USED BOOK CAFE *Books*
☎ 212-334-3324; www.housingworks .org/usedbookcafe; 126 Crosby St; 🕑 10am-9pm Mon-Fri, noon-9pm Sat; 🚇 B, D, F, V to Broadway-Lafayette St
Relaxed, earthy and featuring a great selection of fabulous books

you can buy for a good cause (proceeds go to the city's HIV-positive and AIDS homeless communities), this spacious cafe is a great place to head to if you're looking to while away a few quiet afternoon hours.

🏠 JOHN VARVATOS
Fashion & Accessories
☎ 212-965-0700; 122 Spring St;
🕐 11am-7pm Mon-Sat, noon-6pm Sun;
🚇 R, W to Prince St
One of the city's most coveted menswear designers, John Varvatos creates a classic, timeless look – with a rock 'n' roll soul – in his stylish and handsome-fitting sports coats, jeans, footwear and accessories. Head downstairs for JV's younger, edgier persona.

🏠 MCNALLY ROBINSON
Books, Magazines
☎ 212-274-1160; www.mcnallyrobinson.com; 52 Prince St; 🕐 10am-10pm Mon-Sat, to 8pm Sun; 🚇 R, W to Prince St
Zone out in the cozy cafe (with wi-fi) inside this fully stacked indie store that has books on every conceivable subject – food, fiction, travel, architecture, LGBT, to name a few – as well as magazines and newspapers from around the world.

🏠 ORIGINAL LEVI'S STORE
Fashion & Accessories
☎ 646-613-1847; 536 Broadway at Spring St; 🕐 10am-8pm Mon-Sat, 11am-7pm Sun; 🚇 R, W to Prince St
Stock up on all your favorite Levi's jeans here – 501 button-fly, super-low boot-cut, zip-fly straight-leg cords – plus check out the great selection of Western shirts, tees, sweaters, jackets and always-evolving new styles for both men and women.

🏠 PRADA *Fashion & Accessories*
☎ 212-334-8888; 575 Broadway;
🕐 11am-7pm Mon-Sat, noon-6pm Sun;
🚇 N, R, W to Prince St
Don't come just for the shoes: check out the space. Dutch architect Rem Koolhaas has transformed the old Guggenheim into a fantasy land full of elegant hardwood floors and small dressing spaces. Don't be afraid to try something on – those translucent changing-room doors do fog up when you step inside.

🏠 SIGERSON MORRISON
Footwear
☎ 212-941-5404; www.sigersonmorrison.com; 242 Mott St & 28 Prince St;
🕐 11am-7pm Mon-Sat, noon-6pm Sun;
🚇 6 to Spring St, N to Prince St
Innovation combined with surprising practicality (who would have

thought we could have high-heeled flip-flops, or designer rubber boots to wear in the rain?), plus a love of splashy colors, have made Sigerson a hit. The store also carries Belle, a lower-priced line of its signature high-heeled, glamorous styles.

☐ TOPSHOP *Fashion*
☎ 212-966-9555; www.topshopnyc.com; 478 Broadway at Broome St; ⏰ 10am-9pm Mon-Sat, 11am-8pm Sun; ⊕ 6 to Spring St

The genius of Topshop is that the clothes always find that sweet spot between trendy and wearable. Everything's up-to-the-minute but still flattering and practical for the average person. Three floors for women, one dedicated to men, and all at fairly reasonable prices. Sales can get hectic: be prepared to dig for bargains.

☐ UNIS *Fashion & Accessories*
☎ 212-431-5533; 226 Elizabeth St; ⏰ noon-7pm; ⊕ N, R, W to Prince St

Unis remains a Nolita favorite for its fashionable but functional basics. You'll find slim, nicely cut jeans, soft button-downs and well-made jackets for the men, with feminine dresses and slender tops for the ladies.

☐ UNITED NUDE *Footwear*
☎ 212-274-9000; www.unitednude.m; 268 Elizabeth St near Houston St;

⏰ 11am-7pm Mon-Sat, noon-8pm Sun; ⊕ N, R, W to Prince St

The flagship store is stocked with improbably beautiful and eye-catching footwear – flamboyant, classical, business-oriented and sporty. Whether you want strappy sandals, toweringly high stilettos or a solid pair of wedge-heeled pumps, you'll score here. The store has three basic groupings – Classics, Ultra Collection and Mono Series – and within those categories are a variety of shoe types.

🍴 EAT

🍴 BITE *Organic Snacks* $
☎ 212-431-0301; 335 Lafayette St at Bleecker St; ⏰ 8am-8pm Mon-Fri, noon-8pm Sat & Sun; ⊕ 6 to Bleecker St; ♿ Ⓥ ⚲

Bite specializes in vegan, vegetarian and carnivore-friendly fare perfect for a quick breakfast or lunch. Roll up to the window and get your salad or sandwich to go, or step into the tiny, triangle-shaped shop for a seat.

🍴 BLUE RIBBON BRASSERIE
American Comfort $$
☎ 212-274-0404; www.blueribbonrestaurants.com; 97 Sullivan St near Spring St; ⏰ dinner; ⊕ C, E to Spring St; ♿ Ⓥ ⚲

Going strong since 1992, this comfort-food mecca is still a standout, especially for late-night dining, and the founding Bromberg Brothers have multiple offshoots: **Blue Ribbon Sushi** (119 Sullivan St), just a few doors away, **Blue Ribbon Bakery** (Map pp106–7; 35 Downing St) and **Blue Ribbon Downing Street Bar** (Map pp106–7; 34 Downing St). Blue Ribbon Brasserie's best-known dishes are the succulent, cheesy appetizers and sides; fresh, tangy salads; and delectable seafood, such as sweet and spicy catfish and red trout.

BOND ST *Japanese* $$$
☎ 212-777-2500; www.bondrestaurant. com; 6 Bond St; ⏰ 6-10:30pm Sun & Mon, to 11:30pm Tue-Sat; ⊕ 6 to Bleecker St; ⛧ **V** ⛧
Move over Nobu, this is the new kid in town. Actually, Bond St has been around awhile, but it's been kept a secret by sushi lovers. À la carte rolls include spicy yellowtail with red-pepper miso, spicy tuna with chili mayonnaise, sesame-crusted shrimp with orange curry dressing and hot eel with diced almond. There are also mains, nigiri and sashimi plates, and a full-on tasting *omakase* (chef's choice) menu.

CAFÉ GITANE
Moroccan Bistro $
☎ 212-334-9552; www.cafegitanenyc. com; 242 Mott St; ⏰ 9am-midnight Sun-Thu, to 12:30am Fri & Sat; ⊕ N, R, W to Prince St

Clear the Gauloise smoke from your eyes and blink twice if you think you're in Paris – Gitane has that louche vibe. Label-conscious shoppers love this authentic bistro, with its dark, aromatic coffee and dishes such as yellowfin tuna seviche, spicy meatballs in tomato turmeric sauce with a boiled egg, Greek salad on focaccia and heart-of-palm salad, with plenty of lusty wines.

CECI CELA *Patisserie* $
☎ 212-274-9179; www.cecicelanyc. com; 55 Spring St near Lafayette St; ⏰ 7:30am-8pm Mon-Thu, Sat & Sun, to 10pm Fri; ⊕ 6 to Spring St; ⛧
Tiny and narrow, this French patisserie has all sorts of scrumptious treats: *pains aux chocolats*, *chaussons aux pommes*, *pains aux raisins* and brioches, to name but a few. There's also fruit tarts, pies and crème brûlée – all made with 'pure' butter, the chef says. There's space in the back to sit and eat.

IL BUCO *Italian* $$$
☎ 212-533-1932; 47 Bond St btwn Bowery & Lafayette St; ⏰ lunch & dinner Tue-Sun; ⊕ B, D, F, V to Broadway-Lafayette St, 6 to Bleecker St
This magical nook is a real charmer – it boasts hanging copper pots, kerosene lamps and antique furniture, plus a stunning menu and wine list. Sink your teeth

into seasonal and ever-changing highlights like white polenta with braised broccoli rabe and anchovies, homemade pappardelle with a mélange of mushrooms, and a succulent Dijon-crusted lamb chop.

IVO & LULU Caribbean $
☎ 212-226-4399; 558 Broome St near Varick St; ⏰ dinner (cash only); ◉ C, E to Spring St, 1 to Canal St; ♿ Ⓥ ♨
A tiny storefront shop run by two French Caribbean natives, featuring organic products, quick and simple veggie-friendly dishes and some duck, chicken and seafood specialties. There's no liquor license but you can bring a bottle of whatever you want and they'll uncork it for no fee.

LA ESQUINA Mexican $$
☎ 646-613-6700; www.esquinanyc.com; 114 Kenmare St; ⏰ 24hr; ◉ 6 to Spring St
This mega-popular and quirky little spot is housed in a former greasy spoon that sits within the neat little triangle formed by Cleveland Pl and Lafayette St. It's three places really: a stand-while-you-eat taco window, a casual Mexican cafe and, downstairs, a cozy, overly hip cave of a dining room that requires reservations. Standouts include chorizo tacos, rubbed pork tacos and mango and jicama salads,

among other authentic and delicious options (most of which are also available upstairs at the anyone-welcome area).

PINCHE TAQUERIA
Mexican $
☎ 212-625-0090; www.pinchetaqueria.us; 227 Mott St btwn Prince & Spring Sts; ⏰ 11am-11pm Mon-Thu, to midnight Fri & Sat, to 8pm Sun; ◉ 6 to Spring St; ♨
Dig into authentic Mexican tacos, tostadas, burritos, quesadillas and more (your choice of veggies, fish, chicken or meat), topped with fresh yuca fries and guacamole, and wash it all down with horchata. Crowded and upbeat, Pinche is a great find on a hot, hungry afternoon. Try the Pinche at 333 Lafayette St (situated next to Bite; p85) if this one's too crowded.

TURKS AND FROGS TRIBECA Turkish $$
☎ 212-966-4774; www.turksandfrogs.com; 458 Greenwich St near Desbrosses St; ⏰ lunch & dinner; ◉ A, C, E, 1 to Canal St; ♿
A tongue-in-cheek name that refers to the Turkish and French antiques that decorate this winsome bistro (run by the same folks who own the Turks and Frogs wine bar in the West Village). While the decor is mixed, the food's unabashedly Turkish:

meze appetizers, endless varieties of hummus, eggplant and olives, plus great mains such as ground lamb dumplings, red mullet with arugula, thinly sliced oregano lamb, or chunks of lamb in tomato sauce with baby eggplant.

☖ DRINK
☖ CHINATOWN BRASSERIE
Bar

☎ 212-533-7000; www.chinatown brasserie.com; 380 Lafayette St near Great Jones St; ☺ lunch & dinner; ⑥ 6 to Bleecker St, N, R, W to Astor Pl; ⑤ Ⓥ

The dining areas are huge and sprawling and marked by pagoda decor and hanging Chinese lanterns, and diners can nosh for hours on the dim sum delights. The bar is just as beautiful (and much less taxing on wallet and patience), and the crowd is eclectic and fun.

☖ EAR INN *Bar*

☎ 212-431-9750; http://earinn.com; 326 Spring St btwn Greenwich & Washington Sts; ☺ noon-4am; ⑥ C, E to Spring St

Weekly reading series, live music and history are the main features of this 1817 neighborhood bar. It's in the James Brown House (the James Brown, aide to George Washington, not Soul Brother No 1), and is the preferred dive of sanitation workers, stressed-out Wall Streeters and local folk in need of a drink.

☖ MERCBAR *Bar*

☎ 212-966-2727; www.mercbar.com; 151 Mercer St btwn W Houston & Prince Sts; ☺ 5pm-2am Sun-Tue, to 4am Wed-Sat; ⑥ R, W to Prince St

An intimate hideaway where you can actually hold a conversation without having to scream over the soundtrack is a big draw for the after-work publishing crowd, who like to sip martinis and rub tweedy elbows.

☖ PEGU CLUB *Bar*

☎ 212-473-7348; www.peguclub.com; 77 W Houston St near Wooster St; ☺ 5pm-2am; ⑥ B, D, F, V, 6 to Broadway-Lafayette St

Head on up to the 2nd floor and step inside this naval-themed bar, which prides itself on its out-of-this-world cocktails. Try a Gin Gin Mule, Pisco Sour, Lemon Drop, or any number of martinis, manhattans and vodka mixes.

☖ TOAD HALL *Bar*

☎ 212-431-8145; 57 Grand St near W Broadway; ☺ noon-2am; ⑥ A, C, E, J, M, N, Q, R, W, Z, 1, 6 to Canal St

Old-fashioned hospitality is the norm at Toad Hall (hence the sign in the door: 'Be nice or leave'). There's plenty of wine, beer and good cheer to be had, and if you get hit with the munchies, bartenders have a handy supply of takeout menus on hand to order in.

▼ XICALA *Bar*
☎ 212-219-0599; 151 Elizabeth St;
🕙 5pm-2am; ⊕ 6 to Spring St; ♿

There's a Cuban trio on Wednesday nights who add to the already-festive atmosphere at this quaint, tiny tapas and wine bar. The strawberry sangria is the house signature drink, but the Riojas and Jerez sherries are just as delicious.

★ PLAY

★ ANGELIKA FILM CENTER
Cinema
☎ 212-995-2000; www.angelikafilm center.com; 18 W Houston St at Mercer St; tickets $10-14; 🕙 daily; ⊕ B, D, F, V to Broadway-Lafayette St; ♿ 🚹

Angelika specializes in foreign and independent films and has some quirky charms (the rumble of the subway, long lines and occasionally bad sound). But its roomy cafe is a great place to meet and the beauty of its Stanford White–designed, beaux-arts building undeniable.

★ BOTANICA *Basement Bar*
☎ 212-343-7251; 47 E Houston St btwn Mott & Mulberry Sts; 🕙 daily; ⊕ 6 to Bleecker St, B, D, F, V to Broadway-Lafayette St

Botanica looks like a tough hangout, but in reality it's anything but. Drinks are a bargain, especially during the nightly 5pm to 8pm happy hour, and when the late-night music starts and people start to sway to upbeat tunes, the unpretentious atmosphere gets even more buzzy and stress-free.

★ HERE *Theater*
☎ 212-352-3101; www.here.org; 145 Sixth Ave btwn Spring & Broome Sts; ⊕ C, E to Canal St

An acclaimed and perpetually underfunded theater group that supports the independent, the innovative and the experimental, Here helped develop Basil Twist's *Symphonie Fantastique,* Hazelle Goodman's *On Edge* and Trey Lyford and Geoff Sobelle's *all wear bowlers*. Production times and prices vary, but the onsite cafe offers a great opportunity to check things out.

★ SWAY LOUNGE *Nightclub*
☎ 212-620-5220; www.swaylounge. com; 305 Spring St; cover charge; 🕙 9pm-3am Mon & Thu; ⊕ C, E to Spring St

Seductive and sleek with an elegant Moroccan decor, Sway's got a tough door policy on busy nights (er, pretty much every night). It's small, but there's room to dance to '80s on Thursday nights, rock and hip-hop Fridays, and DJs like Mark Ronson and DJ Herschel other nights.

>EAST VILLAGE

Anarchy still reigns in the East Village, but now the tension is over rents and housing instead of civil rights. Full of punks, NYU students, Wall St brokers, professors, philosophers, poets, hustlers, dancers and ditch-diggers – there are layers of class struggle, class-consciousness and revolutionary leanings. If the cause that everyone rallies behind has more to do with individual survival than universal issues, that's just how it goes in today's East Village, which has traded its hard-core activist roots for some kick-ass nightlife.

But not all is lost: amid the nightly limo crawls up and down Second Ave, the crazy dancing, drinking and dishing, people still step into KGB Bar (former Socialist headquarters) for its weekly reading series, they still attend sit-ins and walk-outs and protest rent hikes, and they still fight against high-rise development with all their might. It's refreshing to know that facades may change, but at least in the East Village, the collective spirit remains the same.

EAST VILLAGE

🅒 SEE
6th and B Garden	1	G4
Colonnade Row	2	B4
Gallery 440	3	B4
Grace Church	4	B3
Merchant's House Museum	5	B5
Russian & Turkish Baths	6	E3
St Mark's in the Bowery	7	D3
Tompkins Square Park	8	F3
Ukrainian Museum	9	C4

🅐 SHOP
Apt 141	10	B2
AuH2O	11	D4
Cadillac Castle	12	D3
John Derian	13	C5
John Derian's Dry Goods	14	C5
Odin	15	D2

Other Music	16	B5
Tokio 7	17	D4
Trader Joe's	18	B1

🍴 EAT
Artichoke Basille's Pizza	19	D1
B & H Dairy	20	D4
Caracas Arepas Bar	21	E4
EU	22	F5
Kanoyama	23	D2
Lavagna	24	F4
Momofuku Ko	25	E3
Momofuku Noodle Bar	26	E3
Momofuku Ssam	27	D2
S'Mac	28	D2
Tuck Shop	29	D6

🍸 DRINK
11th Street Bar	30	F2
Angel's Share	31	C3

Bowery Wine Company	32	C6
DBA	33	E5
In Vino	34	F5
KGB Bar	35	C5
Louis 649	36	G3
Nublu	37	H5

⭐ PLAY
Easternbloc	38	F4
Joseph Papp Public Theater	39	B5
La MaMa ETC	40	C5
Nuyorican Poets Café	41	G5
Orpheum Theater	42	D3
Pyramid Club	43	F4
Webster Hall	44	B2

Please see over for map

◉ SEE

◉ 6TH AND B GARDEN

www.6bgarden.org; E 6th St & Ave B;
🕐 **1-6pm Sat & Sun;** Ⓜ **6 to Astor Pl**
Nature reigns supreme at this quiet corner lot, once a squalid, infested tangle of dirt and roots. Residents turned it into a 17,000-sq-ft section of neat plots, vines, sculptures and flowers. Garden members fought long and hard to keep the city from selling the land out from under them, and now it's a city oasis everyone enjoys.

◉ COLONNADE ROW

428-434 Lafayette St btwn Astor Pl &
E 4th St; Ⓜ **6 to Astor Pl**
Once there were nine Greek Revival mansions in this row; now there are four. All were built in 1833, out of stone, the work done by prisoners from the upstate Sing Sing prison, and all have ornate, detailed touches on their classic facades. Some of the other great buildings you'll see around Colonnade Row are part of Cooper Union, including its great hall, where Abraham Lincoln once made an anti-slavery speech and Barack Obama gave a major economic speech during the 2008 presidential primary.

◉ GALLERY 440

☎ **212-979-5800; www.gallery440**
m; 440 Lafayette St; admission free;
🕐 **10am-6pm Mon-Fri, by appt Sat;**
Ⓜ **6 to Bleecker St**
One-stop shopping for art lovers or art browsers. Located above the famed Wooster Gallery, Gallery 440 has an eclectic roster of artists that it represents, and always has something fresh hanging in its front room.

◉ GRACE CHURCH

www.gracechurchnyc.org; 800-804
Broadway at E 10th St; 🕐 **10am-5pm,**
services daily; Ⓜ **R, W to 8th St-NYU, 6**
to Astor Pl
Nestled into a surprisingly verdant patch of land not far from Astor Pl, Grace Church's ethereal Gothic Revival design is quite an eye-catcher. Designed by James Renwick Jr, it's made of marble quarried by inmates in the upstate Sing Sing prison. Grace Church is also a much-sought-after school, and students love the Harry Potter–esque feel of its hidden nooks, stained-glass windows and old libraries.

◉ MERCHANT'S HOUSE MUSEUM

☎ **212-777-1089; www.merchants**
house.com; 29 E 4th St btwn Lafayette
St & Bowery; adult $10, senior & student
$5; 🕐 **noon-5pm Thu-Mon;** Ⓜ **6 to**
Bleecker St
Get a glimpse of how wealthy businessmen lived in New York in

NEIGHBORHOODS

EAST VILLAGE

the 1800s at this local museum. Drug importer Seabury Tredwell lived in this house (built in 1831), and his family has preserved the original furnishings and clothing, and even his kitchen sink. It's a remarkable glimpse into the past.

☯ RUSSIAN & TURKISH BATHS
☎ 212-473-8806; www.russianturkish baths.com; 268 E 10th St btwn First Ave & Ave A; per visit $30; ☉ noon-10pm Mon, Tue, Thu & Fri, 10am-10pm Wed, 9am-10pm Sat, 8am-10pm Sun; ☺ L to First Ave, 6 to Astor Pl

Since 1892 this has been the place to go for a romp in steam baths, in an ice-cold plunge pool, in a sauna and on a sundeck. All-day access includes the use of lockers, locks, robes, towels and slippers, and an onsite Russian cafe has fresh juices, potato-olive salad, blintzes and borscht. The spas are women-only from 10am to 2pm on Wednesdays and men-only from 8am to 2pm Saturdays.

☯ ST MARK'S IN THE BOWERY
☎ 212-674-6377; http://stmarksbowery .org; 131 E 10th St at Second Ave; ☉ 10am-6pm Mon-Fri; ☺ 6 to Astor Pl, L to Third Ave

Still a working Episcopal church, St Mark's was built in 1799 on farm land owned by Dutch governor

Tompkins Sq Park is a leafy spot with a feisty history

Peter Stuyvesant – he's buried in the crypt below. Sunday services are a big draw, but St Mark's is also revered for its cultural contributions. Regular poetry readings such as **Poetry Project** (☎ 212-674-0910) and dance events like **Danspace** (☎ 212-674-8194) culminate every New Year's Day in a 24-hour nonstop orgy of poetry, song and performance.

⊙ TOMPKINS SQUARE PARK
www.nycgovparks.org; E 7th & 10th Sts btwn Aves A & B; ⏱ 6am-midnight; ⊕ 6 to Astor Pl; ♿
In 1874, 7000 angry workers took on 1600 police in this leafy enclave, and history's been repeated many times since then – Tompkins Sq Park lies at the heart of every East Village rebellion. This wide, pretty, green spot is pastoral by day, communally welcoming at night, and still a bit sketchy in the wee hours.

⊙ UKRAINIAN MUSEUM
☎ 212-228-0110; www.ukrainian museum.org; 222 E 6th St btwn Second & Third Aves; adult $8, senior & student $6, child under 12 free; ⏱ 11:30am-5pm Wed-Sun; ⊕ F, V
to Lower East Side-Second Ave, L to First Ave
Eastern Europeans have a long history in the East Village, and Ukrainians in particular staked a

claim here. The Ukrainian Museum documents that history and showcases its collection of folk art, ceramics, metalwork, woven textiles and traditional Ukrainian Easter eggs.

🛍 SHOP

🛍 APT 141 *Boutique*
☎ 212-982-4227; www.threefreedesign .com; 141 E 13th St; ⏱ noon-8pm Wed-Sat, 1-8pm Sun, appt only Mon & Tue; ⊕ L, N, Q, R, W, 4, 5, 6 to 14th St-Union Sq
Youthful, fresh frocks in vivid prints, attractive stripes and even whimsical polka dots are hand-sewn out of materials like bamboo, silk, linen, lycra and cotton. Apt 141 has a knack for creating flattering urban wrap dresses and well-cut skirts that are the epitome of professional chic.

🛍 AUH2O *Boutique*
☎ 212-466-0844; www.auh2odesigns. com; 84 E 7th St btwn First & Second Aves; ⏱ 1-8pm Tue-Sun; ⊕ N, R, W to 8th St-NYU, 6 to Astor Pl
Owner Kate Goldwater takes recycled shirts, tees and dresses and turns them into lovely one-of-a-kind pieces that she'll custom fit for you (free of charge). Everything is sewn by hand and she frequently adorns her shirts with political slogans (pro-feminist creeds abound).

CADILLAC CASTLE
Fashion & Accessories

☎ 212-475-0406; 333 E 9th St; ☽ noon-8pm; ⓑ 6 to Astor Pl, L to First Ave

Vintage shoes, bags, dresses and accessories at fantastic prices are the big draw at Cadillac Castle (as well as the owner's winsome dog). Lots of big-name merchandise – modern designers as well as the classics like Chanel – to be found.

JOHN DERIAN
Homewares, Curios

☎ 212-677-3917; 6 E 2nd St; ☽ noon-7pm Tue-Sun; ⓑ F, V to Lower East Side-Second Ave

Looking for one-of-a-kind plates, paperweights, coasters, lamps, bowls and vases? Swing by John Derian's shop. The atmospheric store hides many other curiosities, such as T-shirts with roguish 19th-century graphics, handmade terra-cotta pottery, linoleum-cut prints and papier-mâché figurines. For eclectic bed linens and such, visit the nearby **John Derian's Dry Goods** (☎ 212-677-8408; 10 E 2nd St; ☽ noon-7pm Tue-Sun).

ODIN *Fashion & Accessories*

☎ 212-475-0666; http://odinnewyork .com; 328 E 11th St; ☽ noon-8pm; ⓑ L to First Ave, L, N, Q, R, W, 4, 5, 6 to 14th St-Union Sq

Fashion-forward men flock to cheery, chippy Odin, full of artistic

T-shirts and avant-garde designs that are sure to turn heads. Although the atmosphere is definitely downtown chic, you can find anything here, from hippy head gear to Monday-morning suits.

OTHER MUSIC *Music*

☎ 212-477-8150; www.othermusic.com; 15 E 4th St; ☽ noon-9pm Mon-Fri, to 8pm Sat, to 7pm Sun; ⓑ 6 to Bleecker St

An indie-run store that carries new and used offbeat lounge, psychedelic, electronica, indie-rock and more, staffed with helpful, friendly music geeks.

TOKIO 7
Fashion & Accessories

☎ 212-353-8443; 83 E 7th St near First Ave; ☽ noon-8:30pm Mon-Sat, to 8pm Sun; ⓑ 6 to Astor Pl

This revered, hip consignment shop, down a few steps on a shady stretch of E 7th St, has good-condition designer labels for men and women at some fairly hefty prices. Best of all is the selection of men's suits – there's nearly always something tip-top in the $100 to $150 range that's worth trying on.

TRADER JOE'S *Food & Drink*

☎ 212-529-4612; 142 E 14th St; ☽ 9am-10pm; ⓑ L, N, Q, R, W, 4, 5, 6 to 14th St-Union Sq

Most people love Trader Joe's, it seems. It's a slightly smaller

The East Village is full of punks, poets, professors and philosophers, and hats too

version of Whole Foods with fair-trade coffee, organic produce, beef and poultry, and an odd smattering of exotic goods not normally stocked in stores. In fact, so many people love the Trader Joe's on E 14th St that shopping there takes enormous patience; the store is small and awkwardly laid out, and crowds quickly form.

🍴 EAT

🍴 ARTICHOKE BASILLE'S PIZZA Pizza $

212-228-2004; 328 E 14th St btwn & Second Aves; 🕐 lunch & dinner;

⊕ L, N, Q, R, W, 4, 5, 6 to 14th St-Union Sq; 🚻 V 🚻
Some say this pizzeria is in the East Village, others Union Sq but, hey, wherever Artichoke Basille's is, count yourself lucky to be there. Run by two Italian guys from Staten Island, the pizza here is authentic, tangy and piled high with all sorts of toppings. The signature pie is a rich, cheesy treat with artichokes and spinach; the plain Sicilian is thinner, with emphasis solely on the crisp crust and savory sauce. Hours are from around noon to about midnight, but sometimes

B & H DAIRY
Kosher Dairy $

☎ 212-505-8065; 127 Second Ave btwn St Marks Pl & E 7th St; ☾ breakfast, lunch & dinner; ⊕ 6 to Astor Pl; ♿ Ⓥ ⚲

Fresh, vegetarian, homemade Kosher fare, including six types of soup on offer daily with a big knot of challah bread. Join the crowd at the bar and try to grab someone's attention – you've got to speak up here, or you'll go hungry!

CARACAS AREPAS BAR
Arepas, South American $

☎ 212-529-2314; www.caracasarepas bar.com; 93 1/2 E 7th St btwn First Ave & Ave A; ☾ noon-11pm; ⊕ 6 to Astor Pl; ♿ Ⓥ ⚲

Cram into this tiny joint and order a crispy, hot *arepa* (corn tortilla stuffed with veggies and meat) such as the Pepi Queen (chicken and avocado) or La Pelua (beef and cheddar). You can choose from 17 types of *arepa* (plus empanadas and daily specials like oxtail soup), served in baskets with a side of *nata* (sour cream) and fried plantains.

EU
Pan-European Pub Food $$$

☎ 212-254-2900; www.theeunyc.com; 235 E 4th St btwn Aves A & B; ☾ dinner daily, brunch Sat & Sun; ⊕ F, V to Lower East Side-Second Ave

The gastropub craze has come to the East Village, but with a mini-malist twist (in terms of decor). EU (yes, that stands for European Union) has old-world comfort food such as gnocchi with braised capon, boar with Swiss-chard

it doesn't open until 3pm. Lines usually form fast.

YO, MOMOFUKU

New Yorkers can't get enough of David Chang's Momofuku empire, famous for fantastic raw bars, ramen noodles, crispy sweetbreads, grilled octopus salads, grilled beef tongue and those deli-cious *bib bim bap* (rice dish with veggies) lunch boxes. Getting into his most popular incarnation, **Momofuku Ko** (www.momofuku.com; 163 First Ave near E 10th St; ☾ lunch & dinner; ⊕ L to First Ave, 6 to Astor Pl), takes dedication: bookings are done online and a week in advance. There's also **Momofuku Ssam** (207 2nd Ave near E 13th St; ⊕ 6 to Astor Pl), with creative Asian fusion, **Momofuku Noodle Bar** (171 First Ave near E 10th St; ⊕ L to First Ave, 6 to Astor Pl), famous for ramen, and Chang's newest gem, **Ma Peche** (15 W 56th St btwn Sixth & Fifth Aves; ⊕ F to 57th St), a Midtown, French-influenced eatery open for breakfast, lunch and din-ner in the Chambers Hotel. For something sweet, try Chang's **Milk Bar** (at Ma Peche in Midtown & Ssam in the East Village; ☾ 9am-midnight) for its addictive cookies, cakes, pies and shak fondue, and grilled octopus with braised quince. There's plenty of choice beyond the hearty mains, too – like a small tapas menu, a raw bar and a range of charcuterie plates.

KANOYAMA Sushi $
212-777-5266; http://kanoyama.com; 175 Second Ave near E 11th St; dinner; L to Third Ave, L, N, Q, R, W, 4, 5, 6 to 14th St-Union Sq;

No-fuss, no-muss sushi with fresh daily specials in the heart of the East Village, Kanoyama is a local favorite that so far has been overlooked by the city's big-name food critics (that might explain its unpretentious air). You can order sushi à la carte or in rolls, or choose from the many tempura plates.

LAVAGNA Italian $$
212-979-1005; www.lavagnanyc.com; 545 E 5th St near Ave B; dinner; F, V to Lower East Side-Second Ave;

Dark wood, flickering candles and a fiery glow from a somewhat open kitchen help make homey Lavagna a late-night hideaway for lovers. But it's laid-back enough to make it appropriate for children, at least in the early hours before the smallish space fills up. Delicious pastas, thin-crust pizzas and a few eclectic mains, such as rabbit ragout, are standard fare.

S'MAC American $
212-358-7912; www.smacnyc.com; 345 E 12th St at First Ave; 1-10pm Mon, 11am-11pm Tue-Thu & Sun, 11am-1am Fri & Sat; 6 to Astor Pl;

If you're only going to do one thing, you've got to do it well – and S'Mac hits the spot with mac 'n' cheese lovers. The all-American has cheddar and Vermont jack cheese, with bacon if you like. Or, try the Gruyère mac 'n' cheese and the Manchego cheese and Cajun macs.

TUCK SHOP Australian $
212-979-5200; www.tuckshopnyc.com; 68 E 1st St near First Ave; 8am-2am Mon-Thu, 8am-5am Fri & Sat, noon-10pm Sun; F, V to Lower East Side-Second Ave;

Homemade pasties, sausage rolls and sandwiches of all sorts are the rule at Tuck, where everything's done organic and fresh. Daily pie specials include a chook curry pie, shepherd's pie, vegan pie, tiger prawn pie, chili pie and more. Desserts are a treat, including the Dame Edna delight and Peter Allen pie, but perhaps the best is the early morning breakfast: lashings of meat with fresh eggs and cheese, served with steaming cups of fair-trade organic coffee.

DRINK

11TH STREET BAR *Bar*

☎ 212-982-3929; www.11thstbar.com; 510 E 11th St btwn Aves A & B; ⏰ noon-2am; Ⓜ F, V to Lower East Side–Second Ave

Couches, a big bar and a crazy, rowdy clientele made up of East Village hippies and young students make 11th Street Bar the de facto community hangout.

ANGEL'S SHARE *Bar*

☎ 212-777-5415; 2nd fl, 8 Stuyvesant St near Third Ave & E 9th St; ⏰ 5pm-midnight; Ⓜ 6 to Astor Pl

Show up early and snag a seat at this hidden gem, behind a Japa-

nese restaurant on the same floor. It's quiet and elegant with creative cocktails, but you can't stay if you don't have a table, and they tend to go fast.

BOWERY WINE COMPANY *Wine Bar*

☎ 212-614-0800; www.bowerywineco.com; 13 E 1st St; ⏰ 5pm–1am Mon-Thu, 5pm-2am Fri, noon-2am Sat, noon–1am Sun; Ⓜ F, V to Lower East Side–Second Ave

Wine lovers can't be better served than at the Bowery Bar, which offers several dozen delicious vinos – some local, others esoteric – from a rotating menu, plus live jazz, room to dance if the spirit takes you, as well as delightful appetizers.

DBA *Pub*

☎ 212-475-5097; www.drinkgoodstuff .com; 41 First Ave; ⏰ 1pm-4am; Ⓜ F, V to Lower East Side–Second Ave

While you're here, see if you can get owner Ray Deter to tell you if the name stands for 'doing business as,' 'don't bother asking' or 'drink better ale.' The third choice is the most obvious, since Deter specializes in British-style ales in casks. He's got more than 150 at hand, including microbrews like 'High and Mighty Ale.' Other standouts are the single malts and smooth tequilas. A garden in the back doubles as a beer garden.

DBA stands for...

▼ IN VINO *Bar*

☎ 212-539-1011; www.invino-ny.com; 215 E 4th St; 🕐 5-11pm Sun-Thu, to midnight Fri & Sat; ⊕ F, V to Lower East Side-Second Ave

Step off the hectic streets for a second and chill out at In Vino, a cavelike little space with hundreds of Italian wines to choose from and a calm, tranquil atmosphere. Jazzy music is the norm, sometimes live, sometimes piped in, and small plates of Italian snacks – paninis, olives, anchovies – are readily available.

▼ KGB BAR *Bar*

☎ 212-505-3360; 2nd fl, 85 E 4th St near Second Ave; 🕐 5pm-1am; ⊕ 6 to Astor Pl, F, V to Lower East Side-Second Ave

Back in the 1940s, this space housed the local headquarters of a Ukrainian socialist party; its dingy red walls and bright yellow propaganda banners are the real thing. KGB reinvented itself as a literary bar a few years ago and hasn't looked back; its readings are marquee events, and the crowd laps up the vodka.

▼ LOUIS 649 *Bar*

☎ 212-673-1190; www.louis649.com; 649 E 9th St near Ave C; 🕐 6pm-4am; ⊕ L to First Ave

Bronx-born Zachary Sharaga's bar is a local standout in the East Village, beloved by its patrons for the affordable prices and down-home, no-frills decor. Tuesday nights are free tasting nights, when the owner brings in a liquor specialist to talk about their brew and liberally pours free shots. Having done away with its tradition of live jazz, the music's now an eclectic mix of pop, hip-hop and rock from whoever's brought an iPod.

▼ NUBLU *Bar, Club*

☎ 212-375-1500; www.nublu.net; 62 Ave C; 🕐 8pm-4am; ⊕ 6 to Astor Pl, F, V to Lower East Side-Second Ave

Don't back away from the graffiti-scarred exterior – you're at the right place if you see the blue light at the door. Nublu doesn't believe in signage (or paint jobs, apparently), but inside you'll quickly adjust to the hardwood floors, wide-open French doors to a back patio, and chilled-out crowds. On weekends, things get hot and sweaty at night, as the whole club starts to get a little dance-happy.

⭐ PLAY

▣ EASTERNBLOC *Club*

☎ 212-777-2555; www.easternblocnyc.com; 505 E 6th St btwn Aves A & B; 🕐 7pm-4am; ⊕ F, V to Lower East Side-Second Ave

The Red Scare is still among us – at least at Easternbloc, which boasts a kitschy Iron Curtain theme replete with Bettie Page videos, Communist-era posters and adorable Eastern European–looking bartenders. The go-go dancers appear Thursday through Saturday.

⭐ JOSEPH PAPP PUBLIC THEATER *Theater*
☎ 212-260-2400; www.publictheater.org; 425 Lafayette St; ⏱ hours vary; ⓔ N, R to 8th St-NYU, 6 to Astor Pl

Every summer the Papp presents its fabulous, and eagerly awaited, Shakespeare in the Park productions at Central Park's Delacorte Theater – one of its many contributions to the city's cultural tapestry. Established by a wealthy progressive more than 50 years ago, Joseph Papp Public Theater also houses the highly popular Joe's Pub, which has live music and spoken-word performances.

⭐ LA MAMA ETC *Theater*
☎ 212-475-7710; www.lamama.org; 74A E 4th St; ⏱ hours vary; ⓔ F, V to Lower East Side-Second Ave

A long-standing home for onstage experimentation (the ETC stands for Experimental Theater Club), La MaMa is now a three-theater complex with a cafe, an art gallery and a separate studio building that features cutting-edge dramas, sketch comedy and readings of all kinds.

⭐ NUYORICAN POETS CAFÉ *Arts*
☎ 212-505-8183; www.nuyorican.org; 236 E 3rd St; ⏱ 6pm-1am Tue-Sun; ⓔ F to Lower East Side-Second Ave

A legendary club started in 1973 by Miguel Algarin, a Puerto Rican poet, the Nuyorican is home to hip-hop performances, poetry slams, plays, and film and video events. It's a piece of East Village history, but also a vibrant and still-relevant nonprofit arts organization (supported by proceeds from the cafe).

⭐ ORPHEUM THEATER *Theater*
☎ 212-477-2477; www.stomponline.com; 126 Second Ave at E 8th St; ⏱ hours vary; ⓔ F to Lower East Side-Second Ave; ♿ ♨

A Yiddish theater in the beginning of the 20th century, the Orpheum feeds off creative East Village energy. Currently it's home to *Stomp*, a dance-happy beat fest.

⭐ PYRAMID CLUB *Club*
☎ 212-228-4888; www.thepyramidclub.com; 101 Ave A; cover charge $5-10; ⏱ 11pm-4am Mon, 8:30pm-1am Tue & Sun, 9pm-4am Thu & Sat, 10pm-4am Fri; ⓔ F, V to Lower East Side-Second Ave

You'll find red lights strung up along a narrow bar, rather beat-up stools and sticky wooden floors, and if you like cheap drinks, loud bar mates and sweaty, unself-conscious dancing to '80s tunes, then Thursdays are for you. Gay night is on Friday.

⭐ **WEBSTER HALL** *Club*
☎ **212-353-1600; 125 E 11th St near Third Ave;** ⏱ **10pm–4am Thu–Sat;** Ⓜ **L, N, Q, R, W, 4, 5, 6 to 14th St-Union Sq**
The granddaddy of dancehalls, Webster Hall has been around so long it's being considered for landmark status. Following the old 'if it ain't broke, don't fix it' adage, what you'll get here are cheap drinks, eager young things ready to dance, pool tables for the more self-conscious and enough room to really work up a sweat.

>GREENWICH & WEST VILLAGE

Still charming after all these years, Greenwich Village holds a special place in New Yorkers' hearts. This once flamboyant and progressive toehold became a gentle old lady, albeit one with a decidedly unladylike past.

There's no pleasure equal to exploring this twisty little enclave on a sunny afternoon. Its quaint and quirky streets create oddly shaped store-fronts and misshapen cafes, and many of its brick buildings are historic landmarks. Edna St Vincent Millay lived at 75½ Barrow St for a while; her neighbor was William S Burroughs. They'd sometimes stop for a pint at Ear Inn (p88).

There are a few old-style cabaret bars and comedy clubs lining Seventh Ave, and some gay icons – the Duplex, the Monster and Stonewall – are still standing. It's easily the most romantic part of Manhattan.

GREENWICH & WEST VILLAGE

◉ SEE
Christopher Street Piers		
Hudson River Park	1	A5
LGBT Community Center	2	C1
New York University	3	G4
Sheridan Square	4	D3
Washington Mews	5	F3
Washington Square Park	6	F4
West 4th St Basketball Courts	7	E4

🛍 SHOP
CO Bigelow Chemists	8	E3
Duane Reade	9	E3
Ludivine	10	D4
Marc Jacobs	11	B3
Marc Jacobs	12	C3
Mick Margo	13	D4

Murray's Cheese	14	D4
Pleasure Chest	15	C2
Ricky's	16	E2
Verve	17	C3

🍴 EAT
Babbo	18	E3
Blue Hill New American	19	E3
Blue Ribbon Bakery	20	D5
Blue Ribbon Downing Street Bar	21	D5
Caffe Reggio	22	E4
Cru	23	F2
Ditch Plains	24	E5
Mas	25	D5
Minetta Tavern	26	E4
Pearl Oyster	27	E4
Spotted Pig	28	B3

🍸 DRINK
Art Bar	29	B1
Bar Next Door	30	E4
Employees Only	31	C4
Fat Cats	32	C3
Kettle of Fish	33	D3
Sullivan Room	34	F5

★ PLAY
55 Bar	35	D3
Cherry Lane Theater	36	C5
Comedy Cellar	37	E4
Duplex	38	D3
Film Forum	39	D6
Le Poisson Rouge	40	F5
SOBs	41	D6
Village Underground	42	E4
Village Vanguard	43	C2

Please see over for map

SEE

CHRISTOPHER STREET PIERS/HUDSON RIVER PARK

Christopher St & West Side Hwy; 1 to Christopher St-Sheridan Sq

Like so many places in the Village, the extreme west side was once a derelict eyesore used mostly as a cruising ground for quick, anonymous sex. Now it's a pretty waterside hangout, bisected by the Hudson River Park's slender bike and jogging paths, with great sunset views. It's still a place to cruise; now it's just much less dangerous.

NEW YORK UNIVERSITY

☎ 212-998-4636; www.nyu.edu; 50 W 4th St (information center); N, R, W to 8th St-NYU, 6 to Astor Pl

In 1831 Albert Gallatin (buried in the Trinity Church cemetery; p47), Secretary of Treasury under President Thomas Jefferson, founded an intimate center of higher learning open to all students, regardless of race or class. Now it's a mammoth urban campus filled with 50,000 students. Check out the main buildings around Washington Sq Park.

SHERIDAN SQUARE

Christopher St & Seventh Ave; 1 to Christopher St-Sheridan Sq

The shape of a triangle, Sheridan Sq isn't much more than a few park benches and some trees surrounded by an old-fashioned wrought-iron gate. But its location (the heart of gay Greenwich Village) has meant that it's witnessed every rally, demonstration and uprising that has contributed to New York's gay rights movement. It also holds two sets of slender white statues: a male couple and a female couple, holding hands and talking. Known as *Gay Liberation,* they are a tribute to the normalcy of gay life.

WASHINGTON MEWS

btwn Fifth Ave & University Pl & btwn E 8th St & Washington Sq Park; R, W to 8th St-NYU;

Private stables converted into homes line one side of the picturesque Washington Mews. Gaslights and horses have disappeared, but the tiny alley still embodies the essence of old New York. Famous residents have included writers Sherwood Anderson and Walter Lippman, and artist Gertrude Vanderbilt Whitney, founder of the Whitney Museum. It's surrounded now by New York University, which owns some of the properties.

WASHINGTON SQUARE PARK

www.washingtonsquareparkcouncil.org; Fifth Ave at Washington Sq N; A, B, C, D, E, F, V to W 4th St, R, W to 8th St-NYU, 6 to Astor Pl

This crazy place is the heart of what's left of bohemian life in

E 13th St

Newsbar
Internet
Cafe

W 12th St

E 12th St

W 11th St

E 11th St

Broadway

Fourth Ave

Sixth Ave (Avenue of the Americas)

16

W 10th St

E 10th St

Fifth Ave

University Pl

W 9th St

23 ⑂

E 9th St

8

W 8th St

E 8th St

8th St-
NYU

M

Astor Pl

5

GREENWICH
VILLAGE

Astor Pl

Waverly Pl

18

Washington Sq North

Waverly Pl

Colonnade Row

9

Washington Pl

19

Washington Sq West

Washington Sq
Park

Washington Sq East

Greene St

Mercer St

7

6

3

W 4th St

Washington Sq South

W 4th St

E 4th St

W 4th St

87

University Pl

New York
University

NOHO

30

W 3rd St

Great Jones St

42

22

37

See Soho,
Noho & Nolita
Map pp78–9

Minetta La

26

Bond St

Minetta St

34

LaGuardia Pl

40

Bleecker St

Bleecker St

M

MacDougal St

Sullivan St

Thompson St

Mercer St

Lafayette St

24

Sixth Ave (Avenue of the Americas)

W Houston St

Broadway

Broadway-
Lafayette St

M

Prince St

W Broadway

Wooster St

Greene St

Broadway

Crosby St

Jersey St

NEIGHBORHOODS

GREENWICH & WEST VILLAGE

Greenwich Village. But, if the city has its way, the park will undergo a radical redesign: it will have a 4ft fence around it; the famed Garibaldi fountain where, rumor has it, Bob Dylan sang his first folk song will be relocated; and the entire site will be raised 4ft to ground level, disturbing those who were buried underneath it when it was a cemetery and a hanging spot (check out the hanging elm on the northwest corner). Community groups filed a lawsuit and won a stay; the city has appealed, and it will be years before a decision is made. Enjoy it while you can. Regular events are listed on the website.

The one not to miss? Quiet Disco on weekend afternoons – 300 people dancing to iPod tunes only they can hear.

◎ WEST 4TH STREET BASKETBALL COURTS

Sixth Ave at W 4th St; ⏲ **hours vary;** ◉ **A, C, E, F, V to W 4th St**

Don't step into 'the Cage,' as this fenced-in court is called, without bringing your A game; these guys play to win in fierce competitive games. You can have just as much fun watching in the 10-deep crowds that gather, especially on weekends. In summer the W 4th St Summer Pro-Classic League hits the scene.

Washington Sq Park: formerly cemetery, execution site and concert venue – and still an NYC must-see

SHOP

◆ CO BIGELOW CHEMISTS
Drugstore

☎ 212-533-2700; 414 Sixth Ave btwn W 8th & W 9th Sts; 🕑 7:30am-9pm Mon-Fri, 8:30am-7pm Sat, 8:30am-5pm Sun; ⊕ A, B, C, D, E, F, V to W 4th St

There are cheaper and more efficient drugstores all over the city, but none have the charm of Bigelow's, America's 'oldest apothecary' if you believe the managers. It's still got a working pharmacy, but it's most famous for its organic beauty products such as witch-hazel salves and honey-bee balms.

◆ LUDIVINE *Boutique*

☎ 646-336-6576; www.boutiqueludi vine.com; 172 W 4th St btwn Cornelia & Jones Sts; 🕑 11am-7:30pm Mon-Sat, noon-6pm Sun; ⊕ A, B, C, D, E, F, V to W 4th St, 1 to Christopher St-Sheridan Sq

C'est très chic inside this cozy West Village shop, full of lovely items from Et Vous, Vanessa Bruno and Les Prairies de Paris, plus Sissi and designers Chisato and Burfitt.

◆ MARC JACOBS
Fashion & Accessories

☎ 212-343-1490; www.marcjacobs.com; 403, 405 & 385 Bleecker St; 🕑 11am-7pm Mon-Sat, noon-6pm Sun; ⊕ 1 to Christopher St-Sheridan Sq

Marc Jacobs' monster stores domi-nate Bleecker St. Bags and acces-ories at 385, menswear at 403, and his celebrated women's collection holds court at 405.

◆ MICK MARGO *Boutique*

☎ 212-463-0515; www.mickmargo .com; 19 Commerce St; 🕑 noon-7pm Tue-Sat, to 6pm Sun; ⊕ A, B, C, D, E, F, V to W 4th St, 1 to Christopher St-Sheridan Sq

Sharp leather boots by Aigle, crisp Alexander Wang shirts and the latest from designers Rachel Comey, Jerome Dreyfuss and the like. And shoes, bags and sunglasses to accessorize the fantastically feminine clothes.

◆ MURRAY'S CHEESE
Food & Drink

☎ 212-243-3289; www.murrayscheese .com; 254 Bleecker St; 🕑 8am-8pm Mon-Sat, 9am-6pm Sun; ⊕ 1 to Christopher St-Sheridan Sq, A, B, C, D, E, F, V to W 4th St

Founded in 1914, this is repeatedly hailed as the best cheese shop in the city. Owner Rob Kaufelt is, to put it kindly, obsessed with finding the best *fromage* from all over the world, be it runny, firm, mild, sharp or full of holes. There's a Murray's at Grand Central Terminal, too.

◆ PLEASURE CHEST *Sex Shop*

☎ 212-242-2158; www.thepleasure chest.com; 156 Seventh Ave btwn Charles & Perry Sts; 🕑 10am-midnight; ⊕ 1 to Christopher St-Sheridan Sq

No trip to the Village is complete without a stop at the

Pleasure Chest, a gay-friendly, clean, upbeat and inclusive sex shop with zero sleaze factor. Its wildly colorful window displays of creams, oils, funny (and risqué) cards and toys lure a wide variety of shoppers.

🏠 RICKY'S *Drugstore*
☎ 212-924-3401; 466 Sixth Ave at W 11th St; 🕙 9am-11pm Mon-Sat, to 10pm Sun; 🚇 A, C, E to 14th St, L to Eighth Ave-14th St

This is one of the few times in life that stocking up on mundane essentials like toothpaste and hair gel is actually fun. Ricky's is a drugstore that likes to think it's a nightclub – expect pounding music, hot-pink toothpaste tubes, and lots of glitter, faux-color, and outrageous hair and wardrobe selections. In the back you'll find sex toys, of course.

🏠 VERVE *Footwear*
☎ 212-675-6693; www.vervenyc.com; 338 Bleecker St; 🕙 11am-8pm Mon-Sat, noon-6pm Sun; 🚇 1 to Christopher St-Sheridan Sq

The perfect spot for women who like to match their shoes to their bag – Verve carries both. Purses and shoes of all stripes and sizes are temptingly displayed in adorable couplings along the shelf-covered walls. Offerings from shoe wizards like Bettye Muller

and Pura Lopez can be found, and watch out for Verve's sales in January.

🍴 EAT

🍴 BABBO *Italian* $$$
☎ 212-777-0303; www.babbonyc.com; 110 Waverly Pl; 🕙 dinner; 🚇 A, B, C, D, E, F, V to W 4th St, 1 to Christopher St-Sheridan Sq; ♿

Celebrity chef Mario Batali has multiple restaurants in Manhattan, but everyone has a sneaking suspicion that this two-level split townhouse is his favorite. Whether you order mint love letters, lamb's brain *francobolli* (small, stuffed ravioli) or pig's foot *milanese,* you'll find Batali at the top of his innovative, eclectic game. Reservations are in order.

🍴 CAFFE REGGIO *Cafe* $
☎ 212-475-9557; www.caffereggio.com; 119 MacDougal St near W 3rd St; 🕙 8am-3am Mon-Thu & Sun, to 4:30am Fri & Sat; 🚇 A, B, C, D, E, F, V to W 4th St

An echo of old bohemia, this arty cafe is a visual treat of Renaissance paintings and marble-topped tables. Serving fresh pastries, panini, cakes, Italian milkshakes (try the 'delizioso') and delectable coffee since 1927, Reggio's says it invented the cappuccino. True or no, it's wildly popular, and busy all night.

CRU French $$$

☎ 212-529-1700; http://cru-nyc.com; 24 Fifth Ave at 9th St; ☽ 11am-7pm Mon-Sat, noon-6pm Sun; ◎ 1 to Christopher St-Sheridan Sq; ♿

A big hit with the Euro crowd, Cru has more than 150,000 bottles of wine and happily helps you make a good match to dishes like cod with Castelluccio lentils, roasted broccoli ribbons and sautéed cauliflower in lingonberry–red wine jus, and roasted duck-breast braised Romanesco, duck pancetta, maitake mushroom and sweetpotato puree port wine–natural jus. A quick tip: the handsome mahogany bar out front has the same wines and better views to the street, and lets you order à la carte off the menu.

DITCH PLAINS
Seafood $

☎ 212-633-0202; www.ditch-plains.com; 29 Bedford St; ☽ lunch & dinner; ◎ A, B, C, D, E, F, V to W 4th St; ♿ 👶

Ditch Plains' sleek, metallic interior with wood booths and glossy floors is an inviting place to hang out while you inhale celeb chef Marc Murphy's glammed-up seafood shack food: oysters, mussels, fish tacos, fried clams, po' boys and more feed the masses until 2am daily.

EAT LIKE A LOCAL

A pioneer in organic, local eating, **Blue Hill New American** (☎ 212-539-1776; www.bluehillnyc.com; 75 Washington Pl; ☽ dinner; ◎ A, B, C, D, E, F, V to W 4th St) is one of the West Village's hidden treasures. It's linked with the **Stone Barn** (www.stonebarns center.org) upstate, a sustainable Hudson Valley agri-business that shares its seasonal produce between its own on-site restaurant and Blue Hill. Animals are free range and hormone free (and slaughtered in the most humane way possible), and veggies are exploding with freshness. Visitors are welcome at Stone Barn, or you can catch the farm's flavors at Blue Hill.

MAS
New American, French $$$

☎ 212-255-1790; www.masfarmhouse .com; 39 Downing St; ☽ dinner & late-night dinner Mon-Sat; ◎ A, B, C, D, E, F, V to W 4th St; ♿

Chef Galen Zamarra draws heavily from the South of France (in old Provençal a 'mas' is a traditional stone farmhouse), from the solid and ornate oak front door right through to the earthy menu, which features *beau soleil* oysters, braised ribs, flying pig pork belly and wild nettle risotto. Mas is a great option for dining late at night.

▯▯ MINETTA TAVERN
Bistro $$

☎ 212-475-3850; www.minettatavern ny.com; 113 MacDougal St; ☽ dinner daily, brunch Sat & Sun; ⊕ A, B, C, D, E, F, V to W 4th St

Book in advance, or come early to snag a table on a weeknight, because Minetta Tavern is pretty much always packed to the rafters. The snug red leather banquettes, the dark-paneled walls with black-and-white photos, the classic checkered floors, tin ceilings and flaring yellow bistro lamps give it ambience galore. While flavor-filled French-bistro dishes like pig's feet, pan-seared marrow bones, roasted chicken, chocolate soufflé and crème brûlée, plus American faves, such as sirloin steak, crisp fries and big burgers, don't disappoint.

▯▯ PEARL OYSTER
American Seafood $$

☎ 212-691-8211; 18 Cornelia St near Bleecker St; ☽ lunch & dinner Mon-Fri, dinner Sat; ⊕ A, B, C, D, E, F, V to W 4th St; ⅙

People line up for the lobster rolls and oyster rolls and the crowds keep getting bigger, even though Pearl Oyster has now expanded its space twice. The wine list is more detailed than the menu, which consists of fresh fish (catch of the day), Maine lobsters, clams,

shrimp, scallops and thick-hearty New England chowder.

▯▯ SPOTTED PIG
Pub Food $$

☎ 212-620-0393; www.thespottedpig .com; 314 W 11th St; ☽ lunch & dinner to 2am; ⊕ A, C, E, L to Eighth Ave-14th St; ⅙ Ⓥ ⸙

When you belly up for a drink at this bar, don't expect bowls of peanuts. Pub fare here means chicken-liver toast, mozzarella with fava-bean bruschetta, duck egg with tuna *bottarga* (salted tuna roe) and much, much more. Busy at night, much better for children in the day, and with at least two vegan options daily, the Spotted Pig's got something for everyone.

Ⓨ DRINK
Ⓨ ART BAR *Bar*

☎ 212-727-0244; 52 Eighth Ave near Horatio St; ☽ 4pm-4am, happy hour 4-7pm; ⊕ L to Eighth Ave-14th St, A, C, E to 14th St

A decidedly bohemian crowd favors Art Bar, which doesn't look like much up front (oval booths crowded too close to the wooden bar) but has a bit more going on in the back. Grab your beer or one of the house specials (usually martinis) and head for the couches, placed under a huge *Last Supper* mural featuring Jimmy Dean and Marilyn Monroe, among others.

▼ BAR NEXT DOOR *Bar*

☎ 212-529-5945; 129 MacDougal St btwn W 3rd & W 4th Sts; ☾ 6pm-2am Sun-Thu, to 3am Fri & Sat; ⊕ A, B, C, D, E, F, V to W 4th St

One of the loveliest boîtes in the neighborhood, the basement of this restored townhouse is all low ceilings, exposed brick and romantic lighting. You'll find mellow, live jazz nightly, as well as the tasty Italian menu of the restaurant next door, La Lanterna di Vittorio.

▼ EMPLOYEES ONLY *Bar*

☎ 212-242-3021; 510 Hudson St near Christopher St; ☾ 6pm-4am; ⊕ 1 to Christopher St-Sheridan Sq

Duck behind the neon 'Psychic' sign to find this hidden hangout. The bar gets busier as the night wears on. Bartenders are ace mixologists, fizzing up crazy, addictive libations like the 'Ginger Smash' and the 'Mata Hari.' Great for late-night drinking and eating, courtesy of the onsite restaurant that serves past midnight.

▼ FAT CATS *Pub*

☎ 212-675-6056; http://fatcatmusic .org; 75 Christopher St near Seventh Ave; ☾ 2pm-2am Mon-Fri, noon-2am Sat & Sun; ⊕ 1 to Christopher St-Sheridan Sq, A, B, C, D, E, F, V to W 4th St

Crappy and run-down, Fat Cats the place to go for those who ʔnt to hang out, shoot some

pool, play a little chess, Scrabble or backgammon, and maybe even get a Ping-Pong game going. Serious gamers and amateurs get a kick out of this quasi-pool-hall locale, with its live music, cheap beers and no-holds-barred approach to life.

▼ KETTLE OF FISH *Bar*

☎ 212-414-2278; www.kettleoffishnyc. com; 59 Christopher St at Seventh Ave; ☾ 3pm-4am Mon-Fri, 2pm-4am Sat & Sun; ⊕ 1 to Christopher St-Sheridan Sq

Step into this dimly lit spot, full of couches and plump chairs, and prepare to stay for a while because

The Spotted Pig – something for everyone

the crowd is simply beguiling. It's a dive bar, a sports bar and a gay bar in one, and everyone mixes happily. There are stacks of board games like Monopoly and checkers that patrons are encouraged to play, as well as darts, and if you get hungry, the barkeeps will offer menus from nearby restaurants that deliver here. The owner is a Packers fan, so expect raucous activity on game days.

▼ SULLIVAN ROOM *DJ Bar*
☎ 212-252-2151; 218 Sullivan St btwn Bleecker & W 3rd Sts; ⏱ 9pm-5am Wed-Sat; ◉ A, B, C, D, E, F, V to W 4th St
You'll have to look hard to find the entrance to this below-ground hangout, which attracts its share

of the beautiful people with DJ-hosted dance parties, a foreign beer collection and generous mixed cocktails. Best after 1am.

★ PLAY

★ 55 BAR *Jazz Music*
☎ 212-929-9883; www.55bar.com; 55 Christopher St; cover charge $3-15, 2-drink minimum; ⏱ 1pm-4am; ◉ 1 to Christopher St-Sheridan Sq, A, B, C, D, E, F to W 4th St
It's not one of the big players of the jazz scene, but 55 Bar is well known among aficionados who want to hear great music without paying a hefty cover charge. Next to the famous Stonewall Bar (the location of the infamous Stonewall Riot), 55 Bar attracts top-shelf players but doesn't take itself too seriously.

★ CHERRY LANE THEATER *Theater, Arts*
☎ 212-989-2020; www.cherrylane theater.com; 38 Commerce St; ⏱ hours vary; ◉ 1 to Christopher St-Sheridan Sq
A theater with a distinctive charm hidden in the West Village, Cherry Lane has a long and distinguished history. It was started by poet Edna St Vincent Millay and has given a voice to numerous playwrights and actors over the years. It remains true to its mission of creating 'live' theater that's accessible to the public. Readings, plays and spoken-word performances rotate frequently.

UNDER THE RADAR
Some live music venues are so hip they're hidden. Find them, and try them on for size.
Le Poisson Rouge (http://lepoisson rouge.com; 158 Bleecker St, West Village) Only the hippest acts play this 'multimedia cabaret' venue.
Santos Party House (Map pp54–5; www.santospartyhouse.com; 96 Lafayette St, Chinatown) Two large floors, DJs, live music and uninhibited dancing.
Village Underground (☎ 212-777-7745; www.thevillageunderground.com; 130 W 3rd St, Greenwich Village) Dance-fever hits Fridays and Saturdays, open-mic Sundays and live music any night.

⭐ COMEDY CELLAR *Comedy*

☎ 212-254-3480; www.comedycellar
.com; 117 MacDougal St; cover charge
$20; 🕐 shows start approx 9pm Sun-Fri,
7pm & 9:30pm Sat; 🚇 A, C, E, F, S, V to
W 4th St

A Greenwich Village staple for
decades, the Comedy Cellar has
seen quite a few careers come
and go over the years, and is still
filled nightly with wannabes, has-
beens and hot-for-the-moment
comics.

⭐ DUPLEX *Cabaret, Karaoke*

☎ 212-255-5438; www.theduplex.com;
61 Christopher St; cover charge $10-20;
🕐 4pm-4am; 🚇 1 to Christopher St-
Sheridan Sq

Cabaret, karaoke and campy
dance moves are par for the
course at the legendary Duplex.
Pictures of Joan Rivers line the
walls and the performers like to
mimic her sassy form of self-
deprecation, while getting in a few
jokes about audience members as
well. It's a fun and unpretentious
place, and certainly not for the
bashful.

⭐ FILM FORUM *Cinema*

☎ 212-727-8110; www.filmforum.com;
209 W Houston St; tickets $15; 🕐 daily;
🚇 1 to Houston St; 🚻 🚹

The best foreign and domestic
films in the history of cinema get
their treatment at the Film Forum,

which often devotes weeks at a
time to one director or artist's best
works. Buy tickets early, as shows
tend to sell out.

⭐ SOBS *Club*

☎ 212-243-4940; www.sobs.com; 204
Varick St; cover charge $10-20; 🕐 6:30pm-
3am; 🚇 1 to Houston St; 🚻

Shake your hips at SOBs – aka
Sounds of Brazil. Aside from samba
and the lambada, you'll find Afro
Cuban rumba, salsa, reggae and
more. The cheery (if kitschy) decor
and decent food make it a popular
choice for after-work parties; real
dancing doesn't start until 2am.
Sometimes a cover charge applies.

⭐ VILLAGE VANGUARD
Jazz Music

☎ 212-255-4037; www.villagevanguard
.com; 178 Seventh Ave; cover charge $15-
40, 2-drink minimum; 🕐 7pm-1am; 🚇 1
to Christopher St-Sheridan Sq

Possibly the city's most prestigious jazz club, the Vanguard has
hosted literally every major star
of the past 50 years. It started as a
home to spoken-word performances and occasionally returns to
its roots, but most of the time it's
just smooth, sweet jazz all night
long. Mind your step on the steep
stairs, and close your eyes to the
signs of wear and tear – acoustically, you're in one of the greatest
venues in the world.

>MEATPACKING DISTRICT

The Meatpacking District is all about shopping, eating and drinking – and if you enjoy all three, this neighborhood will be nirvana for you.

As you explore this district's wide cobblestone streets, check out three hotels that helped move this area from stodgy to fabulous: Hotel Gansevoort, the Maritime Hotel and the Standard, straddling the High Line; the Standard's large windows let guests look out and park voyeurs peep back. Be sure to stroll the nabe's most famous byway, Gansevoort St, which was a Dutch market, and then a slaughterhouse. It also did a brisk business in prostitution, mostly plied by transsexual or gay men. A holdover from that time is the LGBT Community Center (Map pp106–7), which played a crucial role in forcing discussion of the AIDS epidemic in the 1980s and '90s.

The district's far less rough-and-ready these days. With the coming of the long-awaited High Line, and more incursions from restaurants, galleries and high-end boutiques, this is one neighborhood that's not looking back.

MEATPACKING DISTRICT

◉ SEE
High Line	1	D4
Hotel Gansevoort	2	E3
Maritime Hotel	3	F1
White Columns	4	G3

🛍 SHOP
Adam	5	E3
Alexander McQueen	6	D2
An Earnest Cut & Sew	7	D4
Apple Store	8	E2
Buckler	9	F3
Carlos Miele	10	E3
Catherine Malandrino	11	E3
Helmut Lang	12	D4
Iris	13	D4
Rubin Chapelle	14	D2
Stella McCartney	15	C2

🍴 EAT
5 Ninth	16	E4
Bill's Bar & Burger	17	E3
Paradou	18	D4
STK	19	E4

▼ DRINK
675 Bar	20	E3
Brass Monkey	21	C4
G2	22	E2

★ PLAY
Cielo	23	D4
Griffin	24	D4
Kiss & Fly	25	E3
Sunset Salsa	26	E2

Please see over for m

SEE

⊙ HIGH LINE

☎ 212-500-6035; www.thehighline.org;
Gansevoort St; admission free; ⏱ 7am-
10pm, last entrance 9:45pm; ⊕ A, C, E,
1, 2, 3 to 14th St; &

An old eyesore that's now an airy,
vibrant public park, this renovated
elevated train track is a big hit with
New Yorkers. Full of flowers and
buzzing bees, it will soon extend to
34th St. Wheelchair access at the
14th St and 16th St entrances, and
bike racks at all entrances except
14th St. No alcohol allowed.

⊙ WHITE COLUMNS

☎ 212-924-4212; www.whitecolumns.
org; 320 W 13th St; admission free;
⏱ noon-6pm Tue-Sat; ⊕ A, C, E, L to
Eighth Ave-14th St

Geographically, White Columns is
part of the Meatpacking District,
but aesthetically speaking, it's in
Chelsea. The sedate, four-room
space has ample installations and
exhibits, many of which are by fairly well-known names like Andrew
Serrano, Alice Aycock, Lorna Simpson and a White Columns founder,
Gordon Matta-Clark. One of its
most successful recent installations
came from South London's Studio
Voltaire, which presented different
works all somehow related to the
ᴘublic persona of singer Michael
ᴋ kson.

⌂ SHOP

⌂ ADAM *Fashion & Accessories*

☎ 212-229-2838; www.shopadam.com;
678 Hudson St btwn W 13th & W 14th Sts;
⏱ 11am-7pm Mon-Wed & Fri, 11am-
8pm Thu, 10am-7pm Sat, noon-6pm Sun;
⊕ A, C, E to Eighth Ave-14th St

Oscar de la Renta protégé Adam
Lippes' Meatpacking store is full
of the smart, modern clothes that
have made him a rising star. There's
something for men and women (on
the left and right sides of the store,
respectively) amid the casually
hung chic separates, polos, T-shirts
and sweaters. Emphasis is on un-
usual and sensuous materials, like
buttery suede and plump quilting.

⌂ ALEXANDER MCQUEEN
Fashion & Accessories

☎ 212-645-1797; www.alexander
mcqueen.com; 417 W 14th St; ⏱ 11am-
7pm Mon-Sat, noon-6pm Sun; ⊕ A, C, E,
L, 1, 2, 3 to Eighth Ave-14th St

McQueen's rambunctious outfits
are shown to perfection in his
massive MPD store, and his edgy
creations seem made to be worn
in this fashion-forward district.

⌂ AN EARNEST CUT & SEW
Tailor

☎ 212-242-3414; www.earnestsewn
.com; 821 Washington St; ⏱ 11am-7pm
Mon-Fri, to 8pm Sat, to 7pm Sun; ⊕ A, C,
E, L, 1, 2, 3 to Eighth Ave-14th St

Carlos Miele – adding a little Brazil to NYC

Get your jeans custom made at this ranchero-style store, where denim is cut, hemmed, shaped, trimmed and studded to fit your specific contours.

🏠 APPLE STORE
Computers & Accessories
☎ 212-444-3400; www.apple.com; 401 W 14th St at Ninth Ave; 🕑 9am-9pm Mon-Sat, to 7pm Sun; 🚇 A, C, E, F, V to Eighth Ave-14th St
A gleaming glass-and-chrome presence in an already stylish 'hood, this Apple Store has all the latest tech accessories and trendy Mac products. You can play games or check your email on the MacBooks on the 1st floor, or sweep up the curving staircase to the iPods and 'genius bar' on floors two and three.

🏠 BUCKLER
Fashion & Accessories
☎ 212-255-1596; www.bucklershow room.com; 13 Gansevoort St; 🕑 11am-7pm Mon-Sat, noon-6pm Sun; 🚇 A, C, E, L, 1, 2, 3 to Eighth Ave-14th St
Producing cult menswear that blends 'roguish American icons with British edge,' Buckler's famous for its selection of brash and boyish denim designs. If you like the way Lenny Kravitz and Iggy Pop dress, you've found the perfect store.

🏠 CARLOS MIELE
Fashion & Accessories
☎ 646-336-6642; www.carlosmielebr. com; 408 W 14th St; 🕑 11am-7pm Mon-Sat, noon-6pm Sun; 🚇 A, C, E, L to Eighth Ave-14th St
A bright store for bold shoppers, the cut-out design of Miele's flagship boutique is almost as eye-catching as his sexy, sultry, Carnaval-inspired Brazilian dresses. This is a great place for glamorous gowns that leave you room to dance.

🏠 CATHERINE MALANDRINO
Fashion & Accessories
☎ 212-929-8710; www.catherine malandrino.com; 652 Hudson St; 🕑 11am-8pm Mon-Sat, noon-6pm Sun; 🚇 A, C, E, L, 1, 2, 3 to Eighth Ave-14th

A favorite of curvy girls, Malandrino's city-smart creations are affordable and chic, a slightly younger, hipper version of Donna Karan's sleek, working-woman's clothes.

🏬 HELMUT LANG
Fashion & Accessories

☎ 212-242-3240; www.helmutlang.com; 819 Washington St; 🕐 11am-7pm Mon-Sat, noon-6pm Sun; ⊕ A, C, E, L to Eighth Ave-14th St

Lang's latest outpost is this brick-walled wonder near Little W 12th St, full of dashingly cut men's and women's clothes that have all the style you'd expect but at a somewhat more affordable price than you'll find in his other stores.

👟 IRIS *Footwear*

☎ 212-645-0950; www.irisnyc.net; 827 Washington St; 🕐 11am-7pm Tue-Fri, 10am-7pm Sat, noon-6pm Sun; ⊕ A, C, E, L to Eighth Ave-14th St

All the fine Italian footwear you could ever dream of owning is on display at Iris. Strap on some strappies from Chloe, Viktor & Rolf, Galliano, Marc Jacobs and Branquinho and break out the plastic to pay for it all.

🏬 RUBIN CHAPELLE *Boutique*

☎ 212-647-8636; www.rubinchapelle.
:om; 410 W 14th St; 🕐 11am-7pm Mon-
i, noon-7pm Sat, noon-4pm Sun;
' A, C, E, L to Eighth Ave-14th St

This raw loft space is where celebs go for handmade denim jeans and carefully crafted leather boots cut to their precise fit. You can have them too if you don't mind dallying a month or so until your name pops up on the waiting list. Along with custom-made items, you can find one-of-a-kind, elegant leather bags and silky, floaty dresses.

🏬 STELLA MCCARTNEY
Designer Boutique

☎ 212-255-1556; www.stellamccartney.com; 429 W 14th St; 🕐 11am-8pm Tue-Sat, noon-6pm Sun; ⊕ A, C, E, L to Eighth Ave-14th St

More showroom than full-fledged store, McCartney's Meatpacking outpost has a minimal selection on hand, but oh what a selection it is. Drapy, gauzy, muted in color yet high on femininity, the delicate, ethereal clothes shine in this

NOSHWALKS

Check out the best that New York has to offer in street food on a culinary tour through the city's most delicious neighborhoods. **Noshwalks** (www .noshwalks.com) will take you through the Meatpacking District, Lower East Side, Harlem, and even into truly adventurous territory in Brooklyn and Queens, where you'll likely get tasty Indian, Chinese and Latino food over Jewish and Italian.

pared-down setting. Of course, McCartney's clothes are animal-product free, in keeping with her vegan philosophy.

EAT

5 NINTH
American Nouveau $$

☎ 212-929-9460; www.5ninth.com; 5 Ninth Ave near Gansevoort St; ☺ lunch & dinner; ⓔ A, C, E, L to Eighth Ave-14th St; Ⓥ ♿

A freestanding three-story brown-stone, complete with back porch and pocket-sized garden, makes for a gorgeous dining experi-ence. The menu is inventive and rotates often; you'll find things like roasted black-pepper pork belly braised in garlic, chili jam and anchovy dressing on bib lettuce, a root-vegetable terrine, butternut-squash ravioli, sturgeon, Angus sirloin and Korean-style pork.

BILL'S BAR & BURGER
Burger Joint $

☎ 212-414-3003; www.brguest restaurants.com; 22 Ninth Ave near 13th St; ☺ lunch & dinner; ⓔ A, C, E, L to Eighth Ave-14th St; ♿ Ⓥ ♿

There are ways to navigate around the meat-centric menu at Bill's – a veggie burger, fresh salads, crispy fries – but it's mainly a carnivore's

Treat yourself to fine food in a gorgeous setting at 5 Ninth

kinda place. Classic burgers, bacon-n-cheddar burgers, mushroom 'n' swiss burgers, even a short-rib-style burger are what keep the place hopping. There are also 'disco fries' (smothered in gravy and melted cheese), sweet-potato fries, all types of hot dogs (chili dogs, sauerkraut dogs etc), blackened catfish sammies, chicken wings and apple-crumb pie for dessert.

BEAST

If the Meatpacking District fails you, swing by **BEast** (☎ 212-228-3100; 171 E Broadway near Rutgers St; ⏱ 10pm-4am Thu-Sat). Under a restaurant, this lounge does organic wines, wild music and 'video nights' pairing DJs and visual artists. It's run by the guys who do Santos Party House (p114).

🍴 PARADOU French Bistro $$

☎ 212-463-8345; www.paradounyc. com; 8 Little W 12th St btwn Ninth Ave & Washington St; ⏱ dinner; ◉ A, C, E, L to Eighth Ave-14th St; Ⓥ

This is indeed paradise, which is the literal translation of Paradou in the Provençal dialect. The hydrangea-heavy garden out the back is a mini-miracle in springtime and is the perfect place to share the antipasto plate with artisanal hams, salamis, pâtés, asparagus and haricots verts, or the herbed seared tuna, sardines and smoked trout with baby veggies and saffron aioli. Traditionalists will lick their fingers over the frog's legs with wild mushrooms, fingerling potatoes and paprika crème fraîche.

🍴 STK Steakhouse $$$

☎ 646-624-2444; www.stkhouse.com; 26 Little W 12th St near Ninth Ave; ⏱ dinner until 2am; ◉ A, C, E, L to Eighth Ave-14th St; ♿

An oddly stylized restaurant, with sleek banquettes, metallic and black decor and one kitschy pair of horns protruding from over the bar, STK bills itself as 'not your daddy's steakhouse.' That's why you'll find salads filled with green melon, avocado, mâche greens and kaffir lime, or blue cheese, vine-ripened tomatoes and smoked bacon, plus organic roast chicken, tuna tartare with pineapple, crispy shallots and plantain chips and scallop seviche. But there's still plenty of what you'd expect: T-bones, skirt steaks, filet mignon etc. Portion sizes can be petite, medium or large, and you can add toppings such as black truffles.

🍸 DRINK

🍸 675 BAR Bar

☎ 212-699-2410; www.brguest restaurants.com; 675 Hudson St; ⏱ 8pm-2am; ◉ A, C, E, L to Eighth Ave-14th St

A cavernous below-ground hangout, 675 Bar is a dancehall

(depending on the music/crowd), a cool couples spot (thanks to its private nooks) and a raucous pickup joint (Saturday). No cover, easy-going doormen and a decent DJ.

BRASS MONKEY *Pub*
☎ 212-675-6686; 55 Little W 12th St at Washington St; ✆ 11:30am-4am; ◉ A, C, E, L to Eighth Ave-14th St

An appealing, down-at-the-heels, straightforward pub in a neighborhood of over-the-top 'cocktail bars,' Brass Monkey's for patrons who like to shoot pool, hook their heels over worn-out bar stools, and put more thought into their brew choice than their wardrobe.

G2 *Bar*
☎ 212-807-8444; www.gaslightnyc .com; 39 Ninth Ave at 14th St; no cover charge; ✆ 8pm-4am Mon-Sat; ◉ A, C, E, L to Eighth Ave-14th St

For adult coolness in the hipster-mad Meatpacking District, do your drinking at G2 or its boozy neighbor, Gaslight. G2 is the funkier of the two, with its crazy potted plants, book shelves, marble-topped tables and distressed velvet couches. A DJ spins house, electronica and hip-hop most nights.

⭐ PLAY

⭐ CIELO *Club*
☎ 212-645-5700; 18 Little W 12th St; cover charge $15-25; ✆ 10:30pm-5am

Dance to deep house deep into the night at Cielo

Mon-Sat; **Ⓢ** A, C, E, L to Eighth Ave-14th St

The demise of this house-heavy dancehall has been imminent for years, but so far, Cielo is holding on. The club has still got its 'Deep House' Monday nights and brings in various DJs from Europe who spin entrancing, seductive sounds that pull everyone to their feet.

⭐ GRIFFIN *Club*
☎ 212-255-6676; www.thegriffinny. com; 50 Gansevoort St near Greenwich St; cover charge $20; **Ⓢ** 10pm-2am Wed-Sat; **Ⓢ** A, C, E, L to Eighth Ave-14th St

Come early if you want to actually see the club's glammed-up decor (chandeliers; stuffed, golden banquettes; glittery glass bar-tops and tables; and antique mirrors on the ceilings), because once the people pack in, it's impossible to move around. DJs spin everything from funk to pop to classic rock, and the sweaty crowd goes wild.

⭐ KISS & FLY *Club*
☎ 212-255-1933; www.kissandflyclub. com; 409 W 13th St near Ninth Ave; cover charge $10-25; **Ⓢ** 11pm-4am Wed-Sat; **Ⓢ** A, C, E, L to Eighth Ave-14th St

A heavily European crowd moves and grooves to French electronica and pop into the wee hours at Kiss & Fly, a unique club designed to look a bit like a Roman bathhouse. The circular room flows around a central bar, and arches pull the eye upward to elaborately decorated walls and ceilings.

>CHELSEA

Few neighborhoods are as distinctive as edgy, arty Chelsea – home to New York's club scene, its gallery scene and a large part of its gay scene.

Once a wasteland of empty factories and derelict dumps on the far west side of Manhattan, Chelsea has been transformed over the last 10 years and is now filled almost completely with art galleries, studios and artist collectives. Where once it was hard to find a decent cup of coffee, Chelsea now overflows with cafes, bistros and high-end shops.

It can still feel like a remote region – with its long, sweeping blocks, and brisk westerly winds coming off the Hudson River – but most days you'll find crowds on the streets. If not to see the art, then to hit the clubs – Chelsea's famous for its nightlife, especially from 26th St to around 29th St.

CHELSEA

Please see over for map

SEE

AGORA GALLERY

☎ 212-226-4151; www.agora-gallery.com; 530 W 25th St; admission free; ⏰ 11am-6pm Tue-Sat; ⓜ C, E to 23rd St

A socially progressive gallery open since the '80s, Agora's big white space features international artists with perspectives on global warming, education, feminism, human rights and other issues. It also hosts the annual Chelsea International Fine Arts competition and publishes *ARTis Spectrum* magazine. Recent exhibits include an homage to French painters and sculptors like Laurence Brisson and Elisabeth Guerrier, and a look at the vivid works of Ruth Gilmore Langs. Agora also won raves in 2010 for a long-term exhibit of the Lego art of Nathan Sawaya, who constructed life-sized Lego people for his wacky show.

ALEXANDER & BONIN

☎ 212-367-7474; www.alexanderandbonin.com; 132 Tenth Ave near 18th St; ⏰ 11am-6pm Tue-Sat; ⓜ C, E to 23rd St

Since moving to Chelsea from Soho in 1997, this three-story gallery has made excellent use of its airy space with a stellar roster of artists, including several prestigious Turner Prize winners. In 2010 alone it participated in ARCO 10, Zona Maco, Art 41 and New York's Gallery Week. Carolyn Alexander and Ted Bonin, the

directors, can sometimes be seen at their 2nd-story desks. Recent shows include Willie Cole and the videos of Willie Doherty.

ANDREA ROSEN GALLERY

☎ 212-627-6000; www.andrearosengallery.com; 525 W 24th St; admission free; ⏰ 10am-6pm Tue-Sat; ⓜ C, E, 1 to 23rd St; ♿

Oversized installations are the norm at this spacious gallery, where curators fill every inch of space (and the annex Gallery 2 next door) in interesting ways. Rosen opened her gallery in 1990 and quickly made a name for herself. She's showcased John Currin's 'pale portraits,' Felix Gonzalez-Torres's 'Vultures' and Tetsumi Kudo's oil paintings, to name just a few of her artists.

CHELSEA ART MUSEUM

☎ 212-255-0719; www.chelseaartmuseum.org; 556 W 22nd St; adult $8, student & senior $4, 16 & under free; ⏰ noon-6pm Tue, Wed, Fri & Sat, to 8pm Thu; ⓜ C, E to 23rd St; ♿

Set inside a three-story, redbrick building dating from 1850, and standing on land once owned by writer Clement Clarke Moore, this museum's focus is on postwar abstract expressionism, by both national and international artists. The permanent collection includes works by Antonio Corpora, Laszlo Lakner and sculptor Bernar Venet. It's also the headquarters of the

See Midtown West Map p163

W 30th St
W 29th St
W 28th St

Tenth Ave

Chelsea Park

37

13

W 27th St

39   14
      33
      41

Eleventh Ave

8
1

W 26th St

Ninth Ave

W 25th St

3
7   10

W 24th St   26

Chelsea
Waterside Park

34

London
Terrace
Gardens

W 23rd St   27

Hudson River
Park

30

20

4   11

W 22nd St

17

W 21st St

32   6

Chelsea
Piers

W 20th St   28

Tenth Ave

W 19th St

2

35   36

W 18th St

W 17th St

Hudson River

W 16th St

High Line

Chelsea Market   22

W 15th St

See Meatpacking
District Map
pp118–19

W 14th St

Washington St

MEATPACKING
DISTRICT

Ninth Ave

Hudson St

International art at Gagosian

Miotte Foundation, dedicated to archiving the works of Jean Miotte, a Soho-based artist who has played a big role in the genre of Informel (Informal Art).

CHELSEA HOTEL
☎ 212-243-3700; www.hotelchelsea. com; 222 W 23rd St btwn Seventh & Eighth Aves; ⓒ C, E, 1, 2 to 23rd St
The prime sight on noisy 23rd St is a redbrick hotel with ornate iron balconies and no fewer than seven plaques declaring its literary landmark status. Even before the infamous onsite death of Sid Vicious' girlfriend, Nancy Spungeon, the hotel was famous as a hangout for the likes of Mark Twain, Thomas Wolfe, Dylan Thomas and Arthur Miller. Jack Kerouac allegedly crafted *On the Road* during one marathon session here. Musicians have long favored the Chelsea, and it counts many local eccentrics among its permanent residents. Now under new ownership, it seems the hotel's 'art before profit' attitude is in for a change.

CHELSEA PIERS COMPLEX
☎ 212-336-6000; www.chelseapiers .com; Hudson River at end of W 23rd St; ⓒ C, E to 23rd St
This massive waterfront sports center caters to the athlete in everyone. You can set out to hit a bucket of golf balls at the four-level driving range, ice skate in the complex's indoor rink or rent in-line skates to cruise down to Battery Park along the Hudson Park waterfront bike path. There's a jazzy bowling alley, Hoop City for basketball, a sailing school for kids, batting cages, a huge gym facility with an indoor pool – the works. Kayaks are loaned out free at the Downtown Boathouse just north of Pier 64.

GAGOSIAN
☎ 212-741-1111; www.gagosian.com; 555 W 24th St; admission free; ⏱ 10am-6pm Sat; ⓒ C, E to 23rd St; ♿
International works dot the walls at both the Gagosian in Chelsea and the gallery uptown (Map p183; ☎ 212-741-1111; 980 Madison Ave;

10am-6pm Tue-Sat; 6 to 77th St-Lexington Ave;). The ever-revolving exhibits feature greats like Julian Schnabel, William de Kooning, Andy Warhol and Basquiat.

GREENE NAFTALI
☎ 212-463-7770; www.greenenaftali gallery.com; 526 W 26th St; admission free; 10am-6pm Tue-Sat; C, E to 23rd St;

Sharp, edgy and youth-oriented Greene Naftali has an ever-rotating display of art in all kinds of media: film/video, installation, painting, drawing and performance art. Check out the column running through the gallery's center; it's often used to display pieces.

MATTHEW MARKS GALLERY
☎ 212-243-0200; www.matthewmarks .com; 522 W 22nd St at Tenth Ave; admission free; 10am-6pm Mon-Fri; C, E to 23rd St;

The trendsetter that started the push into Chelsea, Matthew Marks' two galleries (the second is at 523 W 24th St) were once factories. Now they are high-falutin' art houses with shows by the likes of Nan Goldin and Andreas Gursky.

MUSEUM AT FIT
☎ 212-217-5800; www.fitnyc.edu; Seventh Ave at W 27th St; admission free; noon-8pm Tue-Fri, 10am-5pm Sat; 1 to 28th St

The Fashion Institute of Technology is a fashion, design and fine-arts school located on the edge of Manhattan's Fashion District. The best way for a visitor to access its unique riches is to visit its museum, which showcases rotating exhibits on fashion and style, including works by students. Its permanent collection, opened in late 2005, is the country's first gallery of fashion and textile history; it displays rotating items from its collection of more than 50,000 garments and accessories dating from the 18th century to the present.

PAUL KASMIN
☎ 212-563-4474; www.paulkasmin gallery.com; 293 Tenth Ave at W 27th St; admission free; 10am-6pm Tue-Sat, 9am-5pm Mon-Fri Jul & Aug; C, E to 23rd St;

Expect the unexpected at Paul Kasmin. After all, the gallery does represent the legendary Frank Stella. All media are accepted here: collages, paintings, photography, sculptures and more. Shows at this gallery are wide-ranging, expansive and thought-provoking. There's a second branch at 511 W 27th St.

RUBIN MUSEUM OF ART
☎ 212-620-5000; www.rmanyc.org; 150 W 17th St at Seventh Ave; adult $10, student & senior $7, 7-10pm Fri free; 11am-5pm Mon & Thu, to 7pm Wed,

to 10pm Fri, to 6pm Sat & Sun; ⊙ 1 to 18th St

The first museum in the Western world dedicating itself to art of the Himalayas and surrounding regions, Rubin's got an impressive collection. You'll see embroidered textiles from China, metal sculptures from Tibet, Pakistani stone sculptures, intricate Bhutanese paintings and ritual objects and dance masks from various Tibetan regions, spanning from the 2nd to 19th centuries.

🛍 SHOP

📷 192 BOOKS Books
☎ 212-255-4022; 192 Tenth Ave btwn W 21st & W 22nd Sts; ☽ 11am-7pm Tue-Sat, noon-6pm Sun & Mon; ⊙ C, E to 23rd St
This small indie bookstore is located right in the gallery district, with sections on literature, history, travel, art and criticism. The rotating art exhibits – during which the owners organize special displays of books that relate, thematically, to the featured show or artist – are a special treat.

📷 AUTHENTIQUES PAST & PRESENT
Vintage Homewares, Curios
☎ 212-675-2179; 255 W 18th St btwn Seventh & Eighth Aves; ☽ noon-6pm Wed-Sat, 1-6pm Sun; ⊙ 1 to 18th St
Tucked on a quiet side street is this thoroughly dramatic and kitsch-filled vintage shop. Find groovy and colorful lamps from the '50s and '60s, pastel vases and cache pots, quirky barware, nostalgic cartoon figurines, glasses and flashy costume jewelry.

📷 BALENCIAGA
Fashion & Accessories
☎ 212-206-0872; 522 W 22nd St at Eleventh Ave; ☽ 10am-7pm Mon-Sat, noon-5pm Sun; ⊙ C, E to 23rd St
Come and gaze at this cool, gray, Zen-like space. It's the gallery district's showcase, appropriately

ANTIQUES GARAGE FLEA MARKET
The weekend **Antiques Garage Flea Market** (☎ 212-243-5343; 112 W 25th St; ☽ 9am-5pm Sat & Sun; ⊙ 1 to 23rd St) is set in a two-level parking garage, with more than 100 vendors spreading their wares. Antique lovers shouldn't miss a browse here, as you'll find clothing, shoes, records, books, globes, furniture, rugs, lamps, glassware, paintings, artwork and many other relics from the past. If there's not enough here to keep you happy, catch the $1 shuttle to the affiliated Hell's Kitchen Flea Market in Midtown. Or head to the **Chelsea Outdoor Market** (Map p141; 29 W 25th St btwn Fifth & Sixth Aves; ☽ 9am-5pm Sat & Sun; ⊙ L, N, R, 4, 5, 6 to Union Sq) or the **17th Street Market** (W 17th St; ☽ 9am-5pm Sat & Sun; ⊙ L, N, R, 4, 5, 6 to Union Sq).

enough, for the artistic, post-apocalypse, avant-garde styles of this French fashion house. Expect strange lines, goth patterns and pants for very skinny (and deep-pocketed) gals.

BARNEYS CO-OP
Fashion & Accessories

☎ 212-593-7800; 236 W 18th St; ⏰ 11am-8pm Mon-Fri, 11am-7pm Sat, noon-6pm Sun; ⊖ 1 to 18th St

The edgier, younger, less expensive version of Barneys (p187) has (relatively) affordable deals. At this expansive, loftlike space, with a spare, very selective inventory of clothing for men and women, plus shoes and cosmetics, the biannual warehouse sale (February and August) packs the place, with both endless merchandise and mobs of customers.

CHELSEA MARKET
Food & Drink, Market

www.chelseamarket.com; 75 Ninth Ave btwn W 15th & W 16th Sts; ⏰ 7am-9pm Mon-Sat, 10am-8pm Sun; ⊖ A, C, E, L to Eighth Ave-14th St

Gourmet-food fans will think they've died and entered the pearly gates once they've stepped into this 800ft-long shopping concourse bursting with some of the freshest eats in town. But Chelsea Market is part of a larger, million-sq-ft space that occupies a full city block, home to the Nabisco

Knead bread? Visit Amy's Bread at Chelsea Market

cookie factory in the 1930s (which created the Oreo cookie), and current home to the Food Network, the Oxygen Network and the local NY1 news channel. There are more than 25 market food shops, including Amy's Bread, Fat Witch Brownies, the Lobster Place, Hale & Hearty Soup, Ronnybrook Farm Dairy and Frank's butcher shop. These shops are the prime draw for locals.

GIRAUDON *Footwear*

☎ 212-633-0999; 152 Eighth Ave btwn W 17th & W 18th Sts; ⏰ 11:30am-7:30pm Mon-Wed & Fri-Sun, to 11pm Thu; ⊖ A, C, E, L to Eighth Ave-14th St

This small shoe boutique has been selling finely made leather foot sculptures since way before the 'hood was hip. The designs are classic and have a touch of edginess, with both casual and glamorous options. It's a tiny space, but rarely crowded. The staffers are friendly and encouraging.

🏠 HOUSING WORKS THRIFT SHOP *Fashion & Accessories, Bric-a-Brac*

☎ 212-366-0820; 143 W 17th St; 🕙 10am-6pm Mon-Sat, noon-5pm Sun; ◉ 1 to 18th St

This shop, with its swank window displays, looks more boutique than thrift, but its selections of clothes, accessories, furniture and books are great value. All proceeds benefit the charity serving the city's HIV-positive and AIDS homeless communities.

🏠 LOEHMANN'S *Fashion & Accessories*

☎ 212-352-0856; www.loehmanns.com; 101 Seventh Ave at W 16th St; 🕙 9am-9pm Mon-Sat, 11am-7pm Sun; ◉ 1 to 18th St

A starting point for local hipsters looking for designer labels on the cheap (though some may not admit it), Loehmann's is a five-story department store that, it is said, inspired a wee-young Calvin Klein to make clothes. The original store of the successful chain is in the Bronx; see the website for other locations.

🍴 EAT

🍴 202 *Pub Food* $$

☎ 646-638-0115; www.nicolefarhi.com; 75 Ninth Ave; 🕙 lunch & dinner; ◉ 1 to 18th St; ♿ Ⓥ ♨

Now you can shop until you drop...right into a seat at 202, a quasi British/Irish pub set right in the middle of Nicole Farhi's Chelsea Market Store (it's named after Farhi's original London restaurant). Shoppers browse around as you eat your bubble and squeak, fish 'n' chips or full English breakfast. Lunchtimes are busiest, but you can also just swing by the 202 entrance inside the market for counter service and a quick cup of joe (that's coffee in New York).

🍴 BUDDAKAN *Asian* $$$

☎ 646-989-6699; www.buddakannyc.com; 75 Ninth Ave; 🕙 lunch & dinner; ◉ 1 to 18th St; ♿ Ⓥ ♨

Get in early if you want to dine without having to shout to be heard – this cavernous space fills up fast and the buzz starts to get *loud*. Another great find in the Chelsea Market, Buddakan's decor is beyond strange: half movie set, half banquet hall. But put together they produce a jaw-dropping effect. The Asian-fusion cuisine is heavy on seafood infused with delectable flavors and spices.

ⓦ EL QUINTO PINO

Tapas $$

☎ 212-206-6900; 401 W 24th St;
🕒 lunch & dinner; ⓖ C, E to 23rd St;
♿ Ⓥ ⚲

Trolling for tapas is easy enough in small-plate-crazy New York, but true aficionados of the Spanish treats are often disappointed. Not anymore. Now there's El Quinto Pino, a long narrow room ringed with 16 bar stools and no place else to sit; you'll have to lean on the bar like you're in Madrid and snack away on olives, anchovies, sautéed and garlicky shrimp, mini panini, cod sticks, calamari and more. If you must sit down, the owners also run **Tia Pol** (205 Tenth Ave) around the corner; same great food, but with a wee bit more space.

ⓦ GREEN TABLE

Organic $$

☎ 212-741-9174; http://cleaverco.com;
75 Ninth Ave; 🕒 lunch & dinner, closed
Sun Jun-Aug; ⓖ C, E, L, 1, 2, 3 to Eighth
Ave-14th St; Ⓥ ⚲

Another treat tucked inside the Chelsea Market, Green Table uses only organic, local fare trucked in daily from upstate Satur Farms. All the meat, eggs and dairy products are from grass-raised, free-range animals and the many veggie options studding the menu will seduce you with their fresh taste. Menus change daily.

ⓦ KLEE BRASSERIE

Brasserie $$

☎ 212-633-8033; 200 Ninth Ave btwn W
22nd & W 23rd Sts; 🕒 dinner; ⓖ C, E to
23rd St; Ⓥ ⚲

As you'd expect from the name, this brasserie is whimsical and fun with a slight sparkle of romance – and decidedly low-fuss. The open kitchen dishes up wholesome, fresh ingredients: an appetizer salad matches crisp chicory and chanterelle mushrooms with a slow-poached egg, while chicken gets spiced with licorice, and risotto is stud

UPRIGHT CITIZENS BRIGADE

Get some laughs at New York's longest-running comedy and improv theater, founded by famously funny folks like *Saturday Night Live's* Amy Poehler. The standout show at **UCBT** (☎ 212-366-9176; www.newyork.ucbtheatre.com; 307 W 26th St near Eighth Ave; tickets $7-15; 🕒 nightly shows; ⓖ C, E to 23rd St) is the Sunday night laugh-o-rama known as Asscat 3000. It showcases UCBT's most hilarious comedians doing long-form improv, and frequent surprise guests from SNL, *The Daily Show* with Jon Stewart and Conan O'Brien's former show appear. The 7:30pm show costs $10; the 9:30pm show is free but reservations aren't accepted. Tickets are handed out around 8:15pm outside the theater.

NEIGHBORHOODS

CHELSEA

ded with shrimp and lemon. The thoroughly unique herbivore option packs a wide-mouthed jelly jar with a cornucopia of seasonal veggies and a healthy heaping of quinoa.

OMAI *Vietnamese* $

☎ 212-633-0550; 158 Ninth Ave btwn W 19th & W 20th Sts; 🕑 dinner; 🚇 A, C, E to 14th St

Serving Vietnamese delights in a romantic cubbyhole, Omai has cultivated a following for its wok-seared monkfish with peanuts, chili and basil served over sesame rice crackers, crispy rice crepes with shrimp, chicken and bean sprouts, and unexpected combos like grilled shrimp on sugarcane with angel-hair pasta and peanut sauce.

SOCCARAT PAELLA BAR
Spanish $$

☎ 212-462-1000; www.soccaratpaella bar.com; 259 W 19th St near Eighth Ave; 🕑 lunch & dinner; 🚇 1 to 18th St; Ⓥ

A cozy, narrow room dominated by a glass-topped communal table, Soccarat is famous for its heavenly, saffron-scented paellas filled with veggies, seafood and/or meat. Tapas are served too, but nothing compares to the rice. No reservations, but you can wait at the wine bar next door. Lunch is less crowded than dinner.

Check out the wholesome menu at Klee Brasserie (p135)

▼ DRINK

▼ BAR VELOCE *Bar*

☎ 212-629-5300; 176 Seventh Ave near W 20th St; 🕑 5pm-3am; 🚇 C, E to 23rd St

Sip your wine, eat a few panini, watch the well-dressed world walk by, or strike up a conversation with an interesting stranger (or two). What could be better than that? Small and friendly Bar Veloce caters to a fairly sophisticated crowd that likes wine and a few laughs at the end of a hard day.

▼ CHELSEA BREWING COMPANY *Pub*

☎ 212-336-6440; Chelsea Piers, Pier 59, W Side Highway at W 23rd St; 🕑 noon-midnight; 🚇 C, E to 23rd St

Enjoy a quality microbrew, waterside, in the expansive outdoor area of this way-west beer haven – a perfect place to re-enter the world after a day of swimming, golfing or rock climbing as a guest at the Chelsea Piers Complex (p130).

▼ GLASS *Bar*

☎ 212-904-1580; 287 Tenth Ave at W 26th St; 🕑 9pm-4am Wed-Sat; 🚇 C, E to 23rd St

Lots of translucent tiles, bar stools and table tops edged with bright pinks and blues give this glassy bar its name – or maybe it's from the slick crowd. Either way, the cocktails are the big draw: strong

and varied, ranging from blue martinis to deep-green caipirinhas and pretty pink cosmos. It has a small dance floor and sometimes a $10 cover charge at the door, but the egalitarian entrance policy won't leave you waiting in line for hours.

▼ HALF KING *Pub*

☎ 212-462-4300; 505 W 23rd St at Tenth Ave; 🕑 11am-4am Mon-Fri, 9am-4am Sat & Sun; 🚇 C, E to 23rd St

A unique marriage of cozy pub and sophisticated writers' lair, you'll often experience top-notch literary readings in this wood-accented, candlelit watering hole. Its myriad seating-area options are bound to provide one that will seduce you – particularly during warm weather, when a front sidewalk cafe, main indoor room, cozy back section and mellow backyard patio are all open for business.

▼ PARK *Bar*

☎ 212-352-3313; 118 Tenth Ave near W 17th St; 🕑 11am-2am Mon-Wed, to 4am Thu-Sun; 🚇 A, C, E, L to Eighth Ave-14th St

There are plenty of places to get lost in the Park – a sprawling, old-fashioned hangout with a big front room, an even bigger back garden (open year round), an even more cavernous red room (filled with sexy red Chinese lanterns), an airy atrium to drink in, and even a glass-covered rooftop with a hot tub. The garden really looks like an urban park, and there are even a few pretend deer scattered about. The crowd is a varied mix of art-world professionals and fashionistas.

⭐ PLAY

⭐ 1OAK Club
☎ 212-242-1111; 453 W 17th St; cover charge $10-25; 🕑 10pm-4am Tue-Sat; 🚇 A, C, E, L to Eighth Ave-14th St

Part Nordic hunting lodge and part Moroccan hookah lounge, this celebrity favorite has a DJ spinning house and techno tunes, a roaring corner fireplace and bottle service at tables, and it stays packed into the wee hours.

⭐ EAGLE NYC Club
☎ 646-473-1866; www.eaglenyc.com; 555 W 28th St btwn Tenth & Eleventh Aves; cover charge $10; 🕑 10pm-4am Mon-Sat; 🚇 C, E to 23rd St

A bi-level club full of hot men in leather, the Eagle is the choice for out-and-proud fetishists. Its two levels plus roof deck leave plenty of room for dancing and drinking, which are done with abandon at the Eagle. Thursdays are 'code' nights, meaning everyone must meet the dress code (wear leather, or nothing at all). Located in a

renovated 19th-century stable, the inside joke is that 'the studs keep coming.'

⭐ G LOUNGE Bar
☎ 212-929-1085; www.glounge.com; 223 W 19th St btwn Seventh & Eigth Aves; no cover charge; 🕑 4pm-4am; 🚇 1 to 18th St

Glossy and unpretentious, this gay bar is as straight-friendly as they come, and it's really all about the music. DJs rotate daily, but Tuesday is always BoyBox night. Check out the website to find out who's spinning when while you're in town. For heavy drinking and dancing with no cover, you can't beat G – although you may have to wait in line to get in. Dress at G Lounge is refreshingly casual. Cash only.

⭐ HOME Club
☎ 212-273-3700; 532 W 27th St near Tenth Ave; cover charge $20; 🕑 10pm-4am Tue-Sun; 🚇 C, E to 23rd St, 1 to 28th St

Most homes aren't multilevel, cavernous spaces with dark leather couches lining nearly every wall and eerily lit passageways taking you from nook to nook, but maybe that's a growing trend. Either way, there's lots to make you feel comfortable at Home – ample seating and space, and deep electronic, funk and pop coming from the live DJ. Sometimes the doors between

Home and the neighboring club Guesthouse are opened and you can pass from one to the other.

⭐ JOYCE THEATER *Arts*
☎ 212-242-0800; www.joyce.org; 175 Eighth Ave; 🕙 hours vary; 🚇 C, E to 23rd St, A, C, E to Eighth Ave-14th St, 1 to 18th St

An offbeat, intimate venue in Chelsea with clean sight lines from every corner, the Joyce is blessed with annual visits from Merce Cunningham and Pilobolus dance companies, comfortably seen from any of the renovated theater's 470 seats.

⭐ MARQUEE *Club*
☎ 646-473-0202; 289 Tenth Ave btwn W 26th & W 27th Sts; cover charge $20; 🕙 11pm-4am Wed-Sat; 🚇 C, E to 23rd St

Glamorous masses and a fair share of A-listers try to slip past the velvet ropes to get inside, where DJs spin electronica, house and funk all night long. Be prepared to wait to get in unless the doorman takes a shine to you or you are simply born lucky.

⭐ XES LOUNGE *Bar*
☎ 212-604-0212; www.xeslounge.com; 157 West 24th St near Seventh Ave; no cover charge; 🕙 2pm-2am; 🚇 C, E to 23rd St

A divey, fun neighborhood gay bar with a garden out back and a mostly all-male clientele, XES gets rocking late at night (Thursday through Saturday in particular). It's OK to boogie to Beyonce on your table or chair, or even on the dance floor if you prefer. Happy-hour drinks are two-for-the-price-of-one. Karaoke nights are midweek.

>UNION SQUARE, FLATIRON DISTRICT & GRAMERCY PARK

A mid-sized public plaza that's the preferred location for community-led vigils, demonstrations and celebrations, busy, bustling Union Sq is the heartbeat of the city's activist movement. It's also home to the city's best-known greenmarket, a popular weekend shopping choice for New Yorkers.

Gramercy Park, a small stretch of neighborhood just northeast of Union Sq, couldn't be more different. Where Union Sq is egalitarian, Gramercy is exclusive. The tony, brownstone-filled nabe is full of old money and great restaurants, and is dominated by its own lush and beautiful gated park (to be used only by the wealthy few who live on its perimeter).

In contrast, the Flatiron District, directly north of Union Sq, has become a de facto shopping street, full of big-name department stores, such as Home Depot and ABC Carpet & Home.

These three enclaves together are a practical yet wealthy neighborhood that has more than its share of big and expensive restaurants.

UNION SQUARE, FLATIRON DISTRICT & GRAMERCY PARK

👁 SEE
Flatiron Building 1 B4
Madison Square Park 2 B3
Museum of Sex 3 B3
National Arts Club 4 C5
Union Square 5 C6
Union Square
  Greenmarket ....(see 5)

🛍 SHOP
ABC Carpet & Home 6 C5
Chelsea Outdoor
  Market 7 B3

Filene's Basement 8 C6
Nordstrom Rack 9 C6
Shareen Vintage 10 B5

🍴 EAT
15 East 11 B5
Blue Smoke 12 C3
Chocolate by the
  Bald Man 13 C6
Curry in a Hurry 14 D2
Hill Country 15 A3
Shake Shack 16 B4
Steak Frites 17 B5

🍸 DRINK
Black Bear Lodge 18 D4
Flatiron Lounge 19 A5
Heartland Brewery 20 C5
Lillie's 21 B5
Pete's Tavern 22 D5

⭐ PLAY
Irving Plaza 23 C5
Karaoke One 7 ....24 C5
Union Square
  Theater 25 C5

SEE

FLATIRON BUILDING

Broadway, cnr Fifth Ave & 23rd St; ⊖ N, R, 6 to 23rd St

It's a three-dimensional triangle brought to life: the Flatiron Building is a 22-story limestone and terra-cotta structure that was known as 'Burnham's Folly' (after architect Daniel Burnham) when it was built in 1902. Skeptical residents doubted that its odd ironlike shape would hold up. Six feet across at its narrowest point, it's now the defining landmark of the neighborhood.

MADISON SQUARE PARK

www.nycgovparks.org; 23rd to 26th Sts btwn Broadway & Madison Ave; ⊕ 6am-1am; ⊖ N, R, 6 to 23rd St; ♿

You can visit this cute little spot in the Flatiron District for the elegant statues, free summer art programs and the playground for kids. Or you can be like everyone else and come for the **Shake Shack** (☎ 212-989-6600; www.shakeshack.com; 23rd St & Madison Ave; ⊕ 11am-11pm), an environmentally friendly food kiosk that's turned the park's south end into a dining hot spot.

MUSEUM OF SEX

☎ 212-689-6337; www.museumofsex .com; 233 Fifth Ave; adult $16.75, senior & student $15.25; ⊕ 10am-8pm Sun-Thu, to 9pm Fri & Sat (last tickets sold 45min before closing); ⊖ N, R, 6 to 28th St

You do have to be over 18 to visit this museum, but there's nothing particularly illicit about it (sorry, folks). Its mission is more to educate than to titillate, and permanent collections showcase America's various sexual revolutions, from burlesque to gay rights. Some of its visiting and online exhibits are a bit racier, and you can leave with a top-of-the-line sex toy, courtesy of the museum gift store.

GREENMARKETS

Also known as farmers markets, these open-air shopping sprees aim to increase awareness of locally grown produce, mostly from the Hudson Valley. The **Union Square Greenmarket** (17th St btwn Broadway & Park Ave S; ⊕ 10am-6pm Mon, Wed, Fri & Sat) is arguably the most famous, and attracts many of the city's top chefs to its stalls to finger aromatic greens, fresh yellow corn and deep orange squashes. But there are many other greenmarkets around the city on any given day. For more information visit the website of the **Council of the Environment of New York City** (☎ 212-788-7476; www.cenyc.org), which has been organizing the greenmarkets since 1976.

The prow of the Flatiron Building seems set to sail up Broadway

◉ NATIONAL ARTS CLUB

☎ 212-475-3424; www.nationalartsclub
.org; 15 Gramercy Park S; ◉ 6 to 23rd St

Boasting a beautiful, vaulted, stained-glass ceiling above its wooden bar, this club was designed by Calvert Vaux, one of the creators of Central Park. The space holds free art exhibitions, ranging from sculpture to photography. These exhibitions are sometimes open to the public from 1pm to 5pm.

◉ UNION SQUARE

17th St btwn Broadway & Park Ave S;
◉ L, N, Q, R, W, 4, 5, 6 to 14th St-Union Sq

A former 'needle' park opened in 1831, Union Sq has become syn-onymous with protests – starting with the nation's first Labor Day gathering in 1882 and continuing into the present. But the little park was named not for its strong union activities (many labor groups, including the American Civil Liberties Union, Communist and Socialist parties and Ladies' Garment Workers Union, set up offices on its outskirts), but because it was at the 'union' of Broadway and Bowery. It's now home to a fabulous greenmarket (see opposite), several statues (including George Washington *and* Mahatma Gandhi), public works of art, and – after a face-lift on the north end – a new restaurant and playground.

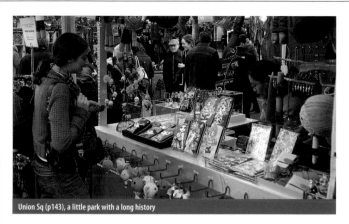
Union Sq (p143), a little park with a long history

🛍 SHOP

🏠 ABC CARPET & HOME
Homewares
☎ 212-473-3000; 888 Broadway;
🕙 10am-7pm Mon-Wed & Fri, 10am-
8pm Thu, 11am-7pm Sat, noon-6pm Sun;
🚇 L, N, Q, R, W, 4, 5, 6 to 14th St-
Union Sq
North of Union Sq there is a
plethora of home-furnishing
stores: besides the museumlike
ABC Carpet & Home, there are
numerous other interior design/
furnishing options stretching
all the way up to 23rd St. ABC's
six stories are filled with home
goods, small and large, including easy-to-pack knick-knacks,
designer jewelry, global gifts and
more bulky antique furnishings
and carpets. Come Christmas
season, the shop is a joy to behold, as the decorators go all out
with lights and other wondrous
touches.

🏠 FILENE'S BASEMENT *Mall*
☎ 212-358-0169; 4 Union Sq; 🕙 9am-
10pm Mon-Sat, 11am-8pm Sun; 🚇 L, N,
Q, R, W, 4, 5, 6 to 14th St-Union Sq
This outpost of the Boston-based
chain is not actually in a basement, but instead three flights
up in the small strip mall that's
sprouted up at the south end
of Union Sq (around the Whole
Foods supermarket). Fashionistas
willing to conduct painstak-
ing explorations could unearth
treasures, including apparel from
Dolce & Gabbana, Michael Kors
and Versace, among others. On

the floors below you'll find cheap chain stores, with the exception of Whole Foods, which is always packed.

NORDSTROM RACK
Department Store
☎ 212-220-2080; www.shop.nordstrom
.com; 60 E 14th St; 9am-10pm Mon-Sat, 11am-7pm Sun; L, N, Q, R, W, 4, 5, 6 to 14th St-Union Sq
A bargain-hunter's dream, this budget Nordstrom's store claims to have 25,000 pairs of discounted shoes, 2000 pairs of designer denim, and 2400 handbags on site. Clothes and accessories from L.A.M.B., Badgley Mischka, Alexander Wang, Nanette Lepore and more are grouped by designer around the store. Discounts range from 30% to 70%, and there's an onsite tailor to make sure what you buy fits just right. Men's and boy's departments too.

SHAREEN VINTAGE
Fashion & Accessories
☎ 212-206-1644; www.shareenvintage.
com; 13 W 17th St near Fifth Ave; 5-10pm Wed & Thu, noon-6pm Sat & Sun; L, N, Q, R, W, 4, 5, 6 to 14th St-Union Sq
Climb to the 2nd floor to check out the racks of fabulous vintage goods. The owner flies to LA frequently to replenish her store, which pops with vivid prints and wild colors from the '60s, '70s and '80s.

EAT

15 EAST *Sushi* $$
☎ 212-647-0015; www.15eastrestaurant
.com; 15 E 15th St; lunch & dinner Mon-Fri, dinner Sat; L, N, Q, R, W, 4, 5, 6 to 14th St-Union Sq; V
Traditional-sushi lovers rejoice: this is your spot. The large, geometric lights that look like massive paper lanterns and sleek, minimalist interior (done in dark brown and creamy white with red flourishes) will transport you right to Japan. Chef Masato Shimizu relies on daily shipments of fresh fish (such as silverfish, salmon, all sorts of yellowtail, mackerel and eel) flown in from his native island to make his delectable sushi and sashimi.

BLUE SMOKE
Southern, BBQ $$
☎ 212-447-7733; www.bluesmoke.com; 116 E 27th St; lunch & dinner; 6 to 28th St;
Lunchtime and early afternoon is your best chance of sneaking in without a wait; Blue Smoke gets busy at night. Downstairs is a bustling jazz club, but the upstairs – spacious and good for groups and children – is where most of the action is. Belly up for old-fashioned appetizers such as hush puppies or mac 'n' cheese, or go straight for the good stuff:

Texas beef brisket, organic grilled chicken, Kansas City spareribs (sweet), Memphis baby back ribs (lean), Texas salt 'n' pepper ribs (smoky and hot) – or try them all in the rib sampler.

🍴 CHOCOLATE BY THE BALD MAN *American Eclectic* $

☎ 212-388-0030; www.maxbrenner .com; 841 Broadway; 🕙 9am-midnight Mon-Thu, 9 to 2am Fri & Sat, to 11pm Sun; Ⓜ L, N, Q, R, W, 4, 5, 6 to 14th St-Union Sq

Sweet-toothed Aussie Max Brenner brought his chocolate empire to Union Sq, and his wildly popular cafe-cum-chocolate-bar, looking from the outside like a gingerbread house, is all the rage.

CURRY HILL

It's not exactly politically correct, but a small four-block section north of Union Sq and Gramercy, traditionally known as Murray Hill, is sometimes also referred to as Curry Hill – a nod to the numerous Indian restaurants, shops and delis that proliferate here. Starting around E 28th St and flowing north on Lexington Ave to about E 33rd St, you'll find some of the finest Indian eateries in town – and most at bargain prices. The all-time local fave? **Curry in a Hurry** (☎ 212-683-0900; 119 Lexington Ave at E 28th St; 🕙 lunch & dinner; Ⓜ 6 to 28th St). It's not fancy, but even Bono of U2 fame has been spotted having a nosh here.

Besides the sweets he's got a full menu (great breakfast) and also does low-cal variations mixed by hand on the spot. Divine!

🍴 HILL COUNTRY *American BBQ* $$

☎ 212-255-4544; 30 W 26th btwn Broadway & Sixth Ave; 🕙 lunch & dinner; Ⓜ N, R, W to 28th St

It's all about the sausage, fatty brisket, beef shoulder and pork ribs cooked Texas-style at Hill Country – named for the area between Austin and San Antonio. You can eat your meat – with sides of smoky baked beans and butter-drenched biscuits – in the large main room dotted with stacks of freshly split wood and brick walls, or drop into the basement for some live honky-tonk music. There are Sunday football games on the big screens and a hoppin' bar that stays open till 2am.

🍴 STEAK FRITES *French Bistro* $$

☎ 212-675-4700; www.steakfritesnyc. com; 9 E 16th St near Union Sq; 🕙 lunch, dinner, brunch Sat & Sun; Ⓜ L, N, Q, R, W, 4, 5, 6 to 14th St-Union Sq; ♿ Ⓥ ♨

The menu's decidely French bistro but the space is all-American: glowing lights, high ceilings, futuristic decor and plenty of elbow room between tables. Daily specials include coq au vin, seared tuna with fennel and olives, all-you-can-eat *moules frites* and ginger-cara-way-covered magret of duck. The namesake dish – steak *frites* – is so tender you won't need a knife and the asparagus risotto is a buttery dish of green heaven. Vegetarians can feast on hearty salads, plus sides like roasted wild mushrooms. Desserts made fresh daily.

Y DRINK

Y BLACK BEAR LODGE *Bar*
☎ 212-253-2974; www.bblnyc.com; 274 Third Ave near 21st St; 🕐 4pm-2am; 🚇 6 to 23rd St

Hunting lodge in Manhattan is the general theme, and if you like sharing picnic tables and $15 buckets of decent beer, here's your go-to place. Black Bear's got darts and board games, but the friendly regulars seem to prefer a rousing session of beer pong.

Y FLATIRON LOUNGE *Bar*
☎ 212-727-7741; 37 W 19th St btwn Fifth & Sixth Aves; 🕐 5pm-2am Sun-Wed, to 4am Thu-Sat; 🚇 F, N, R, V, W to 23rd St

A simple nook with a classic vibe, this mahogany bar from 1927 serves up specialty cocktails made with fresh, seasonal ingredients (pomegranate, Granny Smith apples, mint, lychee nuts) in

a setting that's historic and retro, decorated with red-leather booths and stained-glass lamps. The dramatic entrance, a low-lit archway, only adds to the elegant excitement.

Y HEARTLAND BREWERY
Bar
☎ 212-645-3400; www.heartland brewery.com; 35 Union Sq W at 17th St; 🕐 11am-2am; 🚇 L, N, Q, R, W, 4, 5, 6 to 14th St-Union Sq; ♿

The original Heartland pub is here in Union Sq, and it's still the best in the city for afternoon people-watching and postwork drinks. The outside tables give you a front-row seat for the usual Union Sq zaniness, while inside you can rub elbows with all kinds of New Yorkers while lifting a few specialty brews. Heartland also has an extensive array of tasty bar treats, like wings, cheese sticks and potato skins.

Y LILLIE'S *Irish Bar*
☎ 212-337-1970; www.lilliesnyc.com; 13 E 17th St near Fifth Ave; 🕐 11am-4am; 🚇 L, N, Q, R, W, 4, 5, 6 to 14th St-Union Sq

Awash in Victorian atmosphere, this quaint pub celebrates the life of Lillie Langtry, a former reigning beauty of Ireland. Snag a table or a seat if you can; otherwise stand at the gorgeous mahogany bar (sent

Beer for all at Pete's Tavern

from Ireland) sipping one of many imported Belgian beers.

ⓨ PETE'S TAVERN *Pub*

☎ 212-473-7676; 129 E 18th St at Irving Pl; ⏱ noon-2am; ◉ L, N, Q, R, W, 4, 5, 6 to 14th St-Union Sq

This dark and atmospheric watering hole has all the earmarks of a New York classic – all pressed tin and carved wood and an air of literary history. You can get a respectable burger here, and choose from more than 15 draft beers. The pub draws in everyone from post-theater couples and Irish expats to no-nonsense NYU students. *Gift of the Magi* author O Henry used to drink here.

⭐ PLAY

⭐ IRVING PLAZA *Live Music*

☎ 212-777-6800; 17 Irving Pl at E 15th St; admission $12-35; ⏱ 7pm-midnight Tue-Sat; ◉ L, N, Q, R, W, 4, 5, 6 to 14th St-Union Sq

An old-time hall, Irving Plaza has shows that run the gamut, from classic hard rock to emo to punk (sometimes in the same night, depending on who's opening for whom). U2, Prince, Rufus Wainwright and others have played here. Frequent performers include Sylvain Sylvain and Cheetah Chrome, Ryan Star, Railroad Earth with Donna the Buffalo, Killing Joke and the Dan Band.

⭐ KARAOKE ONE 7 *Karaoke*

☎ 212-675-3527; www.karaoke17.com; 29 W 17th St; ⏱ 4pm-4am, happy hour 2-7pm; ◉ L, N, Q, R, W, 4, 5, 6 to 14th St-Union Sq

If you can remember the song name, you can sing it at Karaoke One 7, which has more than 800,000 titles (and that includes songs in French, Spanish and Tagalog). Join the happy mix of Japanese businessmen, overstimulated NYU students and after-work corporate types blowing off steam. There's a limited bar menu, but you can also bring in food from outside.

⭐ UNION SQUARE THEATER
Theater

☎ 212-674-2267; www.nytheater.com; 100 E 17th St; prices vary; ⊕ L, N, Q, R, W, 4, 5, 6 to 14th St-Union Sq

The coolest thing about this theater is that it's built in what used to be Tammany Hall, seat of the most corrupt Democratic political machine that's ever ruled the city. Now the theater outrages the public in other ways, by hosting searing works like *The Laramie Project*, and the side-splittingly funny (and un-PC) puppet show *Stuffed and Unstrung* (not for children). Campy musicals also pop up sometimes.

>MIDTOWN EAST

Better pack a protein bar for any visit to Midtown East – this fluid space ranges from the Empire State Building at W 34th St to the edge of Central Park at W 59th St and is jam packed with classic New York sights.

Shoppers will revel in the opulence along Fifth Ave, where Prada, Ferragamo, Bulgari and more surround Trump Tower, and just a few blocks east, moneyed Park Ave brings you to the gilded door of a still stunning art deco masterpiece: the Waldorf Astoria Hotel.

You've also got the Chrysler Building, Grand Central Terminal, Rockefeller Center and the UN to explore, not to mention ritzy Sutton Pl, a mini-community of lucky New Yorkers who live along the East River Esplanade from 54th to 59th Sts. The views of the Queensboro Bridge and the East River are amazing – just make sure you've got the stamina to get there.

MIDTOWN EAST

◉ SEE

◎ CHRYSLER BUILDING

405 Lexington Ave at E 42nd St; 🕙 **lobby 9am-7pm;** 🚇 **any train to Grand Central-42nd St**

Feast your eyes on the gorgeous silver spire that most New Yorkers identify as their favorite city symbol. No observation deck here, but the iconic Chrysler Building's art deco lobby and chic wood elevators are sights unto themselves.

◎ EMPIRE STATE BUILDING

☎ **212-736-3100; www.esbnyc.com; 350 Fifth Ave at W 34th St; adult/child 6-12/senior $18.45/$12.92/$16.61;** 🕙 **8am-2am;** 🚇 **B, D, F, N, Q, R, V, W to 34th St-Herald Sq**

The tallest building in New York, this 102-floor steel and brick monster is a sight to behold – and its sunset views of the city are equally stunning. Be prepared to stand in line and expect tight security (hint: buy and print tickets online and you can cut your wait in half). Since 1976 the building's top 30 floors have been floodlit in seasonal and holiday colors (eg green for St Patrick's Day in March, black for World AIDS Day on December 1, red and green for Christmas, and lavender for Gay Pride weekend in June; visit the website for each day's lighting scheme and meaning). As of research time the 86th-floor Observatory tickets

could be bought online, but tickets to the 102nd-floor deck could only be bought on site.

◎ GRAND CENTRAL TERMINAL

☎ **212-340-2210; www.grandcentral terminal.com; Park Ave at 42nd St;** 🕙 **5:30am-1:30am;** 🚇 **any train to Grand Central-42nd St**

The world's largest and busiest train station (76 acres; 500,000 commuters and subway riders daily) is also a gorgeous feat of engineering and architecture. Take in the theatrical beaux-art facade from E 42nd St, particularly luminous at night, and then head inside to marvel at gold-veined marble arches and the bright blue domed ceiling, decorated with twinkling fiber-optic constellations. Don't miss the tiny unrenovated corner of the original ceiling, left alone to acknowledge the size of the job. For a glimpse of how the unfinished ceiling looks underneath all the celestial glitter, find the northwest corner amid the 88,000-sq-ft ceiling, at the very end of the meridian line, and you'll see a small black patch that designers deliberately left there for contrast. Grand Central has an upscale food market, stocked with luxurious delicacies and gourmet goodies like caviar, fine wine and cheese, fresh fish and organic produce.

NEW YORK PUBLIC LIBRARY

☎ 212-930-0800; www.nypl.org; Fifth Ave at W 42nd St; ⏰ 11am-7:30pm Tue-Wed, 10am-6pm Thu-Sat; ⊕ any train to Grand Central-42nd St or Times Sq-42nd St; ♿

A 1911 beaux arts beauty, the New York Public Library's interior is full of molded ceilings, graceful bay windows and ancient marble staircases leading to places like the gorgeous public reading room, with its 52ft-high ceilings, thousands of books, massive chandeliers and comfy chairs by computer stations (next to brass lamps – how quaint). Say hello to the stone lions – Patience and Fortitude – that greet you at the library steps.

RADIO CITY MUSIC HALL

☎ 212-247-4777; www.radiocity.com; W 51st St at Sixth Ave; admission to hall free, shows $15-40; ⊕ B, D, F, V to 47th-50th Sts-Rockefeller Center

This 6000-seat art deco movie palace had a triumphant restoration, returning the velvet seats and furnishings to their original 1932 state. Concerts here sell out quickly, and tickets to the annual Christmas spectacular featuring the hokey but enjoyable Rockette dancers now cost up to $70. You can see the interior by taking a tour, which leaves every half-hour

Creep past Patience and Fortitude at the New York Public Library

V

NEIGHBORHOODS

MIDTOWN EAST

TOP OF THE ROCK OBSERVATION DECK

It's not quite as famous as the Empire State Building, but the views from the top of Rockefeller Center are equally dazzling. **Top of the Rock** (☎ 212-698-2000; www. topoftherocknyc.com; 30 Rockefeller Plaza, entrance on W 50th St btwn Fifth & Sixth Aves; 🕑 8am-midnight, last elevator at 11pm; ⊖ B, D, F to 47th-50th Sts-Rockefeller Center) also has a pre-show on the mezzanine level to entertain you between elevator rides (those elevators, by the way, are super fast and full of neon blue flashing lights, just for a little extra stimulation). The multimedia show talks about the center's history and the legacy of the Rockefellers, and gives you a chance to take a Beam Walk – a simulated example of the narrow steel beams the original Rockefeller construction workers trod every day without harnesses, even at 850ft above the city.

between 11am and 3pm Monday to Sunday. Tickets are sold on a first-come, first-served basis.

◉ ROCKEFELLER CENTER

☎ 212-632-3975; www.rockefeller center.com; btwn Fifth & Sixth Aves & 48th & 51st Sts; 🕑 24hr, times vary for individual stores; ⊖ B, D, F, V to 47th-50th Sts-Rockefeller Center

Built in the 1930s, during the height of the Great Depression in the USA, the 22-acre center gave jobs to 70,000 workers over nine years – and employed many artists who sculpted, painted and otherwise created the numerous works of public art that dot the space, making it an art deco delight. The skating rink is a winter highlight, as is the annual Christmas-tree lighting, but summer sizzles too, as salsa, rock and pop bands take over the space for nightly shows.

You can browse the shops and restaurants or take a guided tour of Rockefeller Center. Tours are also given of NBC studios, and you can join the throngs outside every morning if you want to be in the background of a *Today Show* taping.

◉ ST PATRICK'S CATHEDRAL

☎ 212-753-2261; www.ny-archdiocese .org/pastoral/cathedral_about.html; Fifth Ave btwn 50th & 51st Sts; 🕑 7am-8:45pm; ⊖ V to Fifth Ave-53rd St, 4, 6 to Lexington Ave-53rd St; ♿

Check out the 330ft spires that dwarf everything in the Midtown neighborhood surrounding St Patrick's, including nearby Rockefeller Center. This graceful cathedral, done in Gothic Revival style, is the seat of New York's Roman Catholic Archdiocese, and is used for every major city ceremony.

UNITED NATIONS

☎ 212-963-8687; www.un.org; E 46th St & First Ave; tours adult/child $14/7; ⏱ tours every 45min 9:45am-4:45pm, call for tours in other languages; ⊖ any train to Grand Central-42nd St; ♿

Like a time capsule dug up 40 years after it was buried, the UN is dated, a wee bit irrelevant, and yet somehow captivating. There are guided tours given daily, but you need to call to book ahead, as tickets are limited and sometimes sell out early, and opening hours subject to change. Even in all its fusty, musty 1960s glory, there's no denying the aura of intrigue inside the green-glass Le Corbusier buildings that were built in 1953.

🛍 SHOP

BLOOMINGDALE'S
Department Store

☎ 212-705-2000; www.bloomingdales.com; 1000 Third Ave at E 59th St; ⏱ 10am-8:30pm Mon-Fri, 10am-7pm Sat, 11am-6pm Sun; ⊖ 4, 5, 6 to 59th St, N, R, W to 59th St-Lexington Ave

It's big and brash and full of attitude – beloved Bloomie's is where New Yorkers go to get a major shopping fix. While the store carries plenty of high-end names, it also likes to bring in

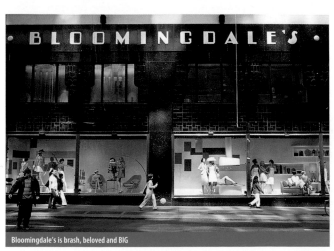

Bloomingdale's is brash, beloved and BIG

NEIGHBORHOODS

MIDTOWN EAST

new designers and right-off-the-runway collections that won't break the bank.

🏠 CALVIN KLEIN
Fashion & Accessories, Homewares
☎ 212-292-9000; www.calvinklein.com; 654 Madison Ave at E 60th St; ☽ 10am-6pm Mon-Sat, noon-6pm Sun; ⊕ 4, 5, 6 to 59th St, N, R, W to 59th St-Lexington Ave Calvin Klein's signature lines fill his flagship Madison Ave store from top to almost the bottom (the lower floor is dedicated to a

surprisingly detailed collection of houseware items, from lamps to linens). On the other floors, you can outfit yourself from head to toe – Calvin Klein sells it all, in materials ranging from denim to lizard skin.

🏠 DIOR *Fashion & Accessories*
☎ 212-931-2950; www.dior.com; 21 E 57th St near Madison Ave; ☽ 10am-7pm Mon-Sat, noon-6pm Sun; ⊕ E, V to Fifth Ave-53rd St, N, R, W to 59th St-Lexington Ave

TOP FIVE ON FIFTH AVENUE
Starting at 59th St and Fifth Ave and heading south, you'll immediately see names like **Trump Towers Galleries** (725 Fifth Ave), **Tiffany's** (727 Fifth Ave), **Louis Vuitton** (1 E 57th St at Fifth Ave) and **Prada** (724 Fifth Ave), but here are five standout shops you don't want to miss.

Bergdorf Goodman (☎ 212-753-7300; www.bergdorfgoodman.com; 754 Fifth Ave; ☽ 10am-7pm Mon-Wed & Fri, 10am-8pm Thu, noon-8pm Sun; ⊕ N, R, W to Fifth Ave, F to 57th St) An otherworldly experience, with separate floors for jewels, fragrance, handbags, menswear, shoes and more, gives you room to browse unhurriedly.

Henri Bendel (☎ 212-247-1100; www.henribendel.com; 712 Fifth Ave; ☽ 10am-7pm Mon-Wed & Fri-Sun, to 8pm Thu; ⊕ E, V to Fifth Ave-53rd St, N, R, W to 59th St-Lexington Ave) The lovely Lalique windows in Henri Bendel frame its quaint little tearoom perfectly; it makes you feel like you're shopping in someone's home.

Jimmy Choo (☎ 212-593-0800; www.jimmychoo.com; 645 Fifth Ave; ☽ 10am-6pm Mon-Sat, noon-5pm Sun; ⊕ E, V to Fifth Ave-53rd St, 6 to 51st St) Sky-high stilettos, sandals and boots galore.

Saks Fifth Ave (☎ 212-753-4000; www.saksfifthavenue.com; 611 Fifth Ave at 50th St; ☽ 10am-8pm Mon-Fri, 10am-7pm Sat, noon-7pm Sun; ⊕ B, D, F, V to 47th-50th Sts-Rockefeller Center, E, V to Fifth Ave-53rd St) A 10-story extravaganza stretching a whole block. Designer goods, casual wear, and an 8th-floor cafe to feed the weary.

Takashimaya (☎ 212-350-0100; www.nytakashimaya.com; 693 Fifth Ave; ☽ 10am-7pm Mon-Sat, noon-5pm Sun; ⊕ E, V to Fifth Ave-53rd St) Seven stories with beauty products, a day spa (top floor), clothes, accessories, home design, floral bouquets and a tea shop.

Stacks of signature Dior sunglasses, handbags and pumps line the walls. Women's clothing and high-end jewelry is in the back; men should head next door to the black-and-white space dedicated to Dior *homme*.

🏠 MULBERRY
Fashion & Accessories

☎ 212-453-4722; www.mulberry.com; 605 Madison Ave near 57th St; ⏰ 10am-7pm Mon-Sat, noon-6pm Sun; 🚇 4, 5, 6 to 59th St-Lexington Ave

High end but not uptight, the friendly staff at Mulberry will help you wade through the designer bags, women's clothes, shoes and other accessories with nary a lifted eyebrow, and gift wrap your purchase too.

🏠 SHANGHAI TANG
Fashion & Accessories

☎ 212-888-0111; www.shanghaitang .com; 600 Madison Ave at E 57th St; ⏰ 10am-6pm Mon-Sat, noon-6pm Sun; 🚇 4, 5, 6 to 59th St, N, R, W to 59th St-Lexington Ave, N, R, W to Fifth Ave-59th St

Asian powerhouse Shanghai Tang is shaking up staid Madison Ave with its bold, patterned and visually arresting designs. Meant to appeal to youthful buyers, this store is as vivid as the clothes, and just as entertaining. Pick up a silk mandarin jacket, beautifully fitted

blouses, daring dresses and much more here.

🍴 EAT

🍴 99 CENT PIZZA *Pizza* $

☎ 212-922-0257; 151 E 43rd St near Third Ave; ⏰ breakfast, lunch & dinner; 🚇 4, 5, 6, 7, S to Grand Central-42nd St; ♿ Ⓥ ♿

Serving up quick and cheap pizza in a city where most slices cost about $2.50, 99 Cent Pizza does a brisk business – always a sign that you've found a good bargain. It's not gourmet and doesn't claim to have fancy toppings, but if you like a good slice with a nice balance of tangy tomato sauce and creamy cheese, 99 Cent won't disappoint. Just don't forget the tax – that'll raise the final price to about $1.10.

🍴 ABURIYA KINNOSUKE
Japanese $$$

☎ 212-867-5454; www.aburiyakinnosuke .com/aburiya.htm; 213 E 45th St near Third Ave; ⏰ lunch & dinner; 🚇 4, 5, 6, 7, S to Grand Central-42nd St; ♿ Ⓥ

Fairly authentic Japanese cuisine (a few nods to American can be found here and there) dished up amid paper lanterns and sleek cherrywood tables tucked behind private screens, or at the open Robata grill at the bar. Sashimi, sake and mains like salmon *harasu* (fatty salmon), dried horse mackerel, organic pork simmered with brown-sugar *soju,* and Japanese-style beef and veggie pot-au-feu dot the menu.

🍴 ARTISANAL
French $$$

☎ 212-725-8585; www.artisanalbistro. com; 2 Park Ave S; 🕐 lunch & dinner; Ⓜ 6 to 33rd St; ♿ Ⓥ

For those who live, love and dream *fromage,* Artisanal is a must-eat. More than 250 varieties of cheese, from stinky to sweet, are on the menu. Along with classic French mains like steak au poivre, you can sample four types of fondue (including chocolate) and *gougères* (little servings) of everything from Brie to Ossau-Iraty.

🍴 DISHES *Fresh Deli* $

☎ 212-687-5511; www.dishestogo.com; 6 E 45th St near Fifth Ave; 🕐 7am-5pm Mon-Fri; Ⓜ S, 4, 5, 6, 7 to Grand Central-42nd St; ♿ 🚻

Not your neighborhood deli at all, Dishes is high-end, haute cuisine with organic/green sensibilities cooked fresh daily for the busy Midtown crowd. It's an overwhelming experience at peak lunchtimes (noon to 1:30pm), when hungry office hordes pour in for the fresh vegan soups, crisp bulgur-wheat-with-goji-berry salads,

Japanese-style sushi and cold sesame noodles, big *sopressata* Italian meat sandwiches, spicy crab cakes with rémoulade, Middle Eastern meze dishes and much, much more.

🍴 GRIFONE
Northern Italian $$$

☎ 212-490-7275; www.grifonenyc.com; 244 E 46th St near Second Ave; 🕐 lunch & dinner Mon-Sat, closed 3-5pm; Ⓜ S, 4, 5, 6, 7 to Grand Central-42nd St; ♿ Ⓥ 🚻

An expensive secret not far from the UN, Grifone is a favorite diplomat hangout. The rich red decor goes hand in hand with the succulent, calorie-laden dishes, heavy on cheeses and sauces, but so finely seasoned that they stop just short of gluttonous. Pasta lovers will swoon at the spaghetti carbonara, with fresh pancetta and parmigiano cheese, and the pesto sauces that are ground and flecked with garlic right under your eyes by chefs working in the open kitchen. There are also tender veal, beef and chicken dishes, and lots of seafood plates.

🍴 ROUGE TOMATE
Belgian $$

☎ 646-237-8977; www.rougetomate .com; 10 E 60th St btwn Madison & Fifth Aves; 🕐 lunch & dinner; Ⓜ F to 57th St, 4, 5, 6 to 59th St-Lexington Ave

Midtown East, home to the five-course business lunch, desperately needed a high-end place that's as easy on the budget as it is on the waistline: voilà Rouge Tomate. This sleek Belgian restaurant eschews french fries and waffles in favor of organic veggies and lean cuts of meat. All the meals – including the $72 prix-fixe with three courses plus dessert – come in at 550 calories or less, but with no sacrifice to flavor or presentation. The chef, formerly of Daniel Boulud's DB Bistro Moderne, works with a nutritionist to count calories (and cooks with olive oil and yogurt over butter and heavy cream), but you won't leave feeling hungry: portions are ample, as Americans like them, and desserts are every bit as decadent as one would hope.

⊞ SIP SAK *Turkish* $
☎ 212-583-1900; www.sip-sak.com; 928 Second Ave; 🕙 lunch & dinner; ⊜ 6 to 51st St, E, V to Lexington Ave-53rd St; ♿ Ⓥ ⛄

Owner Orhan Yeger can usually be found supervising the kitchen, just to make sure everything tastes authentically Turkish (to match the orangey ceiling, bright yellow walls and vivid blue tiles of his restaurant). Lamb and seafood specials never disappoint, but the classic Turkish meze, with

borek filo (dough stuffed with feta cheese), hummus and *cacik* (thick yogurt with garlic and cucumber) is also a winner.

⊞ SOFRITO *Puerto Rican* $
☎ 212-754-5999; www.sofrito.com; 400 E 57th St near First Ave; 🕙 dinner until 2am; ⊜ 4, 5, 6 to 59th St; ♿ Ⓥ ⛄

Pile in for late-night fun (and be prepared to wait) fueled by tasty Caribbean treats like *mofongo* (mashed plantain), *tostones* (mashed, deep-fried plantain), roasted pork with rice and peas, grilled fish dishes, succulent paella, yucca, calamari and more. The ambience is groovy, with the live Sofrito band from Monday to Thursday, and a DJ spinning salsa and hip-hop on other nights.

▽ DRINK
▽ BILL'S GAY NINETIES *Bar*
☎ 212-355-0243; www.billsnyc.com; 57 E 54th St near Madison Ave; 🕙 11am-1:30am Mon-Sat; ⊜ E, V to Fifth Ave-53rd St, 6 to 51st St

Don't let the name fool you – the clientele at this bar are generally as straight as they come. It's all about the Roaring Twenties at Bill's, the decade when original owner Bill Hardy converted the ground floor of his brownstone into a speakeasy. Bill's still retains its illicit aura, in part because you have to traverse hand-carved

NEIGHBORHOODS

MIDTOWN EAST

swinging doors to reach the cavernous inner sanctum, with its high beams, low lights and numerous boxing and racing pictures. It's a great place to unwind, grab a drink and make a new friend.

▼ CAMPBELL APARTMENT *Bar*
☎ 212-953-0409; 15 Vanderbilt Ave at 43rd St; ⏲ noon-1am Mon-Thu, noon-2am Fri, 3pm-2am Sat, 3-11pm Sun; ⓔ S, 4, 5, 6, 7 to Grand Central-42nd St
Take the lift beside the Oyster Bar, or the stairs to the West Balcony, and head out the doors to the left to reach this sublime cocktail spot. This used to be the apartment of a landed railroad magnate and has the velvet, mahogany and murals to prove it. Cigars are welcome, but sneakers and jeans are not.

THE MOVABLE DJ
Greenwich Village native and celebrated New York DJ Danny Krivit brings thousands to his **718 Sessions** (check www .dannykrivit.net for the schedule), frequently heard at clubs like Santos Party House and on his annual 718 harbor boat cruise. To prepare for a 718 Session, hit up **Sunset Salsa at the Triangle** (Ninth Ave & 14th St; ⏲ 6:30pm Thu Jun-Aug) for free salsa lessons and an hour of social dance in the Meatpacking District. All levels, beginner to expert, are welcome to join the gregarious outside dance party.

The Apartment is a great way to enjoy the grandeur of the train station, martini in hand.

▼ MORRELL WINE BAR & CAFÉ *Bar, Cafe*
☎ 212-262-7700; 1 Rockefeller Plaza, W 48th St btwn Fifth & Sixth Aves; ⏲ 11:30am-11pm Mon-Sat, noon-6pm Sun; ⓔ B, D, F, V to 47th-50th Sts-Rockefeller Center
This mega-haven for grape geeks was one of the pioneers of the wine-bar craze that swept through NYC. There are over 2000 bottles of wine to choose from, and there are a whopping 150 wines available by the glass. The airy, split-level room, right across from the famous skating rink at Rockefeller Center, is as lovely as the vino.

 PLAY

☆ **BRYANT PARK**
Outdoor Venue
☎ 212-768-4242; www.bryantpark.org; Sixth Ave btwn W 40th & W 42nd Sts; ⏲ 7am-11pm Mon-Fri, to 8pm Sat & Sun in summer, 7am-7pm Jan-Apr & Sep-Dec; ⓔ B, D, F, V to 42nd St-Bryant Park, 7 to Fifth Ave; ♿
Fashion Week, free films, Latin dancing, concerts and Broadway shows (plus ice-skating in winter): there's always something going on at this grassy haven behind the New York Public Library. With free wi-fi and a cute

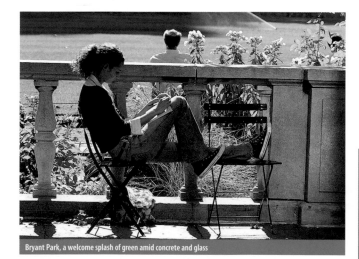
Bryant Park, a welcome splash of green amid concrete and glass

coffee bar, it's everyone's favorite satellite office. Come early for free films in summer – blankets suggested.

⭐ LQ *Club*
☎ 212-593-7575; www.lqny.com; 511 Lexington Ave at 48th St; cover charge $40; ⏰ 5pm-2am Wed-Sat; ⓢ S, 4, 5, 6, 7 to Grand Central-42nd St
Midtown is an odd place for a multistory mega-club, but that doesn't seem to bother the owners of LQ, who have been packing in dance-happy crowds on weekends. The music ranges from salsa to hip-hop and back again, with the odd foray into pop and house. On Latin nights there are often quickie dance lessons on the ground floor to help you find the groove that much faster. The cover can go as high as $60 if you're trying to get in on peak nights.

>MIDTOWN WEST

Teeming Midtown West is full of energy and glaring neon lights, thanks mostly to the frenetic splendors of Times Sq and New York's jaunty Broadway district. It's also filled to the brim with savory food carts, catering to the office crowd rushing along Sixth Ave, and houses the often-overlooked Diamond District, a four-block frenzy of gold and jewel trading.

Shoppers looking for electronic bargains will find a bonanza of discount stores along Seventh and Eighth Aves, and don't be surprised if you hear samba music and Portuguese as you browse: Midtown West also encompasses Little Brazil, an enclave of tasty restaurants and tropical-themed bars. The southern stretch of Midtown West contains the famed Garment District, home to designers' offices, and wholesale and retail shops. The northern tip of this area is Columbus Circle, the gateway to both the Upper West Side and Central Park, backed by the gleaming Time Warner Center.

MIDTOWN WEST

◉ SEE

Herald Square	1	C6
International Center of Photography	2	C4
Museum of Modern Art (MoMA)	3	C2
Paley Center for Media	...4	D2
Times Square	5	C3

🏠 SHOP

B & H Photo-Video	6	A6
Clothingline/SSS Sample Sales	7	B6
Drama Bookshop	8	B5
Duane Reade	9	B1
Macy's	10	C6
Omo Norma Kamali	11	D2
Time Warner Center	12	B1

🍴 EAT

Bann	13	A3
Benoit	14	D2
Best Halal	15	C2
BLT Market	16	D1
Brazil Brazil Grille	17	B4
Empanada Mama	18	A3
Flame Diner	19	A1
Hourglass Tavern	20	A4
Kashkaval	21	A2
Via Brasil	22	D4
Virgil's Real Barbecue	..23	B4

🍸 DRINK

Divine Bar West	24	B2
High Bar	25	B3
Jimmy's Corner	26	C4

⭐ PLAY

Ambassador Theater	27	B3
Birdland	28	B4
Carnegie Hall	29	C2
City Center	30	C2
Don't Tell Mama	31	B4
Little Korea	32	D6
Majestic Theater	33	B4
New Amsterdam Theater	34	C5
New Victory Theater	...35	B4
Samuel J Friedman Theater	36	B3
TKTS Booth	37	C4

Lincoln Center

W 61st St

59th St–Columbus Circle

West Dr

Central Park

See Central Park Map p175

5th Ave–59th St

W 60th St

Columbus Circle

Central Park South

12

16

W 59th St

Columbus Ave

W 58th St

19

9

57th St–7th Ave

W 58th St

W 57th St

57th St

Tenth Ave

W 56th St

Ninth Ave

Eighth Ave

29

Seventh Ave

W 56th St

11

W 55th St

21

30

W 55th St

14

W 54th St

24

W 54th St

Fifth Ave–53rd St

W 53rd St

7th Ave

W 53rd St

3

W 52nd St

NYC & Co

15

4

W 51st St

18

W 51st St

W 50th St

50th St

Radio City Music Hall

Rockefeller Plaza

13 Worldwide Plaza

W 49th St

27

49th St

W 49th St

Rockefeller Center

W 48th St

25 Cyber Café

47th–50th Sts–Rockefeller Center

W 48th St

AAA Dental Care

Fifth Ave

THEATER DISTRICT

36

5

DIAMOND DISTRICT

W 47th St

W 47th St

20

37

W 46th St

31

TIMES SQUARE

Restaurant Row 17

22

W 45th St

W 45th St

HELL'S KITCHEN

28

33

W 44th St

23

26

W 44th St

W 43rd St

W 43rd St

W 42nd St

35

Times Sq–42nd St

5th Ave

42nd St

34

2

42 St–Bryant Park

42 St–Bryant Park

Bryant Park

New York Public Library

Port Authority Bus Terminal

W 41st St

Renwick St

W 40th St

8

W 40th St

W 39th St

W 39th St

GARMENT DISTRICT

W 38th St

W 38th St

Seventh Ave

W 37th St

Sixth Ave (Avenue of the Americas)

W 37th St

Lincoln Tunnel

7

W 36th St

Broadway

0   300 m
0   0.2 miles

W 35th St

34th St–Penn Station

HERALD SQUARE

32

10

1

MIDTOWN

34th St–Herald Sq

W 34th St

6

W 34th St

Empire State Building

W 33rd St

W 33rd St

Tenth Ave

👁 SEE

👁 HERALD SQUARE

cnr Broadway, Sixth Ave & 34th St; 🚇 **B, D, F, N, Q, R, V, W to 34th St-Herald Sq**
Prepare for crowds as you enter the convergence of Broadway, Sixth Ave and 34th St. It's a shopping mecca anchored by a New York landmark of sorts: Macy's department store (p166). The busy square has a small, leafy park offering refuge to foot-sore bargain seekers. South of Macy's on Sixth Ave you'll find an uninspiring string of chain stores, but hidden among them is discount gem Daffy's, stuffed with designer labels that have been (steeply) marked down.

👁 INTERNATIONAL CENTER OF PHOTOGRAPHY

☎ **212-857-0000; www.icp.org; 1133 Sixth Ave at W 43rd St; adult/child under 12 $12/free, voluntary contribution 5-8pm Fri;** 🕑 **10am-6pm Tue-Thu, Sat & Sun, to 8pm Fri;** 🚇 **B, D, F, V to 42nd St-Bryant Park**
It's a museum that doubles as a school, offering classes on all things photography related, while continuously rotating its 60,000 photos, a massive permanent collection spanning from daguerreotypes to modern prints. You'll see some Henri Cartier-Bresson, Man Ray, Matthew Brady, Robert Capa and lots of Weegee, who documented New York's nightlife and crime in the 1930s.

👁 PALEY CENTER FOR MEDIA

☎ **212-621-6800/6600; www.mtr.org; 25 W 52nd St; adult $10, senior & student $8, child under 14 free;** 🕑 **noon-6pm Tue & Wed, Fri-Sun, to 8pm Thu;** 🚇 **E, V to Fifth Ave-53rd St, N, R, W to 49th St, 1 to 50th St, B, D, F, V to 47th-50th Sts-Rockefeller Center;** ♿
Formerly the Museum of Television and Radio, the Paley Center

---

THE MOMA

Japanese architect Yoshio Taniguchi made the most of glass, steel and aluminum when he redid the **Museum of Modern Art** (MoMA; ☎ 212-708-9400; www.moma.org; 11 W 53rd St btwn Fifth & Sixth Aves; adult/student $20/16, 4-8pm Fri free; 🕑 10:30am-5:30pm Sat-Mon & Wed-Thu, to 8pm Fri; 🚇 E, V to Fifth Ave-53rd St, B, D, F to 47th-50th Sts-Rockefeller Center) in 2004. The sumptuous space is its own universe, filled with 100,000 pieces. Most of the big hitters – Matisse, Picasso, Cézanne, Rothko, Pollock – are housed in the central five-story atrium, where peaceful, airy galleries contain works from the departments of Painting and Sculpture, Architecture and Design, Drawings, Prints and Illustrated Books, and Film and Media. The museum's atrium/sculpture garden – returned to its original, larger vision of the early '50s by Philip Johnson – is a joy to sit in.

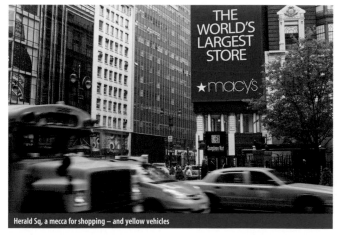

Herald Sq, a mecca for shopping – and yellow vehicles

for Media is dedicated to the small screen and classic radio moments. There are more than 100,000 tapes at your disposal in the archives – pull out that favorite *Star Trek* episode without shame and watch it one more time. There are also retrospective screenings and frequent exhibitions on the rise of modern mass media.

SHOP

B & H PHOTO-VIDEO
Cameras & Accessories
☎ 212-502-6200; www.bhphotovideo .com; 420 Ninth Ave; ☺ 9am-7pm Mon-Thu, 9am-1pm Fri, 10am-5pm Sun; ◉ A, C, E to 34th St-Penn Station

A trip here is an experience unto itself – it's big, buzzy and bristling with every kind of camera, video or DVD equipment you could desire.

CLOTHINGLINE/SSS SAMPLE SALES
Fashion & Accessories
☎ 212-947-8748; www.clothingline .com; 2nd fl, 261 W 36th St; ☺ check website for weekly sales & opening hours; ◉ 1, 2, 3 to 34th St-Penn Station
Line up early to get your hands on designer goods marked down by as much as 75%. Sales happen only on the weekends, and you can find names like Helmut Lang, Rag & Bone, Ben Sherman and others. Check the website to see

what's on the block while you're in town.

☐ DRAMA BOOKSHOP *Books*
☎ 212-944-0595; www.dramabook shop.com; 250 W 40th St; ☼ 11am-7pm Mon-Wed, Fri & Sat, to 8pm (complimentary wine & cheese 6-8pm) Thu; ◉ A, C, E to 42nd St-Port Authority Bus Terminal
Broadway fans will find treasures in print at this expansive bookstore, which has taken its theater (plays and musicals) seriously since 1917. Staffers are good at recommending worthy selections. Check out the website for regular events, such as talks with playwrights.

☐ MACY'S *Department Store*
☎ 212-695-4400; www.macys.com; 151 W 34th St at Broadway; ☼ 10am-8:30pm Mon-Sat, 11am-7pm Sun; ◉ B, D, F, N, Q, R, V, W to 34th St-Herald Sq
Mind your fingers on the old wooden elevators, a highlight of a Macy's trip. The store's goods, mainly linens, clothing, furniture, kitchenware, shoes and more, are affordable and basic. You can lose yourself for hours here, the world's largest department store.

☐ OMO NORMA KAMALI
Fashion & Accessories
☎ 212-957-9797; www.normakamali collection.com; 11 W 56th St at Sixth Ave; ☼ 10am-7pm Mon-Sat, noon-6pm Sun; ◉ N, Q, R, W to 57th St

You won't want to leave the glistening, white-walled, four-story temple that is Norma Kamali's flagship shop. Her one-of-a kind dresses, coats and swimwear hang off dangling mannequins. When you see something you like, a clerk will find it in your size. It's not for bargain hunters, but fashion seekers.

☐ TIME WARNER CENTER *Mall*
☎ 212-484-8000; www.timewarner .com; 1 Time Warner Center; ☼ 10am-9pm; ◉ A, B, C, D, 1 to 59th St-Columbus Circle; ♿
Shop till you drop in Manhattan's glossy urban mall, built to look like a glass-covered mountain and home to more than 40 stores, an organic market, a couple of clubs and theaters, as well as tony residences and $500-a-meal restaurants.

🍴 EAT

🍴 BANN *Korean* $$
☎ 212-582-4446; www.bannrestaurant .com; 350 W 50th St btwn Eighth & Ninth Aves; ☼ lunch & dinner; ◉ C, E to 50th St
You'll have to hunt for the entrance to discreet Bann (tucked inside Worldwide Plaza). A fusion of modern and traditional Korean, Bann lets you do your own BBQ or experiment with some of its offbeat pairings, such as *dak nalke jorim* (spicy chili-glazed chicken

Time Warner Center is a multiuse urban shopping temple

wings with fried plantain) or *cham chi hwe* (ahi tuna tartare served with thinly sliced green apple). The crisp elegance makes it a favorite for business lunches, but the low lights and intimate black tables with granite tops give it a romantic glow at night.

🍴 BENOIT *Bistro* $$
☎ 646-943-7373; http://benoitny.com; 60 W 55th St near Sixth Ave; 🕐 breakfast, lunch & dinner Mon-Sat, brunch, lunch & dinner Sun; ⊖ F to 57th St

Alain Ducasse's New York eatery Benoit is full of bright blond wood, red banquettes, glinting sconces and a more laid-back black-and-white bar. You'll be transported to Paris by fresh-baked croissants,

garlicky escargots, tender duck l'orange, cassoulet and roasted chicken for two. Ducasse fans will also want to check out his more upscale **Adour** (Map p151; ☎ 212-710-2277; 2 E 55th St at Fifth Ave) in the St Regis Hotel; it's got a knockout wine list.

🍴 BLT MARKET
American $$$
☎ 212-521-6125; www.bltmarket.com; 1430 Sixth Ave near W 58th St; 🕐 breakfast, lunch & dinner; ⊖ F, N, Q, R, W to 57th St; ♿

It's in the Ritz-Carlton on Central Park, but aside from that, you might as well be back on the farm. All the food at BLT Market mimics the decor: clean, fresh and changing with the seasons. On a recent visit, chef Laurent Tourondel's organic menu

THE PLATTER CLUB

Known to its many fans as the gyro spot, the chicken and rice plate, or – most famously – the Platter Club, the family-run food cart **Best Halal** (www .53rdandsixth.com; cnr W 53rd St & Sixth Ave; dishes $3-5; ✆ dinner; ☻ B, D, F, V to 47th-50th Sts-Rockefeller Center, E, V to Fifth Ave-53rd St) has long lines stretching down the block every night, well into the wee hours. There's a different cart there during the day but Best Halal moves in at 7pm, and until 4am dishes up succulent rice and chicken, topped with the secret white sauce that many believe is the ingredient that makes this food worth waiting for.

featured seasonal squash and black cod, smoked trout with a cilantro and avocado puree and roasted Hudson Valley duck.

🍴 BRAZIL BRAZIL GRILLE
Brazilian $$

✆ 212-957-4300; www.brazilbrazil restaurant.com; 330 W 46th St btwn Eighth & Ninth Aves; ✆ lunch & dinner; ☻ A, C, E, 1, 2, 3 to Times Sq-42nd St; ♿ 🚻
Most of W 46th St is informally known as 'Little Brazil,' a stretch of businesses, shops and restaurants that cater to the expat Brazilian community. This restaurant, with its relaxed vibe, hefty (and affordable) drinks, live weekend music, and delicious *frango a passarinho* (chicken in white wine, garlic and olive oil), *lula frita* (calamari) and

camarao alhoe (garlic shrimp), is a favorite. Another nearby standout is **Via Brasil** (✆ 212-997-1158; 34 W 46th St near Sixth Ave; ✆ 11am-10pm; ☻ N, R, W, 1, 2, 3 to Times Sq-42nd St); its long room has waving palm trees and super-friendly waiters. The menu's got authentic *feijoada* (beans and meat), *moquecas* (fish stew) and more.

🍴 EMPANADA MAMA
South American $

✆ 212-698-9008; 763 Ninth Ave at W 51st St; ✆ lunch & dinner; ☻ C, E, 1 to 50th St, N, R, W to 49th St; ♿ 🚻 🍴
With its cheery red entrance, long green banquettes down a narrow brick wall, succulent empanadas and great prices, what's not to love about Empanada Mama? The service, unfortunately: it's a little slow and diffident, but these meat-stuffed pastry treats are too addictive to walk away from. You can get wheat, corn and oven-baked empanadas filled with tasty beef or chicken (veggie options too), or *arepas* (stuffed corn patties), or a big plate of *arroz con pollo* (chicken with rice), or shredded beef, or many other South American favorites.

🍴 FLAME DINER *Diner* $
✆ 212-765-7962; 893 9th Ave at 58th St; ✆ 24hr; ☻ A, B, C, D, 1 to 59th St-Columbus Circle; ♿ 🚻
Some people get the appeal of Flame; others don't. It's a classic

New York diner, meaning nobody's going to fawn over you as they take your order. The menu's huge and kind of quirky – shrimp linguine? – but the kitchen does a fine job with fat omelettes, juicy burgers, fries, tuna melts and oozing grilled cheeses, all the requisite dishes for a diner experience.

☷ HOURGLASS TAVERN
Mediterranean $$
☎ 212-265-2060; www.hourglasstavern .com; 375 W 46th St near Ninth Ave; ☽ pre- & post-theater dinner to 4am; ⊕ N, Q, R, S, 1, 2, 3, 7 to Times Sq-42nd St

Truth be told, you're not coming here for the food. The Mediterranean dishes are fine, but the real draw is the old-fashioned New York theater buzz at Hourglass.

DIAMOND DISTRICT
A four-block section of jewelry stores between Fifth and Sixth Aves from W 46th St to W 48th St, the Diamond District is where you can find big bargains on gold and other precious metals. Check out the basics at www.diamond district.org. When you are ready for a break, continue west on 46th St until you hit 'Restaurant Row,' a pretty, tree-lined block between Eighth and Ninth Ave. It's where theater lovers drink and eat pre- and post-shows, and the energy even spills onto Ninth Ave, now alive with its own crop of appealing eateries.

An old townhouse, the 1st floor is romantic (brick walls, lacy tablecloths), the 2nd floor a cool divey bar, and the top floor takes the restaurant overflow from below. Delicious wine list, fabulous staff and after 10pm a lot of Broadway hoofers drift over for a drink. Prix fixe meals are a bargain, served late.

☷ KASHKAVAL *Mediterranean & Cheese Shop* $
☎ 212-581-8282; www.kashkaval.com; 856 Ninth Ave btwn 55th & 56th Sts; ☽ lunch & dinner; ⊕ A, B, C, D, 1 to 59th St-Columbus Circle; ♿

It's not quite clear exactly what type of food Kashkaval serves, except that it's really spectacular. It's a cheese shop in front, and in back a cozy restaurant/bar where you can sip wine and share delicious meze with friends, or fresh panini, fondues, chicken curry salad, chicken caponata and more. Cheese and meat plates, spinach and feta *borek* and creamy white bean *piyaz* are among the eclectic house specialties.

☷ VIRGIL'S REAL BARBECUE
American BBQ $$
☎ 212-921-9494; 152 W 44th St btwn Broadway & Eighth Ave; ☽ lunch & dinner; ⊕ N, R, S, W, 1, 2, 3, 7 to Times Sq-42nd St

Rather than specializing in one specific style of BBQ (styles vary in sauce type and meat base throughout the US), Virgil's celebrates them all. Menu items cover the entire BBQ map, with Oklahoma State Fair corndogs, pulled Carolina pork and smoked Maryland ham sandwiches, and platters of sliced Texas beef brisket and Georgia chicken-fried steak. Meats are smoked with a combo of hickory, oak and fruitwoods, keepin' it all real.

▼ DRINK

▼ DIVINE BAR WEST *Bar*
☎ 212-265-9463; 236 W 54th St near Broadway; ◷ 4:30pm-1am; ◉ F, N, Q, R, W to 57th St, B, D, E to Seventh Ave, C, E to 50th St, A, B, C, D, 1 to 59th St-Columbus Circle

If you worked in Midtown, you'd need a place to blow off some steam too – that's what Divine Bar West offers the buttoned-down business crowd that enjoys its brightly colored chrome bar stools and zebra-patterned seats. It offers a long wine list, extensive beer choices and lots of mixed drinks that you can imbibe over a shared platter of tapas or cheese.

▼ HIGH BAR *Rooftop Bar* $$
☎ 212-229-0010; www.highbarnyc.com; 790 Eighth Ave near 49th St; ◷ open nightly; ◉ C, E to 50th St

Shake your cares away at this lush rooftop hideaway, where you can lounge in breezy comfort on a big plush day bed and sip your martini in peace. Sixteen floors above the city, the High Bar is a sweet escape from the summer heat (in winter the party moves downstairs), even when the dancing starts and things get sticky. High Bar likes the natural look – white canopies, teak and bamboo chairs and tables, and dark slate tile on the floor. When the massive BBQ grill gets fired up and food starts to sizzle it's party time.

▼ JIMMY'S CORNER *Bar*
☎ 212-221-9510; 140 W 44th St near Broadway; ◷ 11:30am-4am; ◉ N, Q, R, S, W, 1, 2, 3, 7 to Times Sq-42nd St, B, D, F, V to 42nd St-Bryant Park

Dive bar or sports bar? The debate rages on. Either way, Jimmy's Corner – long and slender – is bursting with old-time regulars and tons of boxing history, including pictures of owner Jimmy with Ali. A few tables are hidden way in the back, but the most fun is had when you snag a coveted seat at the bar. Mixed drinks abound – including the house special, Jimmy's Hurricane – but the safest bet is to stick to beer.

★ PLAY

◩ AMBASSADOR THEATER
Theater
☎ ticket inquiries 800-927-2770; www.ambassadortheater.com; 219 W 49th St;

🕑 hours vary; Ⓔ C, E to 50th St; ♿ 🚹

Classically horseshoe-shaped, the Ambassador's one of the most intimate large-sized venues on Broadway. If you're in town while *Chicago* is still playing, you'll feel every kick and hear every note Roxie Hart hits, even if you're in the cheap seats in the back.

🌟 **BIRDLAND** *Jazz Music*
☎ 212-581-3080; www.birdlandjazz .com; 315 W 44th St; admission $10-40; 🕑 club from 7pm, shows around 8:30pm & 11pm; Ⓔ A, C, E to 42nd St-Port Authority Bus Terminal

Named for Charlie Parker, or 'Bird,' this jazz club has been turning out big-name acts since 1949 when Thelonious Monk, Miles Davis, Stan Getz and others made music and cut records in front of a live audience. Today you're likely to catch big names from European festivals, like Montreux and North Sea Jazz, and other up-and-coming local talent. Regular performers include the Chico O'Farrill Afro-Cuban Jazz Big Band, Barry Harris and David Berger's Sultans of Swing.

🌟 **CARNEGIE HALL** *Live Music*
☎ 212-247-7800; www.carnegiehall.org; W 57th St & Seventh Ave; 🕑 hours vary; Ⓔ N, R to 57th St

One of the world's most celebrated music halls, Carnegie's not the

biggest, nor the grandest, but definitely one of the most acoustically blessed venues you'll find. Its soaring space still leaves you feeling intimately acquainted with the performers, who can range from jazz greats to opera stars to folk singers like Cesaria Evora.

🌟 **CITY CENTER** *Dance*
☎ 212-581-1212; www.citycenter.org; 131 W 55th St; Ⓔ N, Q, R, W to 57th St; 🕑 hours vary; ♿ 🚹

This red-domed wonder almost went the way of the wrecking ball in 1943, but was saved by preservationists, only to face extinction again when its major ballet companies departed for Lincoln Center. Today, this overlooked treasure hosts the Paul Taylor Dance Company, Alvin Ailey and American Ballet Theater, as well as the New York Flamenco Festival in February and other dance performances.

🌟 **DON'T TELL MAMA** *Cabaret*
☎ 212-757-0788; www.donttellmamanyc .com; 343 W 46th St; 2-drink minimum; 🕑 4pm to 1am; Ⓔ N, R, 1, 2, 3 to Times Sq-42nd St

Piano bar and cabaret venue extraordinaire, Don't Tell Mama is an unpretentious little spot that's been around for more than 25 years and has the talent to prove it. Its regular roster of performers aren't big names, but true lovers

NEIGHBORHOODS

MIDTOWN WEST

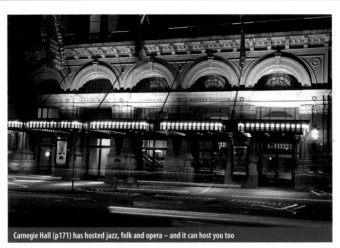
Carnegie Hall (p171) has hosted jazz, folk and opera – and it can host you too

of cabaret who give each show their all and don't mind a little singing help from the audience sometimes. If you want your cabaret a bit more sinister and sexy, head to **The Box** (Map pp64–5; ☎ 212-982-9301; www.theboxnyc.com; 189 Chrystie St; ⊙ F, V to Second Ave). It's risqué and ribald and could get shut down at any moment, but its (very) late-night shows might tickle your fancy.

⭐ LITTLE KOREA *Bars, Karaoke*
Broadway & Fifth Ave & btwn W 31st & W 36th Sts; ⊙ **24hr;** ⊙ **B, D, F, N, Q, R, V, W to 34th St-Herald Sq**
Herald Sq is a bit on the tasteless side when it comes to finding

foodie treats; luckily, you can head for quality refueling at nearby Little Korea, a small enclave of Korean-owned restaurants, shops, salons and spas. It's full of kitschy fun and its late-night hours means it attracts lots of club-goers and party animals seeking Korean BBQ while they drink and sing karaoke into the wee hours.

⭐ MAJESTIC THEATER
Theater
☎ 212-239-6200; www.majestic-theater .net; 247 W 44th St; ⊙ hours vary; ⊙ any train to 42nd St
A fabled performance house that has seen the likes of Angela

Lansbury, Julie Andrews and several Barrymores on its stage, the Majestic is still (still!) selling out every night for *Phantom of the Opera,* 23 years after Andrew Lloyd Webber's creation debuted.

⭐ NEW AMSTERDAM THEATER *Theater*

☎ 212-282-2900; www.newamsterdam theater.net; 214 W 42nd St; 🕑 hours vary; 🚇 any train to 42nd St; ♿ 🚼
If your kids are into theater, watch their eyes pop as they pass through the art deco entrance, into the art nouveau interior of carved and painted plaster, stone, wood, murals and tiles – all of which evoke early-20th-century theater-going – on their way to see *Mary Poppins,* the musical.

⭐ NEW VICTORY THEATER *Arts, Theater*

☎ 646-223-3010; www.newvictory.org; 209 W 42nd St; 🚇 any train to Times Sq-42nd St; 🕑 hours vary; ♿ 🚼
Budding thespians and dancers flock to the upbeat energy of this kid-focused theater. New Victory puts on comedy, dance, music, puppetry and drama shows for the 12-and-under set, and a range of offerings for teenagers.

⭐ SAMUEL J FRIEDMAN THEATER *Theater*

☎ 212-239-6200, 800-432-7250; 261 W 47th St; tickets $50-200; 🕑 show times vary; 🚇 C, E, 1 to 50th St
Formerly the Biltmore Theater, this square, historic building was renamed in 2008; however, its landmarked architectural details remain. Inside you'll find a gorgeous arched dome ceiling, ornate staircases and a gilded 2nd-floor gallery, from its building date in 1925. Notable productions staged here include *No Exit* in 1946, *Billy Budd* in 1951 and *Hair* in 1968.

>CENTRAL PARK

A vast and majestic swath of 843 flowery, tree-filled acres, Central Park (www.centralparknyc.org) is the city's universal backyard, shared equally by billionaires and paupers and everyone in between.

Its glassy lakes, meandering woodlands and lush green lawns offer an unbelievably wide range of physical activities: jogging, skateboarding, cycling, Frisbee-playing, volleyball and more. But cultural fun isn't overlooked either: Shakespeare in the Park, free summer concerts and weekend tango dancing are all part of the Central Park experience.

While sections of Central Park swarm with people, there are also large chunks of land, particularly in the northern section, left untouched. Less populated spots above 72nd St include the Harlem Meer (110th St), the North Meadow Recreation Area (just above 97th St on the west side) and the Ramble (mid-park from 73rd to 79th Sts), a bird-watcher's paradise. Even in winter New Yorkers flock to the park – skiing and snowshoeing if there's snow, and turning out every New Year's Eve for a fast-paced midnight run.

The best subway options are A, B, C, D, E or 1 to 59th St-Columbus Circle, N, R or W to Fifth Ave-59th St or 4, 5 or 6 to 59th St-Lexington Ave.

CENTRAL PARK

👁 SEE
Arsenal 1 C6
Bowling Lawns 2 B5
Central Park Wildlife
    Center 3 C6
Great Lawn 4 B4
Jacqueline Kennedy
    Onassis Reservoir 5 C3
Seneca Village 6 B4
Strawberry Fields 7 B5

Tisch Children's Zoo .....(see 3)
Wollman Skating Rink ...8 C6

🍴 EAT
Central Park
    Boathouse 9 C5
Conservatory Pond
    Kiosk 10 C5
Harlem Meer Kiosk 11 C1
Le Pain Quotidien 12 B5

⭐ PLAY
Belvedere Castle 13 B4
Bike Hire ....(see 9)
Boat Hire ....(see 9)
North Meadow
    Recreation Center 14 B2
Rock Climbing
    Center ....(see 14)
Safari Playground 15 B3

SEE

ARSENAL

E 64th St; admission free; ⏱ 9am-5pm Mon-Fri

Before there was a Central Park there was an armory: the Arsenal, built between 1847 and 1851 to house munitions. The landmarked structure looks like a medieval castle and these days is used by the Central Park Wildlife Center. The reason to visit here is not to see the building, though, but to view Olmsted's original blueprint for the park, treasured here under glass in a 3rd-floor conference room.

BOWLING LAWNS

north of Sheep Meadow at 69th St

There are two 15,000-sq-ft bowling lawns – one for croquet and one for lawn bowling, where members of the 80-year-old New York Lawn Bowling Club still mix it up with tournaments from May to October.

CENTRAL PARK WILDLIFE CENTER

☎ 212-861-6030; www.centralparknyc .org; E 64th St at Fifth Ave; adult/child 3-12/senior $12/7/9; ⏱ 10am-5pm

The feeding hours here are between 10:30am and 4:30pm, which is when the center's penguins, polar bears, rowdy tamarin monkeys and other creatures go crazy – especially the sea lions, who love to chow down. The Tisch Children's Zoo, between 65th and 66th Sts, is perfect for smaller children.

GREAT LAWN

btwn 72nd & 86th Sts

This massive emerald carpet was created in 1931 by filling in a former reservoir. Not far from the actual lawn are several other big sites: the Delacorte Theater, home to the annual Shakespeare in the Park festival, and its lush Shakespeare Garden; the panoramic Belvedere Castle; the leafy Ramble, the epicenter of both birding and gay-male cruising; and the Loeb Boathouse, where you can rent rowboats for a romantic float in the middle of this urban paradise.

JACQUELINE KENNEDY ONASSIS RESERVOIR

For decades the former first lady who lived across Fifth Ave started her day with a brisk walk around this 1.58-mile reservoir. No longer in use as a drinking source, it's become one big reflecting pool, showcasing New York's blue skies and dramatic skyline. The most beautiful time to be here is at sunset, when you can watch the sky turn from brilliant shades of pink and orange to cobalt blue, just as the city's lights slowly flicker on.

Tourie & Damien Escobar, aka Nuttin' But Stringz
Urban rock violin musicians, Emmy winners

How did you two get your signature urban rock sound? We were classically trained, but loved pop and hip-hop and rock. We never really had a plan. We never said let's try and be the next star. We just wanted to play our music and hoped people would like it. At first they didn't, but we went back and rearranged some things, put a beat there, a note here and eventually we started to draw a crowd. **So you played the subways?** Yes, the A and C trains. Also parks, basketball courts, wherever there was people. **Do you still listen to subway music when you're in the city?** Yes, you can definitely hear good music in subways and at sidewalk cafes – and it's free. There are so many talented people out there. Sometimes we just go to open mics to enjoy that. We like to listen to music at the Village Underground (p114) and Brooklyn Bowl (p225), also Alice Tully Hall. **When you aren't performing, where do you go to relax?** We like Play (p197) in Queens and High Bar (p170) in Manhattan.

STATUARY IN THE PARK

Peeking out of unexpected corners are numerous statues and works of art in Central Park that are worth taking a moment to admire.

> **Maine Monument** (at the Merchant's Gate at Columbus Circle), is a tribute to the sailors killed in the mysterious explosion in Havana Harbor in 1898 that sparked the Spanish American War. Ironically, a statue of Cuban independence seeker **José Martí** is just a little further east.

> At Scholar's Gate (Fifth Ave at 60th St), there is a small plaza dedicated to **Doris Chanin Freedman**, the founder of the Public Art Fund, where you can see a new sculpture every six months or so.

> **Angel of the Waters** is an instantly recognizable statue atop Bethesda Fountain, but don't overlook the **Falconer Statue**, tucked away on a rise overlooking the 72nd St Transverse nearby.

◉ SENECA VILLAGE

btwn 81st & 89th Sts

Marked by a simple plaque, Seneca Village was home to Manhattan's first prominent community of African American property owners (c 1840).

◉ STRAWBERRY FIELDS

Standing just across from the famous Dakota building – where *Rosemary's Baby* was filmed in 1967, and where John Lennon was fatefully shot in 1980 – is this poignant, tear-shaped garden, a memorial to the slain star. It's the most visited spot in Central Park, and is maintained with some help from a $1-million grant from Lennon's widow Yoko Ono, who still resides at the Dakota. The peaceful spot contains a grove of stately elms and a tiled mosaic that's often strewn with rose petals from visitors. It says, simply, 'Imagine.'

◉ WOLLMAN SKATING RINK

☎ 212-439-6900; **btwn 62nd & 63rd Sts; adult $10.75 Mon-Fri, $14.74 Sat & Sun, child under 11 $5.50-5.75, skate rentals $8 (cash only);** ☼ **Nov-Mar**

Far less visited than the rink at Rockefeller Center, Wollman's is something to behold during the holiday season, when it's got lights dangling from everywhere. Strap on some rented skates and take a few spins.

🍴 EAT

🍴 CENTRAL PARK BOATHOUSE

Seafood, American Traditional $$$

☎ 212-517-2233; E 72nd St at Park Dr N; ☼ **noon-4pm Mon-Fri, 9:30am-4pm**

> Literary Walk, between Bethesda Fountain and the 65th St Transverse, is lined with statues, including the requisite **Christopher Columbus** and literati such as **Robert Burns** and **Shakespeare**.
> Near Conservatory Pond, kids crawl over the giant toadstools of the **Alice in Wonderland** statue. Replete with Alice of flowing hair and dress, a dapper Mad Hatter and mischievous Cheshire Cat, this is a Central Park treasure and a favorite of kids of all ages. Nearby is the **Hans Christian Andersen** statue, where Saturday story hour (11am June to September) is an entertaining draw.
> **Cleopatra's Needle**, located on the hillock above 82nd St and East Dr, is an obelisk from Egypt, donated in 1877 to the US as thanks for helping build the Suez Canal.
> Near Harlem Meer is a soaring **Duke Ellington** statue, depicting the man and his piano.
> At E 67th St is **Balto** the dog, a replica of an Alaskan sled dog who helped deliver a life-giving serum to a snowbound village suffering a diphtheria outbreak in 1925, an event that captured the world's imagination as people followed his trek by radio.

Sat & Sun Nov 4-Apr 14, noon-4pm & 5:30-9:30pm Mon-Fri, 9:30am-4pm & 6-9:30pm Sat & Sun Apr 15-Nov 3; **V**
Beautifully located on the Park's biggest lake, the Central Park Boathouse offers everything in the way of ambience and setting, but very little in the way of cutting-edge cuisine. It's got a cafe, an outdoor bar and a more formal dining room, all serving up adequate shrimp, calamari and seafood dishes (burgers too).

🍴 KIOSKS
Sandwiches, Snacks S

E 76th St near Conservatory Pond & E 108th St near Harlem Meer; 🕐 11am-8pm Jun-Sep; **V**
When the weather gets warm the Parks Department opens up these small snack shacks. They both sit right on the edge of small ponds,

so you can grab a pretzel on a nice day and then watch the ducks swim your way (hoping you'll share) while you eat.

🍴 LE PAIN QUOTIDIEN
Sandwiches S

www.lepainquotidien.com; 2 W 69th St, north side of Sheep Meadow; 🕐 7am-9pm; 🚇 B, C to 72nd St; 🚹 **V** 🚻
Fresh salads and baguette sandwiches are to be found inside the airy Mineral Springs Pavilion, or outside if you are lucky enough to snag a terrace seat. Other Le Pain treats include organic draft beer and vegan ice cream (plus free wi-fi).

⭐ PLAY
Several of Central Park's most celebrated arts events happen in the summer: Shakespeare in the

Park (www.publictheater.org) and Summerstage (www.summerstage.org) are the two big ones. If you miss those, there are plenty of year-round activities to enjoy.

★ BELVEDERE CASTLE
Bird-Watching

mid-park at 79th St; admission free; ⏱ 10am-5pm Tue-Sun

The castle has a Discovery Room that covers two floors and has an information panel on the trees in the park. More exciting, however, is the display of common birds to be found in the nearby Ramble, and the bird-watching kits you can borrow for free – kids too.

★ BIKING CENTRAL PARK
Cycling

☎ 212-517-2233; www.centralpark.com /pages/sports/bicycle-riding.html; E 72nd St at Park Dr N; adult 1st hr $9, then per hr $5, child 1st hr $6, then per hour $3, incl helmets

There are several places that rent bikes in Central Park, but an easy location to grab one is the Boathouse (p178). Bikes aren't allowed on the small pathways inside the park, but there's a wide road that's easy to follow when circum-navigating the park. Around the reservoir is a dirt track, and around the tennis courts to the north are some family-friendly tracks off the main road. Remember that bike traffic goes counter-clockwise around the park, and you must obey traffic lights.

★ BOATING IN CENTRAL PARK
Boating

☎ 212-517-2233; www.thecentralparkboathouse.com; E 72nd St at Park Dr N; 1st hr $10, then per quarter hr $2.50, $30 deposit, 4 per boat

Set out for a romantic row across Central Park's Boathouse Lake, a tranquil (and fairly shallow) body of water that's home to lots of carp and sun-loving turtles. You'll get to experience the park from a unique point of view.

★ NORTH MEADOW RECREATION CENTER *Sports*

☎ 212-348-4867; www.nyccentralparknyc.org; mid-park at 97th St; equipment free; ⏱ 9am-6pm Mon-Fri, 10am-4:30pm Sat & Sun

---

TANGO IN CENTRAL PARK

It's not quite the docks of Buenos Aires, but pretty darn close. Every Saturday night at 6pm from June to September is tango time in Central Park. Aficionados, neophytes and dabblers gather at the Shakespeare statue near Literary Walk for a little cheek-to-cheek dancing. Even if you aren't one to tango, take a look. You can also swing by a sister event, Tango Porteño, every Sunday night at South Street Seaport (p46). For info and details go to www.newyorktango.com.

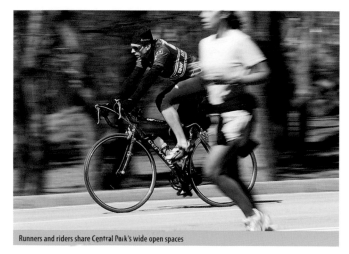

Runners and riders share Central Park's wide open spaces

Trade your ID for a sack full of fun games – baseballs, gloves, bats, Frisbees, basketballs, hula hoops and more. Staff at the NMRC happily lend out their field kits for a day free of charge, but call ahead during busy summer months.

⭐ ROCK CLIMBING CENTRE
Rock Climbing

☎ 212-348-4867; www.nyccentral parknyc.org

New York's urban rock-climbing community flocks to Worthless Boulder (a 10ft-tall rock at the park's north end) near Harlem Meer. Some scaling skills of your own can be harnessed at the supervised **Climbing Wall** (North Meadow Recreation Area; adult/child $7/5; ☽ Tue & Thu evening, Sun), just north of 97th St. Kids can climb on Sundays.

⭐ SAFARI PLAYGROUND
Playground

W 91st St; admission free; ☽ 7:30am-dusk
For kids, there's Safari Playground, a jungle-themed play area featuring 13 hippo sculptures, a tree house and a kiddie jogging path.

>UPPER EAST SIDE

Old money and Irish bars make for strange neighbors on the Upper East Side's leafy, shady blocks, stretching from the lower edge of Central Park to around 96th St.

Its two central avenues – Park and Madison – are generally known as New York's 'Gold Coast,' thanks to the miles of luxury boutiques and jaw-dropping brownstones that line them. As the neighborhood moves further east, along Lexington Ave and all the way to the East River, it gets progressively more working-class, although it's now a world away from the immigrant (and gang-filled) enclave it was four decades ago. The crumbly and ornate buildings show traces of those darker days, but most Upper East Siders are preppy college kids, young families and single 30-somethings.

The neighborhood's cultural interests and nightlife focus on its two greatest assets: Central Park and fantastic museums, most notably the Metropolitan. Those looking for wild drinking and dancing will do better downtown, but for an evening of adult drinking, dining and discussion, the Upper East Side does just fine.

UPPER EAST SIDE

👁 SEE

👁 FRICK COLLECTION

☎ 212-288-0700; www.frick.org; 1 E 70th St at Fifth Ave; adult/senior $18/12, children under 10 not permitted; 🕐 10am-6pm Tue-Sat, 11am-5pm Sun; 🚇 6 to 68th St-Hunter College

Along spectacular Fifth Ave, in what was once known as 'millionaires row,' the private collection of former steel magnate Henry Clay Frick waits to be discovered. His taste in art was as exquisite as his decorating sense; the collection and the home are gorgeous. Look for Jean-Antoine Houdon's stunning figure *Diana the Huntress*, works by Titian and Vermeer, and portraits by Gilbert Stuart, El Greco, Goya and John Constable.

👁 GRACIE MANSION

☎ 212-570-4773 (tour reservations 311 or 212-NEW-YORK outside the city); East End Ave at E 88th St; admission $7; 🕐 tours 10am, 11am, 1pm, 2pm Wed; 🚇 4, 5, 6 to 86th St

This stately mansion is (in theory) the residence of the Mayor of New York – though few of them actually live here – and is worth visiting just for the views. Surrounded by Carl Schurz Park and the East River esplanade, Gracie Mansion is a throwback to American elegance c 1930 and earlier. History buffs should book a tour, but do it at least two months in advance of your trip; the waiting list is long and walk-ins aren't accepted.

The Frick Collection – exquisite art in an elegant setting

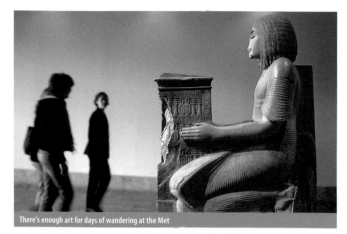
There's enough art for days of wandering at the Met

◉ METROPOLITAN MUSEUM OF ART

☎ 212-535-7710; www.metmuseum.org; Fifth Ave at E 82nd St; admission by suggested donation; ⏱ 9:30am-5:30pm Tue-Thu & Sun, to 9pm Fri & Sat; ◉ 4, 5, 6 to 86th St

What can you say about this gorgeous behemoth? Its size, and the depth and breadth of its collection, simply overwhelms. More than five million come a year for special exhibits, or just to see the cavernous Great Hall entrance, the Temple of Dendur, the Tiffany windows in the American Wing, the collection of African, Oceanian and other works, as well as the famed European Collection on the 2nd floor – it's a city within a city, really, and it's easier to get lost here than in Central Park outside. Avoid rainy Sundays in summer if you don't like crowds. But, during horrible winter weather, you might find the 17-acre museum deserted at night – a real NYC experience. The rooftop garden becomes a wine bar on weekend evenings in the summer.

◉ NEUE GALERIE

☎ 212-628-6200; www.neuegalerie.org; 1048 Fifth Ave at E 86th St; admission $15, children under 12 not admitted; ⏱ 11am-6pm Thu-Mon; ◉ 4, 5, 6 to 86th St

Gustav Klimt, Paul Klee and Egon Schiele are just some of the marquee names hanging on the walls of the Neue Galerie, which opened in 2000 to showcase Austrian and German art. It also boasts a lovely street-level eatery, Cafe Sabarsky (p188), serving Viennese meals, pastries and drinks.

◉ SOLOMON R GUGGENHEIM MUSEUM

☎ 212-423-3500; www.guggenheim .org; 1071 Fifth Ave at E 89th St; adult $18, senior & student $15, child under 12 free, suggested donation 5:45-7:45pm Sat; ☼ 10am-5:45pm Sun-Wed & Fri, to 7:45pm Sat; ◉ 4, 5, 6 to 86th St; ♿

Excellent exhibits from around the world come frequently to the Guggenheim, which is slightly less overwhelming than some other Manhattan museums. Its curving walls bring you in a spiral downward, showcasing Piet Mondrians, Wassily Kandinskys and more.

◉ TEMPLE EMANU-EL

☎ 212-744-1400; www.emanuelnyc .org; 1 E 65th St; ☼ 9am-7pm; ◉ 6 to 68th St-Hunter College; ♿

A premier house of worship, Temple Emanu-El was once part of the Lower East Side Jewish community; as their lot improved, so did the temple's location. It houses a renowned collection of Judaica, and tells the story of its transformation into a ritzy Upper East Side house of worship with murals on the walls.

◉ WHITNEY MUSEUM OF AMERICAN ART

☎ 212-570-3600; www.whitney.org; 945 Madison Ave at E 75th St; adult $18, senior & child $12, suggested donation 6-9pm Fri; ☼ 11am-6pm Wed & Thu, 1-9pm Fri, 11am-6pm Sat & Sun; ◉ 6 to 77th St; ♿

Focused pretty much exclusively on American works, the Whitney pays ample homage to the Rothkos, the Pollocks and the Hoppers in its collection, but also makes room for newcomers and new media. To give you a taste of what you're likely to find, some recent exhibits included a retrospective of William Eggleston

The stunning Guggenheim is itself a work of art

photos (with a nod to his color-saturated influence on modern filmmakers like Gus Van Sant) and a look at the Paris years of sculptor Alexander Calder.

SHOP

☐ ARTHRITIS THRIFT SHOP
Thrift Shop

☎ 212-772-8816; www.arthritis.org; 1430 Third Ave at 81st St; 🕙 10am-6pm Mon-Sat, noon-5pm Sun; 🚇 4, 5, 6 to 86th St; ♿

There are plenty of thrift shops donating to a good cause on the UES; this is the granddaddy of them all. It's been collecting high-end hand-me-downs since 1948, as you'll see from the curious collection of bric-a-brac. Still, there is treasure amid the piles, especially for shoe and handbag fiends (and don't miss a root through the scarf bin). The salespeople maintain a designer rack for couture clothing near the register; that's where to look for your Prada, Balenciaga, Bill Blass, Halston and so on.

☐ BARNEYS *Department Store*
☎ 212-826-8900; www.barneys.com; 660 Madison Ave; 🕙 10am-8pm Mon-Fri, 10am-7pm Sat, 11am-6pm Sun; 🚇 N, R, W to Fifth Ave-59th St

No true shopper could skip a visit to this revered institution, which stretches its youthful apparel, sophisticated looks, designer duds

and cosmetics and accessories over four floors. The best department store in town carries the best of today's designers – Marc Jacobs, Miu Miu, Prada and more. Bargains (comparatively speaking) are on the 7th and 8th floors; or try the Barneys Co-Ops on the Upper West Side, in Soho and in Chelsea (p133).

☐ DONNA KARAN
Fashion & Accessories

☎ 866-240-4700; www.donnakaran .com; 819 Madison Ave at E 68th St; 🕙 10am-6pm Mon-Sat, noon-6pm Sun; 🚇 6 to 68th St-Hunter College

Head to the top floor if you're looking for markdowns, but otherwise

PHARMACIST TO THE STARS

When your clientele consists mainly of fussy Upper East Siders, you know you'd better stock the very best of everything. That's why **Zitomers** (☎ 212-737-2016; www.zitomers.com; 969 Madison Ave at E 76th St; 🕙 9am-8pm Mon-Fri, 9am-7pm Sat, 10am-6pm Sun; 🚇 6 to 77th St), the preferred neighborhood pharmacy to the Upper East Side, carries all things European – including products that aren't exactly (ahem) FDA approved. We're not talking illicit drugs – just high-powered sunscreens and skin-care creams that usually are only available across the pond. This three-story drugstore is sure to have a cure for whatever ails you.

be prepared to pay handsomely for Donna's *tres chic* city-slicker looks. Men won't find many options, but women can dress themselves for life in this three-story store, which has hair pieces, sunglasses, bags, shoes, belts and jewelry to match the wrap jersey dresses and sharp pantsuits that this designer is known for.

🏠 RALPH LAUREN
Fashion & Accessories

☎ 866-606-2100; www.ralphlauren. com; 867 Madison Ave at E 71st St; 🕑 10am-7pm Mon-Wed, 10am-8pm Thu, 10am-6pm Fri & Sat, noon-6pm Sun; ⊕ 6 to 68th St-Hunter College

You'll feel like you've walked into a country estate when you enter this shop, housed in the former Rhine-lander Mansion (an 1898 French Renaissance Revival wonder). Women and men can deck them-selves out in casual wear – jeans, white tops, etc – and more formal wear, with gossamer gowns for the ladies and sleek suits for men.

🍴 EAT
🍴 ANDRE'S PATISSERIE
European/Hungarian Bakery $

☎ 212-327-1105; www.andresnyc.com; 1631 Second Ave; 🕑 9am-11pm; ⊕ 4, 5, 6 to 86th St; Ⓥ ♿

This narrow little cafe/bakery is the perfect antidote to a cold day.

You'll be thoroughly defrosted once you sample the peppery goulashes, homemade stews, warm crepes and the other Old Country favorites that sprinkle the menu. Andre's also has an abundant selection of strudels, chocolate, cinnamon and cabbage kugelhopf, Bavarian chocolates, decadent cakes and more.

🍴 BEYOGLU
Turkish, Middle Eastern $$

☎ 212-650-0850; 1431 Third Ave; 🕑 lunch & dinner; ⊕ 4, 5, 6 to 86th St; ♿ Ⓥ

Best in the summer when you can sit outside, Beyoglu's fresh Turkish cuisine is light and enticing, from the feta-laden salads to the grilled fish and ample meze.

🍴 CAFE SABARSKY
Austrian $$

☎ 212-288-0665; www.wallse.com; 1048 Fifth Ave at E 86th St; 🕑 breakfast, lunch & dinner; ⊕ 4, 5, 6 to 86th St; Ⓥ ♿

It can get a little tight in this popular Neue Galerie cafe on the weekends, but the food and opulent ambience make it worth the fight for a table. Authentic Austrian food – trout-filled crepes, goulash, sausage and strudel – are served on heavy platters and silver cups brought from Vienna.

🍴 CASCABEL
Mexican $-$$

☎ 212-717-7800; www.nyctacos.com; 1542 Second Ave btwn 80th & 81st Sts; 🕑 lunch & dinner; 🚇 4, 5, 6 to 86th St; 🚻 🚼

Inspired by Mexican street food, Cascabel is a classy taqueria joint. Its tacos are a sophisticated step up from traditional *comida de la calle* (street food) but the casual, counter-style atmosphere is laid-back and humorous. Mexican wrestling figures dot the walls, counters and table tops – loads of fun for kids to play with (and there's a kids menu). Adults will appreciate the cold beers, affordable wine by the glass, hot chilies and dishes such as quinoa with frijoles, citrusy fish tacos, tacos with shrimp, or tongue, or slow-roasted Berkshire pork butt, or big platters of roast chicken, rice and beans, and churros (cinnamon doughnuts) for dessert.

🍴 SFOGLIA *Italian*
$$$

☎ 212-831-1402; http://sfoglia restaurant.com; 1402 Lexington Ave at E 92nd St; 🕑 lunch & dinner Mon-Sat, closed 2-5:30pm; 🚇 6 to 96th St; 🚻

A darling of the critics since it opened a few years back, Sfoglia brought its winning combo of fresh seafood and homemade Italian from Nantucket to New York, and its tiny but attractive Upper East Side space is packed every day. Innovative pairings like wild mussels with tomato, garlic, salami and fennel pollen; spinach and ricotta balls cooked in brown butter with preserved lemon; or breaded pork chops with pickled carrots and mustard will have you swooning.

🍴 ZEBU GRILL *Brazilian*
$-$$

☎ 212-426-7500; www.zebugrill.com; 305 E 92nd St near Second Ave; 🕑 dinner daily, brunch Sat & Sun; 🚇 6 to 96th St; 🚻

Rustic wood tables, low lights, potent Brazilian drinks and friendly service make Zebu a great place to end the day. Get the *churrasco* (grilled meat) special for a protein fix, or sample traditional dishes like *feijoada* (black bean stew), *picadinho* (diced beef with a poached egg on rice and beans) or a shrimp *moqueca* (shrimp in coconut milk, lemongrass and sugarcane). There are also typical American plates (salmon, burgers and pastas), plus a few veggie dishes and a prix fixe dinner and brunch for under $30.

🍸 DRINK
🍸 AUCTION HOUSE *Bar*

☎ 212-427-4458; 300 E 89th St; 🕑 7:30pm-4am; 🚇 4, 5, 6 to 86th St

Dark maroon doors lead into a sexy, candlelit hangout that's perfect for a relaxing drink.

NEIGHBORHOODS

UPPER EAST SIDE

BEMELMANS BAR

Listen to the piano man tickle the ivories, sink into deep leather banquettes and take in the glorious 1940s elegance of this fabled bar. The ceilings are 24-carat gold leaf, the ashtrays (artfully displayed, but of course one can't smoke) pure marble, and the mural on the wall is the work of Ludwig Bemelmans, who illustrated the famous *Madeline* books. **Bemelmans** (☎ 212-744-1600; www.thecarlyle. com; Carlyle Hotel, 35 E 76th St; after 9:30pm Sun-Fri $20, after 9:30pm Sat $25; ☷ noon-2am Mon-Sat, to 12:30am Sun; ◉ 6 to 77th St) is a perfect place to canoodle.

Victorian-style couches and fat, overstuffed easy chairs are strewn about the wood-floored rooms. Those looking to mix can gather round the various fireplaces and admire the scene reflected in the gilt-edged mirrors propped up on the walls. The bar's well-crafted martinis taste pretty darn good from the depths of a comfortable chair.

▼ STIR *DJ Bar*
☎ 212-744-7190; http://stirnyc.com; 1363 First Ave near E 73rd St; ☷ 5pm-1am Mon-Wed, 5pm-2am Thu, 5pm-4am Fri, 8pm-4am Sat, 8pm-1am Sun; ◉ 6 to 77th St

A bland entryway turns into a jazzy little bar, with sleek leather banquettes against the wall and fuzzy, brightly colored ottomans to sit on around the room. A DJ spins tunes ranging from '80s alternative to hip-hop and punk on weekends, and a varied local crowd lines up to sample the staple drink: flavored martinis. At happy hour (late afternoon) prices drop as low as two bucks a pop.

▼ UVA *Wine Bar*
☎ 212-472-4552; www.uvawinebar newyork.com; 1486 Second Ave near 77th St; ☷ 4pm-2am Mon-Fri, 11:30am-2am Sat & Sun; ◉ 6 to 77th St

A cozy little wine bar on a quiet UES block, Uva has four graceful tables under a purple awning on the sidewalk and a small, tiny garden out back with French doors and votive candles. Both spaces are pretty, but many find the real gem is the small brick-walled room in between, where couples cuddle on benches along the wall and sip bold and earthy Italian reds and silky, ephemeral whites long into the night.

★ PLAY

☆ 92ND STREET Y *Arts*
☎ 212-415-5500; www.92y.org; 1395 Lexington Ave at E 92nd St; ☷ hours vary; ◉ 6 to 96th St

The Y is a bastion of literary greatness (as well as a venue that caters for music and dance), with its Unterburg Poetry Center hosting frequent readings, plus a Biographers and Brunch lecture series on Sundays, featuring top-shelf authors. Recent appearances have included Paul Auster, Margaret Atwood, Joan Didion and Michael Chabon. Almost all the big-name readings sell out, so if there's a particular author you want to hear, reserve well in advance.

⭐ DANGERFIELD'S
Comedy
☎ 212-593-1650; www.dangerfields
.com; 1118 First Ave at E 61st St;
🕑 shows at 8:45pm Sun-Thu, 8:45pm,

10:30pm & 12:30am Fri & Sat; 🔵 6 to 59th St
New York's oldest and (some claim) funniest comedy club, Dangerfield's is something of an institution. Crowds still pack in for the no-food-or-drink-minimum shows (a rarity in New York, where most clubs make you consume as you laugh), and it features only top-tier talent – no amateur nights allowed. Gone are the days when comedic stars would regularly show up for a cameo, but on the odd occasion an old friend like Jerry Seinfeld, Chris Rock or Jay Leno might pop in.

>UPPER WEST SIDE

Sedate but still charming, the Upper West Side retains its aura of unconventional happiness in the face of increasing gentrification. Its cheery mix of aging liberals, wealthy young families, wide-eyed students and gainfully employed actors and musicians has helped protect the Upper West Side from the ravages of development; stretches of chain stores abound, but plenty of old-school options, such as Zabar's and Barney Greengrass, remain.

Strong on the arts, it houses Lincoln Center, where you can see the Metropolitan Opera House, Jazz at Lincoln Center, the world-famous Juilliard School of Music and, in summer, outdoor performances and free dance nights (mostly salsa, tango and swing, with lessons thrown in).

Nearby Columbia University translates into a college-town feeling on its upper reaches – the bars are plentiful and cheap. It's flanked by two fabulous green spaces that stretch north alongside the neighborhood: Central Park on its east edge and Riverside Park to the west. The plentiful parkland contributes to its friendly, bohemian vibe.

UPPER WEST SIDE

SEE

AMERICAN MUSEUM OF NATURAL HISTORY

☎ 212-769-5000; www.amnh.org; Central Park West at W 79th St; general entrance suggested donation adult $16, senior & student $12, child $9, tickets for interactive exhibits $12-20; ☯ 10am-5:45pm, Rose Center to 8:45pm Fri; ◉ B, C to 81st St-Museum of Natural History, 1 to 79th St

From the outside, it's hard to tell just how massive this museum really is. Its exhibits go on for days through three huge halls, plus there's the Rose Center for Earth and Space (free tapas, jazz and drinks on Friday nights), Imax theaters, a planetarium, and oh, did we mention the special kids section where all exhibits are touchy-feely and interactive? Even experts can't help but be dazzled by the more than 30 million bits and bobs in here.

CHILDREN'S MUSEUM OF MANHATTAN

☎ 212-721-1234; www.cmom.org; 212 W 83rd St btwn Amsterdam Ave & Broadway; admission $10; ☯ 10am-5pm Tue-Sun; ◉ 1 to 86th St, B, C to 81st St-Museum of Natural History

As much for mommy and daddy as the little ones, this museum doesn't talk down to kids. It's got a discovery center, a postmodern media center, and the top-of-the-line Inventor Center where the world's future Bill Gates can prod, poke and disassemble whatever he wants. During summer months, kids can splash around with outdoor waterwheels and boats for lessons on buoyancy and currents. The museum also runs craft workshops on the weekends and sponsors special exhibitions.

DAKOTA BUILDING

1 W 72nd St at Central Park West; ◉ B, C to 72nd St; ♿

Explore the American Museum of Natural History

A turreted, gabled building described in 1884 as so far uptown it was in 'the Dakotas,' this sand-colored gem quickly became the epitome of cool, housing Boris Karloff, Rudolph Nureyev, Lauren Bacall and, most famously, John Lennon, who was fatally shot at its gated entrance.

◉ LINCOLN CENTER

☎ 212-875-5900; www.lincolncenter.org; Lincoln Center Plaza, Broadway at W 64th St-Lincoln Center; ⊙ performance hours vary, tours 10:30am-4:30pm; ◉ 1 to 66th St; ♿ 🚻

Sprawling Lincoln Center is a miniature city in its own right. Avery Fisher Hall, home to the New York Philharmonic, currently undergoing a redesign, sits next to Alice Tully Hall, the locus of the Chamber Music Society. The New York State Theater plays host to the **New York City Ballet** (www.nycballet.com) and the **New York City Opera** (www.nycopera.com). Walter Reade Theater hosts the New York Film Festival and shows quality films daily. There are the Newhouse and Beaumont theaters, Juilliard School and, last but not least, the Metropolitan Opera House, with its sweeping, grand, red-carpeted staircase. Daily tours of the Lincoln Center and theaters are available (tickets adult $15, student & senior $12, child $8; call ☎ 212-875-5350 for tour information).

◉ NEW-YORK HISTORICAL SOCIETY

☎ 212-873-3400; www.nyhistory.org; 2 W 77th St at Central Park West; adult/senior $12/9; ⊙ 10am-6pm Tue-Thu & Sat, 10am-8pm Fri, 11am-5:45pm Sun; ◉ 1 to 79th St, B, C to 81st St-Museum of Natural History

Founded in 1804 to preserve the city's historical and cultural artifacts, this gem is often overlooked by visitors tramping to the nearby American Museum of Natural History. A pity, since its collection of more than 60,000 objects is as quirky and fascinating as NYC itself. Only here can you see 17th-century cowbells and baby rattles and the mounted wooden leg of Gouverneur Morris. The Henry Luce III Center for the Study of American Culture, which opened in 2000, is a 21,000-sq-ft showcase of more than 40,000 objects from the museum's permanent collection, and features items such as fine portraits, Tiffany lamps and model ships. The place always hosts unique special exhibits, too, with recent examples including 'Here is New York: Remembering 9/11' and 'Audubon's Aviary: Portraits of Endangered Species.'

◉ RIVERSIDE PARK

www.riversideparkfund.org; Riverside Dr from W 68th to W 155th Sts; ⊙ 6am-1am; ◉ 1, 2, 3 to any stop btwn 66th & 157th Sts; ♿

Another classic beauty designed by Central Park creators Olmsted and Vaux, this waterside spot, running north on the Upper West Side and banked by the Hudson River, is lusciously leafy and tranquil. Plenty of bike paths and playgrounds make it a family favorite.

SHOP

☐ MAXILLA & MANDIBLE
Novelty Store

☎ 212-724-6173; www.maxillaand mandible.com; 451 Columbus Ave near W 82nd St; ☯ 11am-7pm Mon-Sat, 1-5pm Sun; ◉ B, C to 81st St-Museum of Natural History

'The World's First and Only Osteological Store' has been around since 1983, ideally situated about a block from the Museum of Natural History. Fans of bones, fossils and beetle-studded jewelry will be entranced by the varied goodies on display at this specialty shop. Most people come in to gawk at the dangling skeletons and rows of neatly arranged bones, but few can resist picking up a few novelty items like lucite bracelets filled with brightly colored shield bugs from Thailand. They come in rings and necklaces, too.

☐ OFF BROADWAY BOUTIQUES *Thrift Shop*
☎ 212-724-6713; www.boutiqueoff broadway.com; 139 W 72nd St near

Amsterdam Ave; ☯ 10:30am-8pm Mon-Fri, 10:30am-7pm Sat, 1-7pm Sun; ◉ 1, 2, 3 to 72nd St

Dressing divas since 1970, Off Broadway's clothes are sparkling, vivid and far, far too garish for almost everyone's taste – and yet somehow this thrift shop has stayed in business for 40 years. Maybe it's the odd gem or two tucked into the back section, called Re-Runs, that keeps people flocking in: hidden in the bins are vintage finds by Yves St Laurent, Dior and others. The owner also scours the globe for emerging designers and features their clothes in the front of the shop. There are real bargains to be had, but you'll have to search for them.

☐ WINK *Fashion & Accessories*
☎ 212-877-7727; www.winknyc. com; 188 Columbus Ave near 86th St; ☯ 11am-8pm; ◉ 1 to 66th St

Gorgeous, girly and glamorous, Wink is a favorite for its lush collection of Foley + Corinna bags, Frye and Hunter boots, Dolce Vita, DKNY and House of Harlow shoes – in flats, wedge heels and ankle-twisting stilettos. Pick up some J Brand jeans, Marc Jacobs classics, LaROK eye-candy dresses and LA Made tees and blouses. Wink has also got scarves, bracelets, watches and sunglasses to accessorize your new outfits.

📷 ZABAR'S *Food & Drink*
☎ 212-787-2000; www.zabars.com; 2245 Broadway; ⏱ 8am-7:30pm Mon-Fri, 8am-8pm Sat, 9am-6pm Sun; 🚇 1 to 79th St

An unofficial Upper West Side landmark, Zabar's still has that special 'only in New York' vibe that makes you feel like you're in a Woody Allen movie. People bustle and bump around the gourmet foods discussing their lives, politics and the freshness of the gefilte fish as if they were the only ones in the room.

🍴 EAT
🍴 BARNEY GREENGRASS
Kosher Deli $$
☎ 212-724-4707; www.barneygreengrass.com; 541 Amsterdam Ave at W 86th St; ⏱ breakfast & lunch; 🚇 1 to 86th St; ♿ 🚼

The self-proclaimed king of sturgeon, Barney Greengrass serves up the same heaping dishes of eggs and salty lox, bialys and fishy caviar, and melt-in-your-mouth chocolate babkas that first made it famous when it opened a century ago. Pop in to fuel up in the morning or for a quick lunch; there are rickety tables set amid the crowded produce aisles. Besides salmon and whiting, kippered eggs and other Jewish delicacies, you can of course get a perfect New York bagel.

🍴 CAFE CON LECHE
Cuban, Puerto Rican $$
☎ 212-678-7000; 726 Amsterdam Ave near W 96th St; ⏱ lunch & dinner; 🚇 B, C, 1, 2, 3 to 96th St; ♿ 🚼

A cozy hideaway on the Upper West Side, not far from the

RAINY DAY BARS
It's not all bright skies and sunshine in New York City. When Mother Nature roars, it's good to have a place to go into hiding for a few hours.
> Kettle of Fish (p113) in the West Village is great if there's a football game, and even better if it's the Packers playing.
> Chelsea Brewing Company (p137) is inside the action-packed Chelsea Piers sports complex, which has a skating rink, basketball courts, baseball batting cages and other games.
> Union Hall (p224) in Brooklyn combines bocce ball and beer.
> DBA (p100) in the East Village can keep you amused with its selection of brews, and darts.
> Gutter (p225) in Brooklyn has bowling lanes and kegs. Perfect combo.
> Play (☎ 718-476-2828; www.play-ny.com; 77-17 Queens Blvd in Elmhurst near Albion Ave; ⏱ open nightly; 🚇 R, V to Elmhurst Ave) has chess, pool tables (with lessons), bowling lanes and Ping-Pong tables available for drinking patrons. Divert to this sleek little bar in Queens if your Mets game gets rained out.

NEIGHBORHOODS

UPPER WEST SIDE

SHAKE SHACK OUTPOST
To the delight of moms, pops and kids all over the UWS, organic eats guru Danny Meyer brought the **Shake Shack** (☎ 646-747-8770; www.shakeshack nyc.com; 366 Columbus Ave btwn 77th & 78th Sts; ☼ lunch & dinner; ⊕ B, C, 1, 2, 3 to 72nd St) to their 'hood. The burger stand has sundaes, shakes, thick, fresh burgers and crispy curly fries just like the original in Madison Sq Park (p142).

northern reaches of Central Park and St John the Divine Cathedral, Cafe con Leche's breezy yellow doors lead into a cheery dining room that's short on luxury but long on friendly service. Great Cuban coffee and heaping plates of *arroz con pollo* (chicken and rice), *ropa vieja* (shredded beef) and *mofongo* (a Puerto Rican specialty) keep it busy late into the evening.

FATTY CRAB *Malaysian* $
☎ 212-496-2722; www.fattycrab.com; 2170 Broadway near 77th St; ☼ lunch & dinner; ⊕ 1 to 79th St; ⬤ ⬤
Spicy Malaysian street food is jazzed up with a New York twist at Fatty Crab, known as much for its affordable prix fixe lunch and popular happy hour (drinks half price) as for its chili crab, Singaporean black-pepper mussels, barramundi grilled on banana leaf, short-rib ren-

dang braised with kaffir lime and coconut, chicken claypot and fatty duck with toasted tamaki. There are 20 outdoor seats, plus a long steel bar in the spacious main room.

JOSIE'S RESTAURANT
Health Food $$
☎ 212-769-1212; 300 Amsterdam Ave; ☼ lunch; ⊕ 1, 2, 3 to 72nd St; ⬤ ⓥ ⬤
Organic fare (with its provenance listed on the menu) that satisfies vegans, vegetarians and meat eaters alike has kept Josie's around for more than a decade. Its clean, simple ambience is reflected in the food – steak, salads, gorgeous veggie dishes, but nothing too processed or tortured.

KEFI *Greek* $$
☎ 212-873-0200; www.kefirestaurant. com; 505 Columbus Ave near 84th St; ☼ lunch Tue-Sat, dinner nightly; ⊕ B, C to 86th St; ⬤ ⬤
Acclaimed chef Michael Psilakis opened Kefi a few years ago and almost immediately had to move to a new expanded location, such was the demand for his rustic, Greek cuisine based on childhood favorites like spicy lamb sausage, grilled branzino fish, sheep-milk dumplings, grilled octopus and meatballs in tomato sauce. The white-walled room, with stone floors and stucco, is dominated by a massive, blue wave mosaic,

while rooms above and below handle the overflow. Kids are welcome.

🍴 PIER I CAFÉ Outdoor Cafe $$
☎ 212-362-4450; www.piericafe.com; W 70th St & Riverside Blvd; 🕙 lunch & dinner; 🚇 1, 2, 3 to 72nd St; 👪

A casual cafe along the Hudson River esplanade, Pier i Café is a perfect pit stop for hungry cyclists, runners, strollers and skaters who want to fuel up and catch some rays (or a gorgeous sunset). Live music some nights, big juicy burgers, fries (with garlic if you like), lobster rolls, hot dogs and more (beer and wine), plus an early morning coffee bar (named Klatch), mean the Pier is always packed. It's open daily May through October.

🍴 PIO PIO Peruvian $$
☎ 212-665-3000; 702 Amsterdam Ave at W 94th St; 🕙 lunch & dinner; 🚇 1, 2, 3 to 96th St; 👪

Swallow hard before you order the two-person Matador Combo, which is really enough food to feed you and a bull. It comes with an entire rotisserie chicken – the specialty of the house – plus rice and beans, tostones (deep-fried plantains), a salad and a massive plate of fries. Those without cast-iron stomachs might prefer to just order pieces of rotisserie chicken from the menu. Pio Pio is famous

for its well-marinated and crispy golden birds.

🍸 DRINK
🍸 PROHIBITION Bar
☎ 212-579-3100; 503 Columbus Ave near W 84th St; 🕙 5pm-3am; 🚇 B, C, 1 to 86th St

There's not much that's prohibited at Prohibition – in fact, the bar is nicely set up to accommodate a lot of drinking. There's a live band almost every night up front, but decibel levels are low enough that your ears won't bleed. Those who want to talk can head into the back, which is band-free, and for those who prefer sports, there's a billiard table. Sexy red walls and inventive drinks (lavender martinis and rum mojitos) add a little flair, and the bite-sized burgers are a perfect bar snack.

🍸 WEST 79TH STREET BOAT BASIN CAFÉ Riverside Cafe
☎ 212-496-5542; www.boatbasincafe.com; W 79th St at Henry Hudson Parkway; 🕙 lunch & dinner Apr-Oct, weather permitting; 🚇 1 to 79th St; 👪

Sunsets on the Hudson – it's not quite the same as sundown in the Caribbean, but it's pretty darn good, all the same. This cafe, located on the far west side of Manhattan, offers a great location from which to watch the action, and suck back a cold one while you do it. Come the hot weather, the West 79th Street Boat Basin Café is everyone's favorite evening hangout.

PLAY

⭐ CLEOPATRA'S NEEDLE *Club*

☎ 212-769-6969; www.cleopatrasneedle ny.com; 2485 Broadway btwn W 92nd & W 93rd Sts; 🕑 4pm-late; 🚇 1, 2, 3 to 96th St

Come early and you'll probably make the daily happy hour, when martinis are half price. Cleopatra's Needle (named after the statue in Central Park) is small and narrow, just like its namesake. Grab a small table or sit at the bar to enjoy Mediterranean-style food. There's no cover, but a $10 minimum. If you come early, be prepared to stay late: Cleopatra's famous for all-night jam sessions that hit their peak around 4am.

⭐ IRIDIUM *Jazz Music*

☎ 212-582-2121; www.iridiumjazzclub .com; 1650 Broadway; cover charge $25-40, plus min drink order $10; 🕑 6:30pm-late; 🚇 A, B, C, D, 1 to 59th St-Columbus Circle

Consistently pulling in the biggest names in town, Iridium is pricey and a bit fussy, but it's clear why when you get inside: service, sight lines and acoustics are done to

Music lovers should beat a (rhythmic) path to Jazz at Lincoln Center

perfection, allowing you to slip away on a swell of glossy jazz. Reserve early, especially when the Mingus Big Band is in town.

⭐ JAZZ AT LINCOLN CENTER
Jazz Music

☎ 212-258-9595; www.jazzatlincoln center.org; Time Warner Center, Broadway at W 60th St; ⏰ hours vary; ⊕ A, B, C, D, 1 to 59th St-Columbus Circle
There are three venues that make up Jazz at Lincoln Center: Rose Theater, Allen Room and Dizzy's Club Coca-Cola. The first two are pretty fancy, but it's the last one you're likely to visit because it's got nightly shows year round. Ignore the obnoxious name and focus on the musical talent – it's world class, just like the excellent Central Park views.

⭐ LEONARD NIMOY THALIA
Cinema

☎ 212-864-5400; www.symphony space.org; 2537 Broadway; tickets $7-10; ⏰ daily; ⊕ 1, 2, 3 to 96th St; ♿ 🚻
Name any obscure French or Japanese or Mexican film and you can bet it's been shown here. This secret little cinema can be counted on to show the most eclectic and esoteric films from around the world and through the ages. It's a film buff's fantasy come true.

⭐ SYMPHONY SPACE
Live Music

☎ 212-864-5400; www.symphonyspace .org; 2537 Broadway; ⏰ hours vary; ⊕ 1, 2, 3 to 96th St; ♿ 🚻
Home to National Public Radio's renowned literary readings, Symphony Space is a gem supported by community contributions. It often has three-day series that are dedicated to just one musician, and has an affinity for world music. In the basement is UnWINed, a tapas and vino bar that never charges a cover to listen to its free nightly live band.

>HARLEM

Hip and happening Harlem has held on to its rough edges amid an influx of money and development, and still remains one of Manhattan's most community-oriented neighborhoods. With development surging along the commercial 125th St strip, Harlem's changing one storefront at a time, but not without constant involvement from local leaders determined to keep this Afro-centric nabe's special energy alive.

Settepani's, the iconic Lenox Lounge jazz club, the Malcolm Shabazz Market and other well-known parts of Harlem are along Lenox Ave, the main drag. The west side, by Columbia University, has Riverside Church, the Cathedral of St John the Divine, and Smoke, a funky jazz club. Historic Harlem is along and above the 125th St shopping center, where the Apollo, Studio Museum and the Schomburg Center are located. The east side has El Museo del Barrio, a grassroots museum featuring Puerto Rican, Dominican and Caribbean artists.

HARLEM

SEE
Abyssinian Baptist
  Church **1** B3
Apollo Theater **2** B4
Cathedral of St John the
  Divine **3** A5
El Museo del Barrio **4** C6
General US Grant
  National Memorial **5** A4
Museum of the City
  of New York **6** C6
Riverside Church **7** A4
Schomburg Center for
  Research in Black
  Culture **8** B3
Studio Museum in
  Harlem **9** B4

SHOP
B Oyama Homme **10** B3
Harlem's Heaven Hat
  Boutique **11** B2
Liberty House **12** A5

EAT
Africa Kine **13** B5
Amy Ruth's **14** B5
Caffe Latte **15** B5
Chez Lucienne **16** C4
Community Food and
  Juice **17** A5
El Paso Taqueria **18** C6
El Paso Taqueria **19** D5
Le Baobab **20** B5

Settepani's **21** C4
Society **22** B5
Sylvia's **23** C4

DRINK
Den **24** C3
Nectar **25** B4

PLAY
Lenox Lounge **26** C4
Perk's **27** B4
Shrine **28** B3
Smoke **29** A6

SEE

ABYSSINIAN BAPTIST CHURCH

☎ 212-862-7474; www.abyssinian.org; 132 Odell Pl (W 138th St) btwn Adam Clayton Powell Jr Blvd & Lenox Ave; ⏱ services 9am & 11am Sun; 🚇 2, 3 to 135th St

Founded by an Ethiopian businessman, the Abyssinian Baptist Church began as a downtown institution but moved north to Harlem in 1923, mirroring the migration of the city's black population. Its charismatic pastor, Calvin O Butts III, is an important community activist whose support is sought by politicians of all parties. The church has a superb choir and the building is a beauty. If you plan on visiting with a group of 10 or more, the congregation requests that you call in advance to see if space is available.

APOLLO THEATER

☎ 212-531-5300; 253 W 125th St at Frederick Douglass Blvd; tours weekdays $16, Sat & Sun $18; ⏱ tours 11am, 1pm & 3pm Mon, Tue, Thu, Fri, 11am Wed, 11am & 1pm Sat & Sun; 🚇 A, B, C, D to 125th St

This has been Harlem's leading space for political rallies and concerts since 1914. Virtually every major black artist of note in the 1930s and '40s performed here, including Duke Ellington and Charlie Parker. After a desultory spell as a movie theater and several

The facade of the Abyssinian Baptist Church

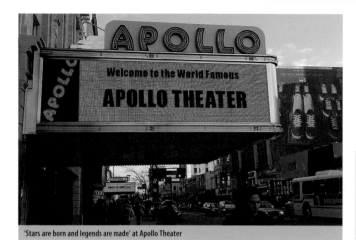

'Stars are born and legends are made' at Apollo Theater

years of darkness, the Apollo was bought in 1983 and revived as a live venue. Now the Apollo interior is more beautiful than ever: gold sconces and balconies, and plush red seats. Its famous weekly Amateur Night, 'where stars are born and legends are made,' still takes place on Wednesdays, with a wild and ruthless crowd that's as fun to watch as the performers.

CATHEDRAL OF ST JOHN THE DIVINE

☎ 212-316-7540, tours 212-932-7347; www.stjohndivine.org; 1047 Amsterdam Ave at W 112th St; ⏰ 7am-6pm Mon-Sat, to 7pm Sun; ⓜ 1 to 110th St; ♿

The Cathedral of St John the Divine is a beloved spiritual and artistic center in Manhattan. Its massive nave is a mix of Romanesque and Gothic Revival styles blended harmoniously together. Started in 1892, the cathedral's still not done – the finishing touches on the towers should be in place by 2050, if workers stay on schedule.

EL MUSEO DEL BARRIO

☎ 212-831-7272; www.elmuseo.org; 1230 Fifth Ave at E 104th St; suggested donation adult $6, senior & student $4, child under 12 free, seniors free on Wed; ⏰ 11am-6pm Wed-Sun; ⓜ 2, 3 to Central Park North-110th St; ♿

Growing out of the Nuyorican and civil rights movement in East Harlem, El Museo remains the only major museum in the city dedicated to Puerto Rican and Latin work, with a permanent collection of pre-Colombian and Taino artifacts, and revolving modern-art exhibits. Through 2012, El Museo is hosting *Caribbean: Crossroads of the World*, with artists from around the globe.

⦿ GENERAL US GRANT NATIONAL MEMORIAL

☎ 212-666-1640; www.nps.gov/gegr; Riverside Dr at W 122nd St; ⊙ 9am-5pm; ⦿ 1 to 125th St

Popularly known as Grant's Tomb, this landmark holds the remains of Civil War hero and president Ulysses S Grant and those of his wife, Julia. Completed in 1897 (12 years after his death), the granite structure cost $600,000 and is the largest mausoleum in the country.

⦿ MUSEUM OF THE CITY OF NEW YORK

☎ 212-534-1672; www.mcny.org; 1220 Fifth Ave at E 103rd St; admission by suggested donation; ⊙ 10am-5pm Tue-Sun; ⦿ 2, 3 to Central Park North-110th St; ♿

This collection spans the past, present and future of the five boroughs in lithographs, photographs, cartoons, clothes and

more. Exhibits cover all facets of city life, from hard-core skaters in Brooklyn to famous city interior designers.

⦿ RIVERSIDE CHURCH

☎ 212-870-6700; www.theriverside churchny.org; 490 Riverside Dr at W 120th St; ⊙ 9am-5pm; ⦿ 1 to 116th St; ♿

Famous for combining its spiritual beliefs with progressive politics, Riverside Church has had Martin Luther King Jr, Fidel Castro and Nelson Mandela holding forth from its pulpit.

⦿ SCHOMBURG CENTER FOR RESEARCH IN BLACK CULTURE

☎ 212-491-2200; www.nypl.org/research /sc/sc.html; 515 Lenox Ave; ⊙ noon-8pm Mon-Wed, 11am-6pm Thu & Fri, 10am-5pm Sat; ⦿ 2, 3 to 135th St

The nation's largest collection of documents, rare books, recordings and photographs relating to the African American experience resides at this center near W 135th St. Arthur Schomburg, born in Puerto Rico, started gathering works on black history during the early 20th century while becoming active in the movements for civil rights and Puerto Rican independence. His impressive collection was purchased by the Carnegie Foundation and eventually expanded and stored in this

Angela Montefinise
Head of public relations for the New York Public Library, native New Yorker, insane Yankees fan

What's your nabe? I live on 110th St near Amsterdam Ave. It's part of Harlem, but we call it Morningside Heights. **What do you like best about where you live?** That it's Manhattan without feeling like the big city. It's bustling, and there are plenty of restaurants and bars and people, but at the same time there are families and parks. **What's an NYC icon worth the admission fee?** Definitely the MoMA (p164). I can spend endless afternoons there. Definitely the Museum of Natural History (p194). Definitely the ball-park and a ride on the Cyclone at Coney Island (p219). And – although it's a bit pricey – the ice-skating rink at Rockefeller Center (p154). I did that for the first time this year, and – it sounds corny – but it was truly magical. Oh, and of course, Yankee Stadium (p230)! Go Yankees! **Got any favorite books about NYC?** Number one is *The Bonfire of the Vanities*. *The Power Broker* is also up there. *Underworld* by Don DeLillo is set in NY and it's brilliant. **What's your favorite guilty NYC pleasure?** No contest, the hot dogs you can get that are wrapped in bacon, smothered in fried egg and cheese, with a side of tater tots. It goes right to the hips, but ohhhh, it's worth it.

branch of the New York Public Library.

☑ STUDIO MUSEUM IN HARLEM

☎ 212-864-4500; www.studiomuseum .org; 144 W 125th St at Adam Clayton Powell Jr Blvd; admission by suggested donation; ⌚ noon-6pm Wed-Fri & Sun, 10am-6pm Sat; ◉ 2, 3, 4, 5, 6 to 125th St; ♿

An eclectic mix of work by African American and Caribbean artists hangs on the walls of the Studio Museum. Exhibits range from abstract expressionism to political cartoons, and they go a long way toward debunking the myth that no great African American artists emerged in the first half of the 20th century.

SHOP

☐ 125TH ST SHOPPING
Various Stores

125th St btwn Frederick Douglass Blvd & Madison Ave; ◉ **A, B, C, D, 2, 3, 4, 5, 6 to 125th St**

Vibrant and buzzing 125th St is a major shopping strip in Harlem, full of big-name chain stores like Carol's Daughter, American Apparel, H&M and The Body Shop, and some quirky old holdouts selling incense and African goods. Harlem's best-kept secret is the big department store, Marshall's,

on Lenox Ave and 125th St (across from the popular Starbucks); it's full of deeply discounted clothes, shoes, housewares and more.

☐ B OYAMA HOMME
Fashion & Accessories

☎ 212-234-5128; www.boyamahomme .com; 2330 Adam Clayton Powell Jr Blvd at W 136th St; ⌚ 2-8pm Mon, 11am-8pm Tue-Fri, 10:30am-6pm Sat; ◉ C to 135th St

Bernard Oyama is the 'Haberdasher of Harlem,' and one look at his wing-tipped shoes, two-tone suits and sleek fedoras and you'll get an urge to shoot your cuffs, too. His boutique sells tailor-cut suits, an assortment of shirts, and items like ties, pocket squares, gloves, cuff links and suspenders.

☐ HARLEM'S HEAVEN HAT BOUTIQUE *Hats*

☎ 212-491-7706; www.harlemsheaven .com; 2538 Adam Clayton Powell Jr Blvd at W 147th St; ⌚ noon-6pm Tue-Sat; ◉ 3 to Harlem-148th St

Evetta Petty's been designing custom hats from her Harlem location for more than 15 years – and if you've been looking for just the right hat for Easter Sunday, or a day at the races, Evetta's got many, many options for you. There are also some fantastic retro creations, glittering and fancy fedoras, some men's hats and a great treasure trove of vintage brooches, sunglasses and earrings.

LIBERTY HOUSE
Arts & Crafts, Fashion & Accessories

☎ 212-932-1950; http://libertyhousenyc
.com; 2878A Broadway near W 112th St;
☻ 10am-6:45pm Mon-Sat, noon-5:45pm
Sun; ⊕ 1 to Cathedral Parkway-110th St

A 1960s grassroots cooperative designed to promote the work of American artisans and farmers, Liberty House retains its ecofriendly mission even in today's global economy. Women and children can pick up organic, natural-fiber clothes (no sweatshop labor here, thank you very much!) and its imported goods are bought directly from artists and artisan collectives who use only recycled or non-endangered woods and materials.

🍴 EAT

🍴 AFRICA KINE
Senegalese, Moroccan $

☎ 212-666-9400; www.africakine.com;
2nd fl, 256 W 116th St; ☻ lunch & dinner;
⊕ B, C to 116th St; ♿

One of the first African restaurants to open up along the stretch of W 116th St now known as Little Senegal, Kine's succulent lamb and fish dishes, with big bowls of brown rice, garlicky veggies and sometimes couscous, bring in a big lunchtime crowd. Kine doesn't look like much from the

outside, but it's a real treat for Africa aficionados. For hard-core Senegalese fans, check out nearby **Le Baobab** (☎ 212-864-4700; 120 W 116th St near Lenox Ave; ☻ lunch & dinner; ⊕ B, C to 116th St). It's a small hole in the wall with minimal decor, mostly doing takeout for taxi drivers, but the food is authentic and flavorful. House specialty *poulet yassa* (spicy lemon chicken with rice) sells out fast; call ahead if you want it for dinner.

🍴 CAFFE LATTE *Cafe* $

☎ 212-222-2241; www.ilcaffelatte.com;
189 Lenox Ave near 119th St; ☻ breakfast, lunch & dinner; ⊕ 2, 3 to 116th St;
Ⓥ ♿

Full of students, seniors, old Harlem and new Harlem, Caffe Latte is fast becoming the place to meet and hang in the 'hood. Breakfasts feature deep rich coffee, omelettes, granola, pancakes and more – organic and some vegan options are offered too (and a lot of baked goods). Lunch and dinner lean toward Italian cuisine, with lots of pastas, raviolis and baked zitis, plus organic burgers.

🍴 CHEZ LUCIENNE
French $$

☎ 212-289-5555; www.chezlucienne.
com; 308 Lenox Ave at 125th St; ☻ lunch
& dinner; ⊕ 2, 3 to 125th St; ♿

Fans of classic French fare won't be disappointed in Chez Lucienne.

SOUL FOOD

The reigning queens of Harlem soul food are alive and well:

Amy Ruth's (☎ 212-280-8779; www .amyruthsharlem.com; 113 W 116th St near Lenox Ave; ☼ lunch & dinner; ◉ 2, 3 to 116th St) Delicious collard greens, mac 'n' cheese, fried chicken and biscuits.

Sylvia's (☎ 212-996-0660; www .syvliassoulfood.com; 328 Lenox Ave; ☼ lunch & dinner; ◉ 2, 3 to 125th St) All the same fixins as Amy Ruth's, plus chicken-n-waffles, Southern gravy and more.

The traditional bistro dishes like coq au vin, tender *steak au poivre*, escargot with parsley and butter and *moules frites* balance nicely with a juicy Kobe burger, Cobb salad and other American standbys. The small but attractive dining room, with low lights and black banquettes, fills quickly with a diverse Harlem crowd. Weekend reservations are a good idea.

🍴 COMMUNITY FOOD AND JUICE
American Comfort $$

☎ 212-665-2800; www.community restaurant.com; 2893 Broadway near W 113th St; ☼ breakfast, lunch & dinner; ◉ 1 to 116th St-Columbia University; Ⓥ ♿

At long last, a green restaurant in northern Manhattan. The

energy-saving kitchen equipment, recycled wood tables, and filtered water (not bottled) speak to the owners' green ethos, but the real showstopper is the food and wine: organic, biodynamic, locally grown and bought at peak freshness, rotating with the changing seasons. Weekend brunches, with light blueberry pancakes, veggie scramble and warm faro porridge, are insanely popular. Mains include warm lentil salad, 'bowl of beets' (with pistachio nuts, goat cheese and balsamic vinegar), country fried chicken or a grass-fed-beef burger.

🍴 EL PASO TAQUERIA
Mexican $

☎ 212-860-9753; www.elpasotaqueria .com; 237 E 116th St; ☼ lunch & dinner; ◉ 6 to 116th St; ♿ Ⓥ ♿

There are three of these fantastic Mexican joints around town, all of them in upper Manhattan. The one in **East Harlem** (☎ 212-831-9831; 1643 Lexington Ave near 105th St) has a garden, and a pretty main room with *azulejos* (tiles). The **original El Paso Taqueria** (☼ 212-996-1739; 64 E 97th St) is a few blocks south. The newest one, at 116th St in Harlem, offers the same authentic Mexican food as its sibling locations: fresh *flautas* (long, thin stuffed tortillas), bangin' burritos and a variety of chicken, pork and beef mole dishes that are *muy, muy, muy bueno*.

NEIGHBORHOODS

HARLEM

🍽 SETTEPANI'S
American, Italian $

☎ 917-492-4806; www.settepani.com; 196 Lenox Ave; ☺ lunch & dinner; 🚇 2, 3 to 116th St; 🚻 Ⓥ ♿

Pretty Settepani's is a glorious sight on a warm day – its rust-colored awning flutters in breezes that flow up and down broad Lenox Ave, and people of many different backgrounds enjoy fresh salads, sandwiches, quiches and desserts. It's one of several bright coffee hangouts springing up in Harlem. The service is sometimes a little slow, but people are rarely in a rush to leave anyway.

🍽 SOCIETY *Coffee Shop* $

☎ 212-222-3323; www.cupofnyc.com; 2104 Frederick Douglass Blvd at W 114th St; ☺ 7am-10pm Mon-Thu, 7am-midnight Fri, 9am-midnight Sat, 9am-9pm Sun; 🚇 2, 3 to 116th St; ♿

A sleek, brick-walled, wooden-table-filled coffee shop that's a popular Harlem hangout, especially among young students who make liberal use of its free wi-fi. The weekend brunches are a madhouse; at quieter times you can sit for hours sipping your latte or glass of wine and nibble on all sorts of cakes and snacks while soaking in the relaxed, comforting ambience.

Drop in to Settepani's for coffee, quiche and dessert

DRINK

DEN *Bar*
☎ 212-234-3045; www.thedenharlem
.com; 2150 Fifth Ave near E 132nd St;
⏲ 6pm-2am Mon-Fri, 8pm-4am Sat,
11am-5am Sun; ⊕ 2, 3 to 135th St

This is a very sexy place, visited by some very sexy people who like to laugh, drink and eat, as well as share the stage on Kill Karaoke night (Tuesday). Part art gallery (the work of local painters is shown on the walls), part gin joint (sip your Uncle Tom Collins with your tongue in cheek) and part soul restaurant (with pulled pork and sushi on the menu), the Den is also gorgeous to look at. It's located on the 1st floor of a restored brownstone, where you'll feel right at home. Wednesday, Friday and Saturday nights you'll get live hip-hop and blues.

NECTAR *Wine Bar*
☎ 212-961-9622; www.nectarwinenyc.
com; 2235 Frederick Douglass Blvd near
121st St; ⏲ 4pm-1am; ⊕ A, B, C to
125th St

Slide inside this modernist wine bar, where one wall is covered with bottles of the good stuff, and prepare to be charmed. Nectar is low key and relaxed, pairing its selection of red, white and dessert wines with panini and artisanal cheeses from around the world (helpfully described on the menu).

PLAY

LENOX LOUNGE
Jazz Music, Lounge
☎ 212-427-0253; www.lenoxlounge
.com; 288 Lenox Ave btwn W 124th &
W 125th Sts; ⏲ noon-4am; ⊕ 2, 3 to
125th St

The classic art deco Lounge, which frequently hosts big names, is an old favorite of local jazz cats, though it's a beautiful and historic house for anyone who wants a nice place to imbibe. Don't miss the luxe Zebra Room in the back.

PERK'S *Club*
☎ 212-666-8500; 553 Manhattan Ave at
W 123rd St; ⏲ 4pm-4am Mon-Sat; ⊕ 2,
3 to 125th St

On the weekends, Perk's is packed with hip-swinging dancers who take over the floor and move to the fusion sounds produced by the DJ. On weeknights this sedate-looking club pulls in the best local jazz artists to play live sets. You can't go wrong either way.

SHRINE *Live Music*
☎ 212-690-7807; www.shrinenyc.com;
2271 Adam Clayton Powell Jr Blvd near
134th St; ⏲ 4pm-4am; ⊕ 2, 3 to 135th St

All kinds of people pack in here every night for the vivacious happy hour, plus the eclectic live music, which can be reggae, rock or jazzy/bluesy tunes, even karaoke or poetry depending what night you visit.

It's a big draw for Harlem's West African community, but everyone is welcome to enjoy the cover-free bands and amiable atmosphere. Bar food and weekend brunch served.

⭐ SMOKE *Club*
☎ 212-864-6662; 2751 Broadway near W 106th St; 🕐 5pm-4am; 🚇 1 to 103rd St

Smoke has defied the odds of its no-man's-land location (not deep in Harlem but north of the Upper West Side) and flourished as an intimate and welcoming club. Its long dark drapes and fluffy sofas give it a homey feel, and the low covers appeal to the local student population.

>BROOKLYN

New York City's most densely populated borough is a sprawling amalgamation of brownstones, skyscrapers, cobblestone streets and narrow highways, with an eclectic mix of hipster yuppies, working-class Latino and Caribbean families, and a surging influx of Eastern European immigrants.

It's mesmerizing, overwhelming and ripe for exploration. Start with the warren of reclaimed factories in Dumbo, then explore the old brownstones of Carroll Gardens, Red Hook or Cobble Hill, also renowned for fabulous restaurants. Park Slope is a laid-back, gay-friendly neighborhood mirroring Manhattan's upscale lifestyle. For a singular experience, head to Coney Island and check out the freak shows and 1926 roller coaster.

Closest to Manhattan – in price and lifestyle – is hip Williamsburg, a former industrial area now embraced by recent grads and 30-somethings. The incoming wave of condos has yet to eclipse the old-school Polish community who lived and worked here for generations, so for now it's still possible to bar-hop along Bedford Ave while peering into myriad offbeat and avant-garde stores and art galleries.

BROOKLYN

🔵 SEE
111 Front Street
  Galleries **1** H4
Brooklyn Museum of
  Art **2** E3
Coney Island Boardwalk ..**3** A6
Dumbo Arts Center **4** H4
New York Transit
  Museum **5** G5
Pierogi 2000 ....**6** G2
Prospect Park **7** E3

🔵 SHOP
Asha Veza **8** G6
Brooklyn Flea Market
  (Boerum Hill) **9** G6

Brooklyn Flea Market
  (Fort Greene) **10** G6
Butter **11** G5
Cloth **12** G6
Jacques Torres
  Chocolate **13** H4
Sahadi's **14** G4
Thistle & Clover **15** H6

🍴 EAT
Al Di La Trattoria **16** F6
Grimaldi's **17** H4
Habana Outpost **18** G6
Nathan's Famous
  Hot Dogs **19** A5
River Cafe **20** H4
Totonno's **21** A5

🍸 DRINK
68 Jay St **22** H4
Henry Street Ale
  House **23** G4
Last Exit **24** G4
Union Hall **25** F6

⭐ PLAY
Barbes **26** E6
Brooklyn Bowl **27** G2
Gutter **28** G2
St Ann's Warehouse **29** H4

Please see over for map

NEIGHBORHOODS

BROOKLYN

SEE

111 FRONT STREET GALLERIES

111 Front St near Washington St; ⏰ **hours vary;** Ⓜ **A, C to High St**

Local artists exhibit their latest works in this orange-colored mega-gallery – a restored factory that actually houses about 11 galleries and ateliers. There's also a dash of international flair from visiting artists-in-residence; Dumbo runs several such programs a year.

BROOKLYN MUSEUM OF ART

☎ **718-638-5000; www.brooklynmuseum .org; 200 Eastern Parkway; suggested donation $8;** ⏰ **10am-5pm Wed-Fri, 11am-6pm Sat & Sun;** Ⓜ **2, 3 to Eastern Parkway**

Perched on the edge of Prospect Park, this 560,000-sq-ft beaux arts museum is full of dazzling diversity. Its permanent collections include ancient Egyptian and Assyrian masterpieces, plus an entire floor dedicated to the sculptures of Rodin. Innovative rotating exhibits range from studies of the feminist experience to explorations of Jesper Just's *Romantic Delusions*. On 'First Saturdays' (the first Saturday night of every month), the museum throws a dance party, and locals show up to boogie down.

The Brooklyn Museum of Art – you don't have to be in Manhattan to see great art in New York

Alexandra Poolos
Producer for Anderson Cooper's 360° at CNN

What do you like best about your nabe and why? I love the street life in Brooklyn. It's very relaxed and vibrant. **Where do you work and what are your hangouts in that neighborhood?** I work at Time Warner Center (p166) in Columbus Circle. I love Kashkaval (p169), a place with great fondues and wines in Hell's Kitchen. **Where do you go when you need good food in a hurry – like say when you're rushing against a deadline?** I like Le Pain Quotidien (p179), which is also a great place to hang out, drink coffee and read the paper. **What's a Brooklyn bar you recommend?** My favorite bar is Union Hall (p224) in Park Slope. Great bar with a bocce court inside. **Where do you go when you want to blow off steam?** I go dancing in the Lower East Side. **What's a tourist trap you think is worth the price?** Carriage rides in Central Park are totally worth it. **Know any hidden treasures of Brooklyn – places you think are great but aren't public knowledge?** There is a fantastic organic ice-cream truck that parks on 7th Ave in Park Slope on the weekends.

CONEY ISLAND BOARDWALK

www.coneyisland.com; 1000 Surf Ave; D, F, N, Q to Coney Island-Stillwell Ave

Change is on the horizon for Coney Island. As of press time, a major developer was preparing to start the first phase of a sweeping overhaul of the boardwalk area, but just exactly when it will begin (and how much of the historic area will be included) was still being worked out with the city. Until then, the kitschy and somewhat dissolute charm of Coney Island remains intact, along with the stunning Atlantic views and surrounding Russian community.

DUMBO ARTS CENTER

☎ 718-694-0831; www.dumboartscenter .org; 30 Washington St; noon-6pm Thu-Mon; A, C to High St

Stop by this Dumbo nerve center and learn all about the artist community – who works where and is planning what exhibit. This center plans the annual Dumbo art festival and is home to a great local gallery.

NEW YORK TRANSIT MUSEUM

☎ 718-694-1600; www.mta.info/mta /museum; Boerum Pl at Schermerhorn St; admission $5, some tours $15; 10am-4pm Tue-Fri, noon-5pm Sat & Sun; 2, 3, 4, 5 to Borough Hall, M, R to Court St

Occupying an old subway station built in 1936 (and out of service since 1946), this museum takes on 100-plus years of getting around the Big Apple. Kids love the models of old subway cars, bus drivers' seats and the chronological display of turnstiles from the late 19th century. Best is the downstairs area, on the platform, where everyone can climb aboard 13 original subway and elevated-train cars, dating from the 1904 wicker-seat, army-green-and-crimson Brooklyn Union Elevated Car.

PIEROGI 2000

☎ 718-599-2144; 177 N 9th St btwn Bedford & Driggs Aves; 11am-6pm Tue-Sun; L to Bedford Ave

A gallery that's grown in reputation and scope since its start in 2000, Pierogi 2000 handles about 1000 artists from Williamsburg and elsewhere, displaying most of their works in the front room. People can flip through drawings and other artist renderings in the back room if they wish. The back room is also a community center/meeting space for cultural gatherings.

PROSPECT PARK

www.prospectpark.org; Grand Army Plaza; 5am-1am; 2, 3 to Grand Army Plaza, F to 15th St-Prospect Park;

Although not as famous as the iconic Central Park, this lush green oasis is considered an equal masterpiece

NEIGHBORHOODS

BROOKLYN

from designers Olmsted and Vaux. Its 585 acres contain the gorgeous Brooklyn Botanical Gardens, numerous lakes, bike paths, meadows and running routes. The soaring arched entrance at Grand Army Plaza, not far from the Brooklyn Museum of Art and next to the Brooklyn Public Library, is one of the borough's most celebrated sights.

SHOP

☐ ASHA VEZA
Fashion & Accessories
☎ 718-783-2742; www.ashaveza.com; 69 Fifth Ave, Park Slope; ☽ noon-7pm Wed-Fri, 11am-7pm Sat, noon-6pm Sun; ⊕ F, M, R to Fourth Ave-9th St
Graceful designs from global dressmakers, including fashion-forward lines from new talent in Eastern Europe and Southeast Asia. The store owner tries to buy directly from designers wherever they are in the world and avoids big brands.

☐ BROOKLYN FLEA MARKET
Flea Market
www.brooklynflea.com; 176 Lafayette Ave in Fort Greene, One Hanson Pl in Boerum Hill; ☽ outdoors at Fort Greene 10am-5pm Sat Nov, inside at One Hanson Pl 10am-5pm Sun Nov; ⊕ A, C to Lafayette Ave in Fort Greene, 2, 3, 4, 5 to Atlantic Ave in Boerum Hill; ⓰
Too bad this flea market only takes place on weekends (Saturdays

at Fort Greene and Sundays in Boerum Hill) because a lifetime isn't long enough to wade through all the riches here – and you'll definitely want to check out the food stalls, many stocked with delectables from standout local restaurants.

☐ BUTTER *Fashion & Accessories*
☎ 718-260-9033; 389 Atlantic Ave near Bond St; ☽ noon-7pm Mon-Sat, to 6pm Sun; ⊕ A, C, G to Hoyt-Schermerhorn
The best of local designers share space with more experimental goods from Dries, Margiela, Rick Owens and others at Butter.

☐ CLOTH *Fashion & Accessories*
☎ 718-403-0223; www.clothclothing .com; 138 Fort Greene Pl; ☽ noon-8pm; ⊕ B, Q, 2, 3, 4, 5 to Atlantic Ave
Modern clothes for 20- and 30-somethings at bargain prices, located in a quaint store not far from the Brooklyn Academy of Music.

☐ JACQUES TORRES CHOCOLATE *Food & Drink*
☎ 718-875-9772; www.mrchocolate.com; 66 Water St, Dumbo; ☽ 9am-8pm Mon-Sat, 10am-6pm Sun; ⊕ A, C to High St
Serious chocolatier JT runs this European-style store with a three-table cafe, filled with the most velvety and innovative chocolates ever crafted. Take a few to the nearby Empire Fulton Ferry State Park for a snack and a view between the

Art you can eat at Jacques Torres Chocolate

Brooklyn and Manhattan Bridges. It also has internet access, and makes its delicacies available at Chocolate Bar in the Meatpacking District.

SAHADI'S Food & Drink
☎ 718-624-4550; www.sahadis.com; 187 Atlantic Ave near Clinton St; ⏱ 9am-7pm Mon-Sat; 🚇 2, 3, 4, 5 to Borough Hall
Kalamata olives, fresh hummus, sweet figs and dates, and briny pickles – all sorts of Middle Eastern treats are sold at this specialty store, run by a Middle Eastern family.

THISTLE & CLOVER
Fashion & Accessories
☎ 718-855-5577; www.thistleclover .com; 221 Dekalb Ave; ⏱ noon-8pm

Mon-Fri, 11am-7pm Sat & Sun; 🚇 G to Clinton-Washington Aves
Started by two young shopaholics who met at a Scotland flea market, Thistle & Clover's making a name for itself with stellar offerings of contemporary women's clothes and vintage jewelry. Sunday nights there's free nibbles and sometimes a party in the back garden.

EAT
AL DI LA TRATTORIA
Northern Italian $$
☎ 718-636-8888; www.aldilatrattoria .com; 248 5th Ave near Carroll St; ⏱ lunch & dinner; 🚇 M, R to Union St
Run by a husband-and-wife team from Northern Italy, this trattoria

NEIGHBORHOODS

BROOKLYN

is proud of its handmade pastas and pizzas. Cheery Al Di La is also famous for savory beet ravioli, risotto nero, sweet pea tortellini, braised rabbit and rich, buttery polenta.

🍴 GRIMALDI'S *Pizza* $
☎ 718-858-4300; www.grimaldis brooklyn.com; 19 Old Fulton St; ⏲ lunch & dinner; 🚇 A, C to High St; ♿ Ⓥ 👶
Legendary pizza with perfect crust and spicy sauces, topped with bubbling cheeses of all types. If the 'no reservations' policy creates long lines, everybody stops complaining once the pizza's dished up.

🍴 HABANA OUTPOST *Latin* $
☎ 718-858-9500; www.cafehabana. com; 757 Fulton St; ⏲ noon-midnight; 🚇 C to Lafayette Ave; ♿ Ⓥ 👶
A solar-powered and self-styled 'eco-eatery,' Habana's a smallish cafe with a big courtyard and delicious Latin fare. Side dishes of plantains, yellow rice and grilled corn go perfectly with burritos, quesadillas and enchiladas. Goes without saying that the food is organic.

🍴 NATHAN'S FAMOUS HOT DOGS *Hot Dogs* $
☎ 718-946-2202; 1310 Surf Ave; ⏲ breakfast, lunch & dinner

River Cafe, a floating wonder with great food and beautiful views till late; 🚇 D, F to Coney Island-Stillwell Ave

If you eat em, this is the place for an all-beef dog with sauerkraut and mustard. A frightening time to visit is July 4, when Nathan's holds a hot-dog-eating contest (the record stands at Joey Chestnut's 68 in 10 minutes).

🍴 RIVER CAFE
American $$$
☎ 718-522-5200; www.rivercafe.com; 1 Water St; 🕐 lunch & dinner daily, brunch Sat & Sun; 🚇 A, C to High St; Ⓥ ♿

It takes a beating from purists who sniff the words 'tourist trap,' but they've probably never actually been to this floating wonder with beautiful views from under the Brooklyn Bridge. The seared mahimahi with almond crust and scallop seviche are just two of many innovative dishes the kitchen produces, and River Cafe's brunches are legendary for their Bloody Marys and perfect eggs.

🍴 TOTONNO'S *Pizza* $
☎ 718-372-8606; 1524 Neptune Ave near W 16th St; 🕐 noon-8pm Wed-Sun; 🚇 D, F, N, Q to Coney Island-Stillwell Ave; ♿

Open daily as long as there's fresh dough – when it goes, the shop closes for the day. It's part of the only-do-it-when-it's-fresh ethos

that's run this place for decades. The crust tastes better and the sauce sweeter, making the experience worth a Coney Island trip.

🍸 DRINK

🍸 68 JAY STREET *Bar*
☎ 718-260-8207; 68 Jay St; 🕐 2pm-3am; 🚇 A, C to High St

Paint-spattered but still elegant, with rounded arches and a big columned doorway, 68 Jay Street is a rarity among bars – it turns the music down to a comfortable level for discussion among patrons. Consequently, you hear a lot of art-world buzz as the regulars – all members of said world – dish the dirt over drinks.

🍸 HENRY STREET ALE HOUSE *Pub*
☎ 718-522-4801; 62 Henry St near Orange St; 🕐 4pm-4am; 🚇 A, C to High St, 2, 3 to Clark St

Steps from the subway, this near-perfect pub serves gourmet cheese, fresh apple slices and other fragrant snacks with its 16 varieties of beer.

🍸 LAST EXIT *Bar*
☎ 718-222-9198; http://lastexitbar .com; 136 Atlantic Ave near Henry St; 🕐 4pm-4am; 🚇 2, 3, 4, 5 to Borough Hall, M, R to Court St, F, G to Bergen St

Sometimes the laid-back bartenders put on a pub quiz; other times

NEIGHBORHOODS

BROOKLYN

a DJ shows up to spin. Most of the time it's locals unwinding over beers, happy to talk to strangers and let the night slip away.

☒ UNION HALL *Bar*
☎ 718-638-4400; 702 Union St btwn Fifth & Sixth Aves, Park Slope; ⏰ 4pm-4am Mon-Fri, noon-4am Sat & Sun; ◉ M, R to Union St, 2, 3 to Bergen St, F to Seventh Ave

Up front, leather settees and arm-chairs sit next to the masculine full-wall bookshelves and the fireplace makes the Hall feel like an old-world gentleman's club during gentler times. Things get busy-rowdy later on, with a clanking bocce court in back and an

indie-rock stage in the basement. If you're thinking of clanking the bocce ball, prepare to wait an hour or two. Good snacks.

☆ PLAY

☆ BARBES *Live Music, Arts*
☎ 718-965-9177; www.barbesbrooklyn .com; 376 9th St at Sixth Ave; no cover charge for bar, suggested $10 donation for live music; ⏰ 5pm-2am Mon-Thu, noon-4am Fri & Sat, noon-2am Sun; ◉ F to Seventh Ave

This bar and performance space, owned by two French musicians and longtime Brooklyn residents, is named after the North African enclave of Paris. It hosts music,

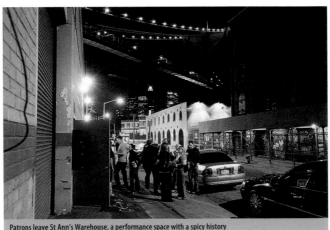

Patrons leave St Ann's Warehouse, a performance space with a spicy history

readings and film screenings in the back room, and plays eclectic music, ranging from Lebanese diva Asmahan to Mexican *bandas,* Venezuelan *joropos* and Romanian brass bands.

⭐ BROOKLYN BOWL *Music*
☎ 718-963-3369; www.brooklynbowl. com; 61 Wythe Ave near N 12th St; 🕑 daily; 🚇 L to Bedford Ave
Fill up on Blue Ribbon mac 'n' cheese then catch DJs like Sam Ronson and ?uestlove, or live bands like Dinosaur Feathers, The Fiery Furnaces, Glint and Destroy Baby-lon (part of a Clash tribute night).

⭐ GUTTER *Bowling*
☎ 718-387-3585; 200 N 14th St btwn Berry & Wythe Sts; 🕑 4pm-4am Mon-Thu, noon-4am Fri-Sun; 🚇 L to Bedford St

An unself-conscious and un-hip bar (designed to look so un-hip, in fact, that it had to be on purpose), this refurbished old warehouse is now a bar/bowling alley, with eight working lanes to play on. Beer comes in pitchers, you've got to put on bowling shoes, and the loser buys (house rules).

⭐ ST ANN'S WAREHOUSE *Arts*
☎ 718-254-8779; www.stannsware house.org; 38 Water St btwn Main & Dock Sts; 🕑 hours vary; 🚇 A, C to High St
This avant-garde performance company took over an old spice mill and turned it into an excit-ing venue for the arts. Now the cavernous space regularly hosts innovative theater and attracts the Brooklyn literati crowd.

In a city with endless possibilities, it can be hard to find the neighborhood offering the best options for what interests you. Here's a breakdown to make it easy.

Live music, free concert, great setting – Dumbo (p22)

ACCOMMODATIONS

There's no shortage of great hotels in New York City, just a lack of space for more rooms! You'll get lots of bang for your buck in terms of service at most locations, but truly spacious accommodations are pretty much a rarity unless you're willing to dig out the pocketbook.

For relaxing, family-friendly, old-fashioned hotels, great for visitors wanting to visit museums and cultural highlights, try the Upper West and East Sides. Boutique-hotel lovers can pick and choose from among the classic, super-stylish hotels around Union Sq, Bryant Park and Times Sq, or the slightly edgier downtown hotels. Business travelers and Broadway aficionados tend to stick to Midtown. You can find bargains in older hotels in Chelsea and among the B&Bs of Greenwich Village and the East Village.

Accommodations in New York fall into five broad categories. Book yourself into a B&B and you'll likely end up in an old brownstone or converted loftlike flat. Rooms tend to be bright and spacious, but bathrooms are usually shared, as are all common spaces. B&Bs can save you money as long as you don't mind early morning chatter over a communal breakfast table.

Boutique hotels tend to have mini-rooms tricked out like glam jewel boxes. Colors are seductive, as are amenities – expect brand names likes Bulgari and high-end linens, plus a celebrity-filled basement or rooftop bar.

Classic hotels, like the Waldorf Astoria, are a throwback to the days of Coco Chanel and W Somerset Maugham, when travelers came with trunks and entourages and booked suites to stay for months. You'll find big ballrooms, grand and sweeping staircases, gilt-covered wall hangings and dangling chandeliers – and usually smallish rooms with deep carpeting and lots of knick-knacks to distract from the hotel's somewhat faded glory.

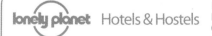 **Hotels & Hostels**

Need a place to stay? Find and book it at lonelyplanet.com. Over 110 properties are featured for New York City – each personally visited, thoroughly reviewed and happily recommended by a Lonely Planet author. From hostels to high-end hotels, we've hunted out the places that will bring you unique and special experiences. Read independent reviews by authors and other travelers, and get practical information including amenities, maps and photos. Then reserve your room simply and securely via Hotels & Hostels – our online booking service. It's all at www.hotels.lonelyplanet.com.

Manhattan also has a few 'travelers' hotels. These are European-style locales with mini-kitchenettes in rooms, beds plus pull-out sofas (to pack in a third or fourth guest) and lots of floral-print bedspreads. Some rooms will have private baths and others will share toilets with the whole floor.

Hostels are dormlike rooms with bunk beds stacked one over the other. Decor is minimal to nonexistent in the dorms, but often the hostels have backyard gardens, quaint surroundings and a cheery clientele.

Good resources to use include Lonely Planet's Hotels & Hostels (www .hotels.lonelyplanet.com), Just New York Hotels (www.justnewyorkhotels .com), New York Deals on Hotels (www.newyork.dealsonhotels.com), New York City Hotels Today (www.newyorkcityhotelstoday.com) and NYC Hotels (www.nyc-hotels.net). Hotels sometimes offer special internet-only deals too. Priceline (www.priceline.com), Hotwire (www.hotwire.com), Orbitz (www.orbitz.com), Hotels.com (www.hotels.com), Hoteldiscounts .com (www.hoteldiscounts.com) and Travelzoo (www.travelzoo.com) all claim prices that are up to 70% less than standard rates.

BEST NEWCOMERS
> The Standard (www.standardhotels.com)
> Greenwich Hotel (www.greenwichny hotel.com)
> Cooper Square Hotel (www.thecooper squarehotel.com)
> Ace Hotel (www.acehotel.com)
> Stay Hotel (www.stayhotelny.com)

BEST BOUTIQUES
> Mercer (www.mercerhotel.com)
> 60 Thompson (www.60thompson.com)
> Gansevoort (www.hotelgansevoort. com)
> Casablanca Hotel (www.casablanca hotel.com)
> Gild Hall (www.thompsonhotels.com)

Sitting outside the Mercer, one of the city's best boutique hotels

SPORTS & ACTIVITIES

Baseball aficionados will know that New York's two most successful sporting franchises have transitioned into new homes: the Yankees and the Mets, the city's major-league teams, now play in spanking-new stadiums.

The House that Ruth Built, old Yankee Stadium, is no longer. A similar, but larger and more glamorous, stadium went up across the street in late 2009, and the old building was torn down and sold off for memorabilia and scrap metal. The land is supposed to become a public park, but as of research time plans hadn't yet moved forward. The Mets' beloved Shea Stadium met a similar fate in 2009. The Mets are now playing in CitiField, their glitzy new stadium, where the likes of Jerry Seinfeld (an old Queens boy) have luxury boxes. Both teams attract high-profile fans (not all of them are boy-toy Alex Rodriguez' A-list girlfriends either), and you never know who will be joining you in the stands. How all this will affect New York's World Series–dominating Yankees is anybody's guess; one can only hope it improves the luck of the perennially second-placed Mets.

The New York Knicks, who haven't brought glory to their city in a distressingly long time, still play in Madison Sq Garden, which is also home to the far more successful women's pro-team, the New York Liberty, and the New York Rangers hockey team from October to April. It's also the city's biggest concert venue, where bands like U2 and the Jonas Brothers have played.

New Jersey's Nets basketball team was slated to move to Brooklyn in 2010, but the stadium under development for them there hasn't gone ahead at all, thanks to the distressed economy and very determined resistance from some local residents.

NY Giants football tickets sell out years in advance, but tickets to New York Jets football games are easier to come by. Both teams now share a new mega-stadium in the Meadowlands, NJ. To finance the ritzy new digs, the teams adopted a controversial pricing plan that requires season-ticket holders to pony up thousands of dollars for lifetime rights to their seats. That's on top of paying $700 a season for tickets. But all is not lost for the average fan; one-time ticket buyers can sit in nosebleed sections for $100 to $200.

The US Open is the year's final Grand Slam tennis event (spanning the Labor Day weekend) and is held at Flushing Meadows in Flushing, Queens. Reserved tickets are only required for Arthur Ashe Stadium, which usually sells out far in advance of the tournament. Day-session ground passes are sold on the morning of each day's play; get in line before 9am.

An easy way to book sports tickets is through **Ticketmaster** (☎ 800-745-3

ARCHITECTURE

New York is still a city of varied scale, although increasingly it is turning tall and vertical. You can see its colonial past in a few quaint structures – short, squat rows of Federalist-style houses – in Lower Manhattan, and Colonnade Row (p91) along Astor Pl is a great example of pre-1900s architecture. Sadly, fires wiped out most of New York's early housing stock; later, developers switched to less flammable materials.

The city's love of art deco is visible in the Chrysler Building, Grand Central Terminal's interior, and the Empire State Building. Inside Rockefeller Center you'll find the GE Building, another art deco construction that's lauded for the frieze over the main entrance depicting Wisdom.

The Time Warner Center, a mixed-use building at Columbus Circle, was the first major skyscraper built in the city after September 11. Its striking, black-glass exterior and sloping facade are considered an architectural feat and it's one of the city's toniest addresses.

By far the most common facade in the city, however, is beaux arts, used on the New York Public Library and the thousands of huge, solid apartment buildings that sprang up pre- and post-WWII. They line the large avenues running up both the Upper East and West Sides, done in an off-white stone, with great flourishes carved around windowsills and under the eaves.

ICONIC BUILDINGS
> Empire State Building (p152)
> Colonnade Row (p91)
> Dakota Building (p194)
> Time Warner Center (p166)
> Chrysler Building (pictured left; p152)

HISTORIC & RELIGIOUS BUILDINGS
> Cathedral of St John the Divine (p205)
> Federal Hall (p44)
> St Paul's Chapel (p46)
> St Patrick's Cathedral (p154)
> St Patrick's Old Cathedral (p80)

BARGAIN & SOUVENIR SEEKING

What could be better than a good bargain? That's why the weekend market was invented. New Yorkers love to amble around the city's parks and squares, eyeing other people's cast-offs and hand-me-downs.

Chinatown and Times Sq are famous for T-shirts. Shops around here are generally open from 10am to 8pm daily, with stores owned by Orthodox Jews closing Fridays and reopening Sunday mornings.

For real finds, dig through Chelsea's Antiques Garage Flea Market, the affiliated Hell's Kitchen Flea Market, the Chelsea Outdoor Market or the 17th Street Market: all of them are open weekends and full of gently used hand-me-downs (see p132 for more information).

Tribeca, Soho and Lower Manhattan are great for window-shopping and browsing. Mainstream department-store offshoots like Soho Bloomingdale's abound, but you'll also find quirkier options around Nolita, the Lower East Side, and Greenwich and East Villages.

Don't forget to check for sample sales while you're here; www.dailycandy.com has a page devoted to nothing else. Other good sources to check include www.lazarshopping.com, www.nysale.com and *New York Magazine*'s rundown at http://nymag.com/shopping.

WHERE TO FIND BARGAINS
> Orchard Street Bargain District (p68)
> Century 21 (p48)
> Chinatown (p56)
> Barneys Co-Op (p133)
> Arthritis Thrift Shop (p187)

BEST DEPARTMENT STORES
> Takashimaya (p156)
> Macy's (p166)
> Barneys (p187)
> Filene's Basement (p144)
> Pearl River Mart (pictured above; p57)

BARS

There's no shortage of cool places to wet your whistle while in New York. Whether you're a whiskey freak or a brandy snob, or just a plain old beer drinker, you can find a bar to make you feel at home.

Experimental types should try some of the legendary cocktails: they're constantly evolving into something new. You can get the classics – a martini, a sidecar and, of course, the Manhattan – but you can also find drinks with a twist. Pomegranate, sake, passionfruit and honey are the latest 'must-mix' ingredients; there's always a race on to create the next big winner.

Old-school Irish pubs can be found all over the city, usually with the doors thrown wide and a soccer or football game on. Microbreweries exist at Chelsea Piers and Union Sq and in Brooklyn. Chelsea is where to go for the *dernier cri* in chic drinks, but there's sure to be a secret bar somewhere on the Lower East Side thumbing its nose at that crowd and serving up the anti-cocktail.

For those who don't care what's in or what's out, the laid-back pubs in Greenwich Village that value conversation over trends are the best bet.

Many bars, particularly those downtown, have late-afternoon happy hours, when drinks are half their regular price, and some clubs repeat the fun after midnight, all the better to draw in the club-hopping crowd.

QUIET DRINK SPOTS
> Bemelmans Bar (p190)
> Whiskey Ward (p73)
> Park (p137)
> Campbell Apartment (p160)
> Bill's Gay Nineties (p159)

BEER & WINE BARS
> Jimmy's Corner (p170)
> DBA (p100)
> Morrell Wine Bar & Café (p160)
> Chelsea Brewing Company (p137)
> Bar Veloce (p137)

CLUBBING & NIGHTLIFE

Despite a strong challenge from the Meatpacking District, clubbing in New York is still all about the wild, wild west – west Chelsea, that is.

New York's clubs tend to open and shut doors with alarming frequency, as cops periodically crack down on underage drinking and notorious drug dealing. But, for the most part, Chelsea is still the magnet, since owners can switch locations fairly easily just by moving a few blocks north or south if they have to.

Smaller, slightly more intimate clubs are the norm in the Meatpacking District, where recent hot spots include G2. Kiss & Fly is a Euro-dancehall kind of vibe, breezy and fun, where nobody takes the scene too seriously.

The Lower East Side is also vying for attention with The Box, a bizarre, late-night supper/cabaret club.

To get on top of the options that are out there, grab the Sunday and Friday editions of the *New York Times,* and the weekly editions of *New York Magazine, Time Out New York* and the *New Yorker*. The *Village Voice* has good information on dance clubs and a weekly column (Fly Life) that runs down where the best DJs are playing. Also try **Clubfone** (☎ 212-777-2582; www.clubfone.com).

BIG CLUBS
> 675 Bar (p123)
> Griffin (p125)
> Santos Party House (p114)
> Eagle NYC (p138)
> Home (p138)

DANCE SPOTS
> Cielo (p124)
> BEast (p123)
> G2 (p124)
> Kiss & Fly (p125)
> 10ak (p138)

COMEDY & CABARET

Life is a cabaret, old chum, except in New York City, where an old Prohibition-era law actually makes it illegal to have more than three people dancing in a club unless the owner has applied for a (very hard to get) special license.

For some reason that arcane legislation is still on the books, but no worries: everyone ignores it. Cabaret is alive and well, from the classic shows put on at Café Carlyle to the raucous burlesque-like performances at The Box, and the laugh-till-it-hurts cabaret/comedy that has kept the Duplex in business for 40 years. These plucky establishments, like Don't Tell Mama, manage to hang in there even as popular taste has moved away from the ribald, Broadway-esque performance style.

Comedy clubs are also enjoying a bit of a comeback, although they're nowhere near as popular as they were in the 1980s, when Jerry Seinfeld, Chris Rock and the Belushi brothers were on the circuit. Dangerfield's and Comic Strip Live still fill the room with their nightly shows on the Upper East Side. Caroline's, Gotham Comedy Cellar and Laugh Factory New York dominate the Midtown action. Clubs usually have two showings nightly; your ticket price gets you in for a full set (usually three or four comics), but there's often a two-drink minimum on top of that for table service. Most clubs now also serve food so you can nosh while you laugh.

BEST COMEDY & CABARET
> Duplex (p115)
> The Box (p172)
> Don't Tell Mama (p171)
> Upright Citizens Brigade (p135)
> Dangerfield's (p191)

BEST LOUNGE ACTS
> Bemelmans Bar (p190)
> Lenox Lounge (p212)
> Bar Next Door (p113)
> Sway Lounge (p89)
> Divine Bar West (p170)

FASHION & COUTURE

There are two – possibly three – places in New York where devotees of fashion and haute couture tend to congregate: the Upper East Side and the Meatpacking District. Occasionally a few forward-thinking fashionistas will venture downtown to the less stylized boutiques of Tribeca.

The 'Gold Coast' along Madison Ave is a 40-block stretch of big-name designers: Armani, Kors, Ferragamo, Bulgari, Prada and much more. The few thrift shops that populate this area, as you can imagine, have waiting lists to inspect the merchandise: these stores get last year's cast-offs from the well-heeled, and the working-class girls line up waiting to buy.

In the Meatpacking District, the aura is a little less rarified, but the focus is still on high-end fashion. Edgier, more youthful names like Malandrino (p120), Miele (p120) and McQueen (p117) are all the rage.

Downtown in Tribeca is where almost-but-not-quite-discovered young models like to browse; the flashy boutiques are more willing to take a chance on the latest European and Asian imports.

Don't forget to sign up for a list of the day's sample sales at www.daily candy.com and at http://nymag.com/shopping before you go.

BEST SHOPPING SPOTS
> Fifth Ave (p156)
> Madison Ave (p155)
> Chinatown (p56)
> Gansevoort St (p117)
> Orchard Street Bargain District (p68)

TOP SHOPS
> Donna Karan (p187)
> Issey Miyake (p48)
> Carlos Miele (p120)
> Topshop (p85)
> Apt 141 (p95)

FOOD SHOPPING

Green, leafy things are sprouting all over New York, thanks to the new local and organic food craze that's taken hold in the city. If you're in town during the warmer months, seek out the network of greenmarkets that populate Manhattan. The main one is in Union Sq – it sometimes doubles as a craft market – and you'll often spot five-star chefs there early in the morning, planning the day's menu.

If outdoor markets are too rustic for you, there are plenty of big chains and revered mom-and-pop-type bodegas to be found. Check out the many Whole Foods stores around the city for the best in fair-trade and organic eats. Trader Joe's, another high-end gourmet organic shop, is two doors down from Whole Foods in Union Sq. If you're looking for old-school New York, it's Zabar's on the Upper West Side. Gourmet Garage all over, or the quaint, upscale market inside Grand Central Terminal. Chelsea Market on the West Side is great if you get hungry while shopping; it also houses a slew of delectable restaurants.

BEST FOOD STORES

- › Andre's Patisserie (p188)
- › Chelsea Market (p133)
- › Trader Joe's (p96)
- › Whole Foods at Filene's Basement (p144)
- › Zabar's (pictured above; p197)

BEST SPECIALTY SHOPS

- › Murray's Cheese (p109)
- › Barney Greengrass (p197)
- › Union Square Greenmarket (p142)
- › Grand Central Market (p152)
- › Canal St stalls in Chinatown (p56)

FOOD

New York's constant influx of world-class chefs means plenty of first-rate cooking for those who lust after a truly inimitable dining experience. Classic diners, brasseries and intimate bistros stud the entire city, and original restaurants with ties to foreign lands are practically ubiquitous.

It's not a question of whether you want Chinese tonight, but do you want Szechuan or Mandarin? French Thai or traditional? Big, bean-filled burritos from Northern Mexico or spicy, sauce-laden concoctions with mole and chilis from the Oaxaca region? Every budget and preference can be accommodated in New York City.

Some places are so hot you can only book online (ahem...Momofuku; p98). New Yorkers are addicted to **Open Table** (www.opentable.com), which lets you read reviews, follow the 'buzz,' and book and instantly confirm reservations at hundreds of eateries.

To help you navigate your way through New York's rich foodie pickings, grab a copy of *Time Out New York*, which reviews 100 restaurants in every issue, or a Zagat guide at any newsstand. The *Village Voice* also has a database of cheap eats on its website (www.villagevoice.com). With so much to choose from, you definitely won't go hungry.

HARD TO GET RESERVATIONS
> Momofuku (p98)
> Il Buco (p86)
> Sfoglia (p189)
> Bond St (p86)
> Minetta Tavern (p112)

COUPLE SPOTS
> Benoit (p167)
> BLT Market (p167)
> Pier i Café (p199)
> Schiller's Liquor Bar (p72)
> Al Di La Trattoria (p221)

GOOD DEALS
> Bite (p85)
> Cascabel (p189)
> Fatty Crab (p198)
> Hourglass Tavern (p169)
> Zebu Grill (p189)

WORTH FINDING
> Chez Lucienne (p209)
> Kashkaval (p169)
> Shanghai Kitchen (p59)
> Pinche Taqueria (p87)
> Georgia's East Side BBQ (p71)

op left **Get a seat at David Chang's Momofuku Ko (p98), if you can** Above **Schiller's Liquor Bar (p72) – warm** cor, cold beer

GAY & LESBIAN NEW YORK

Gay Pride is a month-long celebration in June of the city's long-standing and diverse queer communities, and an apt description of New York's gay and lesbian lifestyle: unabashedly out and empowered in a city noted for its overachievers. For more details on Gay Pride, check out www.heritageofpride.org.

New York doesn't differentiate much between heterosexual and homosexual – at least, not when it comes to dancing, drinking and eating. Chelsea, Greenwich Village, Jackson Heights and Park Slope are famously gay-friendly communities, but there's hardly any establishment in town where gays and lesbians wouldn't feel welcome. The one rule to remember is that the age of consent in New York for sex (of any kind) is 17.

The magazines *HX* and *Next* are available at restaurants and bars, or pick up *LGNY* and *NY Blade* from street-corner boxes and the lifestyle magazine *Metrosource* at shops and the LGBT Community Center. *Time Out New York* features a good events section. Useful counseling, referral and information centers include the **Gay & Lesbian Hotline** (☎ 212-989-0999; glnh@glnh.org) and the **LGBT Community Center** (Map pp106-7; ☎ 212-620-7310; www.gaycenter.org; 208 W 13th St at Seventh Ave; ☽ 9am-11pm).

Above **Statues of two gay couples by George Segal in Sheridan Square** (p105)

LITERARY NEW YORK CITY

Here's a funny tidbit: most of New York's most celebrated living authors reside in Brooklyn. How's that for a switch? Actually, it's not all that new. Isaac Bashevis Singer, Truman Capote, Norman Mailer and William Styron all lived there. Today, Brooklyn hosts a new generation of writers, including Jonathan Safran Foer, Jonathan Lethem and Colson Whitehead.

But perhaps no other place has the celebrated history of Greenwich Village. Edna St Vincent Millay, EE Cummings, James Baldwin, William S Burroughs, Mark Twain, Edith Wharton, Henry James and other great writers have lived in that neighborhood. In contrast, the East Village favors nonfiction: the roiling socialist speeches of Emma Goldman and pro-birth-control advocate Margaret Sanger were handed out on seditious pamphlets.

The Oak Room in the Algonquin Hotel is also hallowed ground (Dorothy Parker drank here), and Harlem resounds with the energy of Ralph Ellison, Zora Neale Thurston, Langston Hughes and others.

The 92nd Street Y (p190) stages the most interesting author events north of 14th St. Bluestockings (p68), a LES bookstore, is your best bet for face-to-face time with an author. And KGB Bar (pictured below; p101) has a weekly reading series. For the inside scoop, visit www.clubfreetime.com.

CLASSIC NEW YORK READS
> *Just Above My Head*, James Baldwin
> *The Mambo Kings Sing Songs of Love*, Oscar Hijuelos
> *Motherless Brooklyn*, Jonathan Lethem
> *Lush Life*, Richard Price
> *Rise and Shine*, Anna Quindlen

NEW YORK IN HISTORY
> *Low Life*, Luc Sante
> *Bonfire of the Vanities*, Tom Wolfe
> *The Tenement Saga*, Sanford Sternlicht
> *The Gangs of New York*, Herbert Asbury
> *Gay New York: Gender and Urban Culture*, George Chauncey

V

SNAPSHOTS

LIVE MUSIC

Catching a live band in New York is easy – just head toward the sound of music. In the summer and spring, New Yorkers take the party outside. Listen to bluesy jazz on the lawn in Battery Park (p44), salsa and swing at South Street Seaport (p46) and Lincoln Center (p195), all kinds of bands at Central Park Summerstage, and somewhat unplanned but free (and very popular) breakout performances at 400 Carroll St in Brooklyn (www.sundaybestnyc.com).

To stay on top of what's happening year-round, check out www.whatsupnyc.com, which posts tips about spontaneous performances in the city that aren't promoted anywhere but passed around by word of mouth (like the surprise early morning show once put on by His Purpleness, Prince, in Brooklyn's Prospect Park).

There are still plenty of old jazz haunts in the West Village and Harlem, and some laid-back dive bars paying homage to punk and grunge on the Lower East Side and in Hell's Kitchen. Lincoln Center has set the standard for high-quality performances for decades now and continues to showcase artists from all genres. Symphony Space (p201) on the Upper West Side is known for live world music from under-appreciated performers.

BEST BARS FOR ROCK
> Arlene's Grocery (p74)
> Brooklyn Bowl (p225)
> Living Room (p74)
> Pianos (p75)
> Village Underground (p114)

BEST BARS FOR ECLECTIC SOUNDS
> 55 Bar (p114)
> Le Poisson Rouge (p114)
> Mercury Lounge (p75)
> Shrine (p212)
> Smoke (p213)

MUSEUMS & GALLERIES

Art is everywhere in New York City, from huge institutions like the Metropolitan (p14), the MoMA (p15) and the Guggenheim (p186) to avant-garde ateliers in Chelsea, Dumbo and the Lower East Side. And now there's a newcomer: the New Museum of Contemporary Art (p67).

Chelsea, from about 21st to 26th Sts on 10th and 11th Aves, is one long strip of salons, shops, art dealers and galleries. Midtown Manhattan has also become an art-world offshoot. The Lower East Side is the new place to showcase up-and-coming artists; Dumbo is where they work and live.

New York Magazine's free online reviews (www.nymetro.com), *Time Out New York*'s comprehensive listings (www.timeoutny.com) and the *Gallery Guide* in major galleries are indispensable in sorting through your options. The *New York Times*' weekend edition and the venerable *Village Voice* (www.villagevoice.com) are your backup sources, and www.westchelseaarts.com provides an exhaustive database of current galleries. The city's **Department of Cultural Affairs** (www.nyc.gov/html/dda) maintains an event calendar and allows you to search for galleries and attractions by art type and borough. If you're pressed for time, head out on a comprehensive tour through Chelsea and Soho by calling **New York Gallery tours** (☎ 212-946-1548; www.nygallerytours.com).

FIVE MUST-SEE SPOTS
> Agora Gallery (p127)
> White Columns (p117)
> New Museum of Contemporary Art (p67)
> Greene Naftali (p131)
> Gagosian (p130)

EAST-SIDE STANDOUTS
> Gallery OneTwentyEight (p63)
> Participant Inc (p68)
> Lower East Side Tenement Museum (p66)
> ABC No Rio (p67)
> Nuyorican Poets Café (p102)

The New Museum of Contemporary Art (p67), designed by Sejima + Nishizawa/SANAA

SNAPSHOTS

NYC FOR KIDS

New York is a blast for kids. They have their own museums, restaurants and theaters, and even a few after-hours hangouts they can call their own.

The American Museum of Natural History is a real kid-friendly standout, as is the Children's Museum. Young children are generally welcome in upscale dining rooms as long as it's on the early side, but there are plenty of quirky diners and bistros that cater to kids.

Parents might find moving about the city a bit stressful at first: squeezing strollers in and out of ill-configured subway stops isn't easy. Don't panic if someone grabs your stroller from behind as you're hauling it up the subway steps: New York etiquette mandates that weighted-down parents get a helping hand. The too-skinny-turnstiles at subway exits and entrances are another problem; catch the attention of the station clerk to get buzzed through the larger gates to the side. A few Manhattan museums don't allow strollers on certain days but will give you baby carriers to make up for it.

To make the cultural capital your personal playground, pick up a *Time Out New York Kids,* published four times a year and available at newsstands. It has tons of fabulous information and listings. **GoCity Kids** (www.gocitykids.com) is a useful online reference, as is **New York Kids** (www.newyorkkids.net).

FUN PLACES FOR KIDS
> American Museum of Natural History (p194)
> Children's Museum of Manhattan (pictured above; p194)
> Safari Playground (p181)
> Central Park Wildlife Center (p176)
> South Street Seaport (p46)

FAMILY FRIENDLY EATS
> S'Mac (p99)
> Tuck Shop (p99)
> Cafe Con Leche (p197)
> Pio Pio (p199)
> Shake Shack (p198)

NYC FOR LOVERS

It's not all bottom lines and boardroom deals in hard-nosed New York: there's room for love too. Where else can you get the romantic thrill of rowing across the lake in Central Park (p180), canoodling on the roof of the Empire State Building (p152) or dining in the bright lights of Broadway (p16)? Nowhere – so you better take advantage while you're here.

There's no need to be shy about your affection. New Yorkers are quite accustomed to seeing couples – same-sex or otherwise – walking arm-in-arm, holding hands, trading smooches and even snuggling closely while enjoying an outdoor concert at night. Just don't block the sidewalk when you're moving in tandem – that might net you some annoyed stares.

Famously romantic NYC experiences include a ride around Central Park in a horse-and-buggy, a kiss in the middle of blaring Times Sq (p16), dressing to the nines for a concert at Lincoln Center (195), hand-holding across the table at a dark and secluded jazz club, and sharing a drink at a sexy rooftop bar.

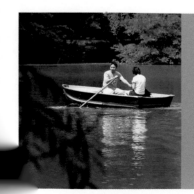

BARS FOR CANOODLING
> Happy Ending (p73)
> Apotheke Bar (p60)
> Macao (p51)
> Auction House (p189)
> Park (p137)

CLASSIC DATE BARS
> Bemelmans Bar (p190)
> High Bar (p170)
> Den (p212)
> Bacaro (p61)
> Campbell Apartment (p160)

PARKS & GREEN SPACES

Not all parks have to be used for exercise: New Yorkers have perfected the art of turning their green spaces into multi-use common areas. Consider these summer activities: Monday night outdoor films in Bryant Park, Shakespeare in the Park in Central Park, Central Park's Summerstage concerts, Battery Park's Hudson River Park concerts and its River to River Festival, and the Lincoln Center Dance Nights (OK, that one will definitely get your heart rate going). And don't forget the city's two roving outdoor tango parties: Saturday nights in Central Park and Sunday at the South Street Seaport.

It just goes to show there are plenty of ways to enjoy New York's more than 28,000 acres of greenery. While you're here, you are welcome to make use of any of the city's 614 baseball fields, 550 tennis courts, numerous basketball courts, golf and track courses, as well as its indoor and outdoor swimming pools: just go to www.nycgovparks.org for locations and details.

BEST PARKS
> Central Park (p174)
> Riverside Park (p195)
> Prospect Park (p219)
> Governor's Island (p47)
> Battery Park (p44)

BEST PARK ACTIVITIES
> Cycling in the Hudson River Park (p105)
> Walking the Jacqueline Kennedy Onassis Reservoir in Central Park (p176)
> Boating in Prospect Park (p219)
> Picnicking in Battery Park (p44)
> Strolling above the city on the High Line (p13)

SPAS

Picture this heavenly scenario: a few hours of shopping, light tea and then a blissful spa treatment that leaves you glowing and refreshed. Divine, right?

Well, that's now the standard at several high-end New York department stores: Takashimaya, Saks Fifth Ave and Bloomingdales all want you to go for the trifecta of pampering while you're in their stores.

But let's say you're only in town for a short visit. No problem: go to **Juvenex** (☎ 646-733-1330; www.juvenexspa.com; 5th fl, 25 W 32nd St btwn Fifth & Sixth Aves), an Asian-themed 24-hour spa in Little Korea. Its primary clientele are the dancers and performers from Broadway shows (hence the flexible hours) and it's also got special treatments for couples that involve hot tubs and rose petals (book those treatments in advance).

A visit to the spa means different things: a simple and straightforward after-work-out massage, a mani-pedi (manicure and pedicure), a waxing (bikini, Brazilian or otherwise), any number of different facials and topical skin treatments, or a combination of minimally invasive procedures to erase fine lines, peel away surface layers of old skin, zap broken capillaries, and so on and so on. Most spas have also picked up on the organic craze and are offering biodegradable wraps, chemical-free creams and soaps, and scenting your steam room with fresh, citrusy smells that won't irritate sensitive sinus tissues.

And spas are not just for women: several cater exclusively to men, and even unisex places offer male facials and 'handshake upkeep' treatments.

THEATER

Though some longtime favorites recently ended their runs, the big Broadway show is still king in New York.

There are 38 Broadway theaters that put on the lavish, million-dollar spectacles that enthrall crowds. Upkeep on these grande old dames (the theaters, not the stars) is steep, hence the hefty price of many Broadway tickets: sometimes $100 or more. However, there are ways to get half-price tickets. Run by the Theatre Development Fund (www.tdf.org), New York has three discount TKTS booths that sell steeply discounted seats to same-day Broadway shows. The main booth is in Times Sq, with another at South Street Seaport, and a third in Brooklyn (see the website for details). Most evening curtain calls are at 8pm, with Wednesday and weekend matinees starting at 2pm.

Besides the heavy hitters on Broadway, there's experimental theater on the Lower East Side, world-class ballet at Lincoln Center, or a low-key, nonprofit production of Chekhov, Stoppard or Miller in downtown revival theaters.

To keep track of it all, start with the Sunday and Friday editions of the *New York Times,* as well as the weekly editions of *New York Magazine, Time Out New York* and the *New Yorker.* The *Village Voice* has good information on alternative and off-off-Broadway productions. The **Department of Cultural Affairs** (☎ 212-643-7770) has a hotline that lists events and concerts at cultural institutions, while **NYC On Stage** (☎ 212-768-1818), a 24-hour information line, publicizes music, theater and dance events. Other good sources include **All That Chat** (www.talkinbroadway.com/allthatchat), **NYC Theater** (www.nyc.com/theater) and the **Broadway Line** (☎ 888-276-2392).

CELEBRATED THEATERS
> Joseph Papp Public Theater (p102)
> Ambassador Theater (p170)
> New Amsterdam Theater (p173)
> Newhouse at Lincoln Center (p195)
> Harry de Jur Playhouse at Abrons Art Center (p74)

POPULAR SHOWS
> *Wicked* (www.wickedthemusical.com)
> *Chicago* (www.chicagothemusical.com)
> *Billy Elliott* (www.billyelliotbroadway.com)
> *The Lion King* (www.disney.go.com)
> *Avenue Q* (www.avenueq.com)

VISTAS & VIEWPOINTS

Doesn't matter whether you're 100 stories above street level, or three levels below in the subway stations, there's always something to see. There are a thousand ways to observe the city as it goes by in a flash: from the swaying top of the Empire State Building (p152), from the back of a zippy pedicab, even as you clip-clop along in a hansom cab.

The views from the top seem to be the most sought after, but Manhattan can be entrancing from alternative angles. Take a trek to the New York Transit Museum (p219) and take its tour through a defunct section of the subway system to see how the city looks from the bottom up.

More scenic options can be found in Central Park, especially at its gorgeous central fountain located at Bethesda Terrace, near the Ramble. (The adjacent Bow Bridge is a popular place to pop the question, by the way.)

Harlem Meer is a scenic pond with honking geese and weeping willows, and Battery Park (p44) offers gorgeous views of New York Harbor. For the best sunset, take the Staten Island Ferry (p46): time the return trip right and you'll catch the glowing sun as it dips behind Manhattan's skyscrapers.

WHERE TO FIND GREAT VIEWS
> High Bar (p170)
> Crossing the Brooklyn Bridge (pictured above; p22)
> Taking a water taxi (p262)
> Cycling the Hudson River Park (p105)
> Ferry to Governor's Island (p47)

PICTURE-PERFECT NEW YORK STATUES
> José Marti (Columbus Circle)
> George Washington (Federal Hall)
> Duke Ellington (Harlem)
> Giovanni da Verrazano (Battery Park)
> Eleanor Roosevelt (Riverside Park)

SNAPSHOTS

FREE NYC

It's a bit counterintuitive, but there are a few things that don't cost an arm and a leg in this town – the trick is finding them. For that, New Yorkers have a few tools: www.lifebooker.com, www.freenyc.net, www.clubfree time.com and www.freeinnyc.net. These four websites can provide you with free events for a month of Sundays, and then some. LifeBooker is actually a booking service that hooks you up with last-minute, half-price spa services, hair cuts, manicures and pedicures at salons; the theory being that it's better to have someone pay half-price and fill an empty chair than get nothing. Clubfreetime lists all kinds of cultural, social and intellectual events in up-to-the-moment postings; Freenyc and Freeinnyc do much the same, and add in things like free yoga in the park and free gallery events.

Don't forget that most museums (with the exception of the Metro-politan, which is always suggested donation) have at least one evening a week where they drop their entry fee and take suggested donations. Also consider buying a CityPass (www.citypass.com), which can get you steeply discounted admission into seven major attractions.

TOP FREEBIES
> Staten Island Ferry (pictured above; p46)
> Museum of Modern Art on Friday evenings (p164)
> Shakespeare in the Park (p176)
> River to River Festival (p51)
> Summerstage (p179)

BEST HAPPY HOURS
> Cleopatra's Needle (p200)
> DBA (p100)
> Whiskey Ward (p73)
> Henry Street Ale House (p223)
> Stir (p190)

>BACKGROUND

Grand Central Terminal (p152) functions like clockwork

BACKGROUND

HISTORY

Long before Giovanni da Verrazano sailed by Staten Island in 1524, or Henry Hudson came looking for land to claim for the Dutch East India Company in 1609, great numbers of Algonquin-speaking people had made the Manhattan area their home.

The Lenape Native Americans fished New York Bay for oysters and striped bass, and laid down well-worn trading routes across the hilly island (Manhattan means 'island of hills' in one native dialect); those same routes later became Broadway, Amsterdam Ave and other large city thoroughfares. Legend says that Dutch trader Peter Minuit bought the island from the Lenape for trinkets worth about $24, but historians say it's unlikely the Lenape agreed to anything of the sort, since it was a culture that didn't adhere to the idea of private property. In any case, the Dutch assumed control of the island and by 1630 the colony numbered 270, with a number of Belgians (Walloons), French Huguenots and English mixed in.

Peter Stuyvesant arrived to impose order on the unruly colony of New Amsterdam in 1647, but his intolerant religious views led to unrest. Few resisted the bloodless coup by the British in 1664, and the colony was renamed New York. It became a British stronghold and remained steadfastly loyal to George III through much of the Revolutionary War in the 1770s. George Washington's ragtag army of farm boys was almost wiped out by Britain's General Cornwallis and his troops in what is currently Brooklyn Heights – only a daring, all-night march north saved them.

Post-Revolutionary times were good for most New Yorkers, even though the founding fathers disliked the bustling seaport city. The capital moved further south, to Washington DC, but the masses didn't go with it, and by 1830 the population had expanded to 250,000, mostly composed of immigrants working in dangerous factories and living in tenements on the Lower East Side. At the same time, corrupt politicians bilked millions from public works projects and industrial barons amassed tax-free fortunes. A lack of space forced building sprawl upward rather than outward; skyscrapers peppered the horizon and the city continued to expand its network of subways and elevated trains. In 1898 the independent districts of Staten Island, Queens, the Bronx and Brooklyn merged with Manhattan into the five 'boroughs' of New York City. With wave after wave of immigrants arriving, the population reached three million in 1900.

AFRICAN BURIAL GROUND

Africans have been in New York City since the 17th-century Dutch era. Brought over as slaves, they built many of the colonial attractions of Lower Manhattan. Their contributions were largely forgotten as slavery disappeared from the north, but the African Burial Ground (www .africanburialground.gov) – the final resting place of some 400 slaves taken mostly from Ghana that was discovered accidentally in 1991 – is a poignant reminder of their suffering. The site is at Duane and Elk Sts, adjacent to 290 Broadway, and a permanent exhibition is on display at the Schomburg Center for Research in Black Culture (p206) in Harlem.

Speakeasies, flappers, gangsters, the 19th Amendment (which gave women the right to vote) and a Harlem Renaissance brought incredible vitality to New York in the years before and after WWI. Margaret Sanger preached about birth control in Washington Sq Park, Wall St made golden boys out of hayseeds, and F Scott Fitzgerald chronicled it all in *The Great Gatsby*. When the stock market crashed on Black Tuesday (October 29, 1929), the apparently limitless future of New York was smashed overnight. Hard times followed, and even though Manhattan was the nation's premier city after WWII, economically things continued to stagnate. Only a massive federal loan program rescued the city from bankruptcy in the 1970s.

LIFE AS A NEW YORK RESIDENT

New York City is the original 'melting pot,' the term used by the nation's leaders to encourage mixing between old settlers and new arrivals at the turn of the 20th century. Popular theory held that incoming immigrants would assimilate to the dominant culture (which was primarily Anglo-Saxon at the time) and create a unified population free of ethnic and class divisions. Instead, the opposite happened: Italians coming into New York City didn't settle in the Irish enclave of Greenwich Village or the Eastern European Jewish communities of the Lower East Side. They established their own beachhead, which became known as Little Italy, and proudly spoke their language and practiced their traditions. Dominicans of the 1950s and 1960s settled in what became Spanish Harlem, and Puerto Ricans still own most of the Bronx. Along the way other nationalities arrived and rubbed shoulders and traded quips, and if the perfect homogeneity the city planners envisioned never materialized, well, nobody misses it because a vibrant hybrid culture of multi-culti influences has taken its place. No matter what their ethnic roots, your average New Yorker today knows a smattering of Spanish or another foreign language (or is perfectly bilingual), has a good sense of the Chinese lunar calendar (how else to know when the Chinese New Year is coming with its fabulous dragon parade?) and can order a bagel with a *schmear* (dab of cream cheese) without batting an eye.

Which is not to say that all New Yorkers live together in perfect harmony – in a city of about nine million, there are bound to be a few problems. Politicians are expected to resolve most of these conflicts and if they don't, they can kiss that second term goodbye. When it comes to the city's overall well-being, New Yorkers have no problem banding together in amazing displays of solidarity.

New Yorkers do everything double-time, and exchanging one-liners while on the fly is a highly prized skill. You'll hear such exchanges everywhere ('How you doin,' 'Hey, what's happening,' 'You got the time, buddy?'), so don't hold back if someone sends a well-meaning inquiry your way. Politeness – please, thank you, etc – is also important, and displays of class status, such as slighting the taxi driver or doorman, do not go over well in democratic Manhattan. There are a few things that raise local ire: do not exit the subway stairs and stop to pull out your map, thereby blocking those behind you. Move to the corner and then look. Don't go into an eatery during the busy lunch hour rush and keep everyone waiting while you decide. Hang back until you are ready to order. A jacket and tie are expected at upscale restaurants, but otherwise feel free to wear what you wish.

GOVERNMENT & POLITICS

New York City has five borough presidents, a city-wide comptroller, a public advocate and a 51-member city council to balance mayoral power. Buoyed by the November 4, 2008, election of Democrat Barack Obama to the presidency, Democrats in New York made significant gains in upstate territories and State Legislature races. For the first time in generations, New York State has a Democratic majority in its legislature, and a Democratic governor. Only New York City – traditionally the bluest region of the whole state – didn't put a Democrat in power in 2009. But that's because billionaire Mayor Mike Bloomberg successfully repealed a law prohibiting third terms for local officials. He ran as an Independent and won, but had to spend millions on his re-election campaign, and barely squeaked by in the end. With the city's economic fortunes on the wane in late 2008, Bloomberg instituted a round of cost-saving measures, scaling back city services and agencies. Housing remains a hot issue, with a grassroots push to improve housing options for the low-income and working-class families who have been priced out of Manhattan and practically all of the surrounding boroughs. America's ongoing debate on immigration reform has also fired up pockets of resistance in New York City, home to some of the largest émigré communities in the country. Local politicians pressured to take a stand have come out in favor of amnesty programs that would grant legal status to longtime undocumented residents.

ECONOMY

At press time, the US was grappling with its first major recession in more than a decade, and New York hadn't escaped the downturn. Workers' salaries haven't kept pace with inflation, and most of the middle and upper-middle class have been priced out of the city. For a while New York looked immune to the economic woes, thanks largely to the influx of foreign cash from bargain-seeking tourists. But all that changed in late 2008, when a series of Wall St and bank meltdowns (Bear Stearns laid off most of its staff, Lehman Bros crashed completely) rocked the foundation of the city's finances and set off a global economic crisis. With Wall St in turmoil, the city lost its largest source of tax revenue almost overnight, abruptly putting an end to what formerly seemed to be an invincible run of good fortune.

Still, hopes are high among New Yorkers that the nation's president will find a way to turn the country's situation around. Many New Yorkers are also reassured by a third term of Mayor Bloomberg's strict fiscal policies. He has ruthlessly tightened the belt on city spending, threatened to cut some firehouses and taken aim at liberal pension and sick-leave policies for many unionized workers. He's slashed his staffer salaries too. New Yorkers, already looking at likely subway-fare hikes and increased costs on water and heating bills, won't react kindly to any increases in property or state income taxes. Already the question hovering on most people's lips is: 'how can I afford to live here?' With Democrats in charge of the nation and now New York State, residents are looking to that party for answers after almost a decade of Republican rule.

ENVIRONMENT

New Yorkers are increasingly worried and affected by the environment, and have taken proactive steps to try and make a difference. Many restaurants have stopped serving bottled water and now offer their own filtered and recycled *agua fresca* in place of plastic or glass bottles.

Mayor Bloomberg won kudos from most city residents for his proposal to bring congestion pricing to the city; his idea got shot down by state lawmakers, but various versions to limit traffic jams are still on the table. More New Yorkers are turning to bicycles to navigate the city; it's a novel way to get around, and with subway fares increasing and quality of service decreasing, many prefer to pedal. It's still not as smooth riding around New York as it is in Paris or Copenhagen: bicyclists have to be on the defensive, be supremely careful and obey all traffic laws.

City residents are also worried about development encroaching on the Croton Watershed, a pristine and delicate wetland system that cleans much of the rainwater that flows into the city and into New Yorkers' taps. Environmentalists have held off the worst of the development, but it's a battle that will intensify in coming years. The dangers of too much building can be seen in the Gateway National Park in Jamaica Bay, Queens. The once massive wetland system has been reduced to just a few miles of shoreline, and Army Corp of Engineer scientists predict the marshland – dying of unknown reasons – will be gone entirely in 25 years. The city has recently taken steps to limit building on the marshy edges, but many fear it's too little too late.

FURTHER READING
NYC IN LITERATURE

Bonfire of the Vanities (Tom Wolfe; 1987) Delve into the status-obsessed '80s with this gripping novel of an uptown investment banker's entanglement with the world of the black South Bronx.

Go Tell It on the Mountain (James Baldwin; 1953) A day in the life of 14-year-old John Grimes, bringing readers into Harlem during the Depression.

The Invention of Everything Else (Samantha Hunt; 2008) The Brooklyn author goes back to the 1940s, creating historical fiction out of the adventures of scientist Nikola Tesla, who lived in the Hotel New Yorker.

Jazz (Toni Morrison; 1992) Pulitzer Prize–winner Morrison explores the Harlem Jazz Age through the tales of three tragic, intersecting lives.

Lush Life (Richard Price; 2008) Screenwriter and novelist Price tackles the gentrification of the Lower East Side and the lives of three friends who witness a shocking murder.

Motherless Brooklyn (Jonathan Lethem; 1999) This oddly compelling tale – of grown-up orphan Lionel Essrog, a detective with Tourette's syndrome who is investigating the death of his boss – explores crevices and histories of north Brooklyn 'hoods that newcomers never knew existed.

Push (Sapphire; 1996) A wrenching modern-age story about an abused young Harlem woman, 16-year-old Precious Jones.

Small Town (Lawrence Block; 2002) A chilling thriller about one man's response to losing his wife in the September 11 attacks: by becoming a serial killer on a vengeance spree.

MUSIC UNDER NEW YORK
Every year the MTA invites the best talents in New York City to play in the subway system. Violinists, barbershop quartets, Chinese dulcimer players, Haitian folk singers, cellists, jazz ensembles, salsa bands, opera singers and hip-hop dancers are just a small sampling of the kinds of shows you could be in for. Artists have to audition before becoming part of the official lineup. For a list of participating locations, visit www.mta.info/mta/aft/muny.

The Story of Junk (Linda Yablonsky; 1997) Years after her grim existence as a heroin junkie living in the down-and-out, pregentrified artists' Lower East Side, Yablonsky recalls all the shocking, seedy details.

FILMS & TV

American Gangster (2007) A Harlem-based drug drama, this one deals with heroin importation and an alliance with the Mafia, as well as the tale of one very honest policeman. It's based on a true story.

Fatal Attraction (1987) This psycho thriller is about a happily married man whose one-night stand turns into a series of run-ins with his lover-turned-stalker. Catch great glimpses of the pregentrification Meatpacking District.

Kids (1995) Shot in documentary style and starring a bunch of then-unknowns who include Rosario Dawson and Chloë Sevigny, this chilling tale tackles sexual promiscuity, drugs and AIDS.

Law & Order Dick Wolf's long-running series about the city's criminal justice system, set and shot in New York, and using real-life stories ripped from the headlines in — where else? — New York.

Manhattan (1979) Directed by and starring Woody Allen, as well as Diane Keaton and Mariel Hemingway. A divorced New Yorker dating a high-school student (the adorable, baby-voiced Hemingway) falls for his best friend's mistress in what is essentially a love letter to NYC.

Party Monster (2003) Macaulay Culkin plays the crazed, famed, murderous club kid Michael Alig in this disturbing look into the drug-fueled, club-kid era of the late '80s in downtown NYC.

Project Runway Heidi Klum and adorable Tim Gunn shepherd would-be designers to New York's best fabric stores in the Fashion District as they compete to win $100,000 in this New York–based reality show.

Saturday Night Fever (1977) John Travolta is the hottest thing in bell-bottoms in this tale of a streetwise Brooklyn kid who becomes king of the dance floor.

Sex and the City (2008) The eagerly awaited big-screen continuation of the cult-TV favorite catches up with the famous foursome, all as witty as ever, as their lives are filled with dramas that include cheating, jilting and kids.

Spider-Man 3 (2007) Tobey Maguire is battling villains with NYC as a backdrop in the darkest, most action-packed film of the three Spideys.

Taxi Driver (1976) Robert DeNiro is a mentally unstable Vietnam-war vet whose urges to lash out are heightened by the high tensions of a much grittier city.

What Not to Wear Shot at Silvercup Studios in Queens, where more than 30 other NY-centric shows are filmed, this reality show teaches women what flatters them most during a Tribeca shopping spree.

DIRECTORY
TRANSPORTATION
ARRIVAL & DEPARTURE
AIR

Multiple direct flights from just about every major city in North and South America and western Europe arrive in New York daily, as do many stopover flights from Asia. Most domestic air travel goes to LaGuardia, international tends to go to John F Kennedy (JFK) and a third, often easier option is Newark Liberty International in New Jersey, only a short drive from Manhattan.

John F Kennedy International Airport

In the far reaches of Queens, **John F Kennedy International Airport** (www .kennedyairport.com) is about 15 miles from Midtown, but it can take 45 to 75 minutes by car, and longer

Travel to/from JFK

	AirTrain/Subway	Taxi	Bus	Car Service
Pickup point	look for AirTrain signs at terminals that take you to the Rockaway subway station; from there take the A train into Manhattan	outside any terminal; look for the lines, as there are specific pickup points under 'Taxi' signs	outside any terminal; buses run every 15-20min to midnight	at any JFK terminal
Drop-off point	anywhere on the A train line	anywhere you want	Penn Station, Port Authority Bus Terminal and Grand Central Terminal	anywhere in Manhattan
Cost	AirTrain/subway $5/2.25	$45 to Manhattan and most of Brooklyn	$12-15 1-way	$50-75
Duration	1hr	1-2hr	allow 60-75min	1hr
Contact	www.airtrainjfk.com, www.mta.info		for express bus service, ☎ 718-875-8200; www.nyairportservice .com	operators include Big Apple (☎ 718-232-1015), Carmel (☎ 212-666-6666), Dial (☎ 718-743-2877) and Tel Aviv (☎ 212-777-7777)

Travel to/from LaGuardia

	New York Airport Service	Taxi	Train/Subway
Pickup point	to LaGuardia, buses leave every 20min between 6am and midnight from Penn Station, Port Authority Bus Terminal and Grand Central Terminal	outside any terminal. From the airport, take the M60 to W 106th St and Broadway; the M60 also connects with trains and the subway into Manhattan	a taxi can take you to the N and W trains in Astoria Queens, the A, B, C, D, 2, 4, 5, 6 subways along 125th St and the 1 subway at 116th/110th Sts and Broadway
Cost	$15	$15-30	$2.25
Duration	1hr	20-40min	allow 1hr
Contact	☎ 718-875-8200; www .nyairportservice.com		www.mta.info

in peak traffic. Useful numbers for this airport:

General inquiries (☎ 718-244-4444)
Hotel bookings (☎ 212-267-5500)
Lost and found (☎ 718-244 4225/6)
Medical services (☎ 718-656-5344)
Parking info (☎ 718-244-4444)
Traveler's aid (☎ 718-656-4870; ☒ 10am-6pm) Located in the arrival areas of terminals 1, 3, 4, 6, 7, 8 and 9; helps stranded travelers.

LaGuardia Airport

In northern Queens, **LaGuardia** (www.laguardiaairport.com) is about 8 miles from Manhattan, but traffic can turn that into a two-hour drive. Normally it's not more than 20 minutes. The car services available at JFK airport are also available at LaGuardia (see the table opposite). Useful numbers for this airport:

General inquiries (☎ 718-533-3400)
Lost and found (☎ 718-639-1839)
Parking info (☎ 718-533-3400)

TRAIN

Amtrak trains come right into Midtown, and you can pick them up in Boston, Philadelphia and Washington DC, as well as at smaller stops along the way. Long-distance Amtrak and Long Island Rail Road trains arrive at **Pennsylvania (Penn) Station** (☎ 212-582-6875, 800-872-7245; W 33rd St btwn Seventh & Eighth Aves). Commuter trains (MetroNorth) use **Grand Central Terminal** (Map p151, B4; ☎ 212-532-4900; Park Ave at E 42nd St). **New Jersey PATH trains** (☎ 800-234-7284) stop at the World Trade Center site, Christopher St, 14th St, 28th St and 34th St.

PASSPORT

Visitors are now required to have a passport that's valid for at least six months after their intended stay in the USA.

VISA

There are 27 countries whose residents can enter the US without a visa, provided they have a passport and will only stay 90 days. These countries include Australia, France, Germany, Italy, Japan, the Netherlands, Switzerland and the UK (for a complete list, visit www. cbp.gov). Under this program you must have a round-trip ticket that is nonrefundable in the USA, and you will not be allowed to extend your stay beyond 90 days.

Residents of other countries should apply for a visa at the nearest US embassy or consulate to their home before hitting the road. Most applications can be done through the mail. Many of the application forms and further information can be found at the website of the **US State Department** (http://travel.state.gov/visa).

CUSTOMS & DUTY FREE

If you are carrying more than $10,000 in US and/or foreign cash, traveler's checks or money orders when you enter the USA, you must declare it. You can import 1L of liquor (if you are over the age of 21); 200 cigarettes, 50 cigars (provided they are not Cuban) or 2kg of tobacco; and gifts up to a total value of $100 ($800 for US citizens). If you're bringing prescription drugs, make sure they're in clearly marked containers. For updates, check www.cbp.gov.

SECURITY

Security is very visible and tight at all three airports. Allow extra time for check-in and always have your identification on hand. Don't try to carry on metal nail files, Swiss Army knives, pocketknives, razors, corkscrews or any other sharp implements. Of course, any kind of firearm or other weapon, explo-

NEWARK LIBERTY INTERNATIONAL AIRPORT

Although it's in another state (New Jersey), many travelers find Newark easier to fly into than either of the very busy New York airports. If traffic is bad, traveling from Newark into Manhattan can take an interminably long time, but public transportation is quick and efficient. Take the **Monorail** (☎ 973-275-5555; www.njtransit.com; tickets $15; ⏰ 6am-9pm) from the airport to the NJ Transit train station. From there take a train to Newark's Penn Station (not Manhattan's Penn Station) and get on a **PATH Train** (tickets $2; ⏰ 24hr) into Manhattan. There's also the **Coach/Olympia Express Bus** (☎ 877-8-NEWARK; www.coachusa. com; tickets one way $15, round trip $25; ⏰ 24hr) which departs from Newark airport to Manhattan, but it could get you stuck in traffic if you take it at peak hour.

CLIMATE CHANGE & TRAVEL

Travel – especially air travel – is a significant contributor to global climate change. At Lonely Planet, we believe that all who travel have a responsibility to limit their personal impact. As a result, we have teamed with Rough Guides and other concerned industry partners to support Climate Care, which allows people to offset the greenhouse gases they are responsible for with contributions to energy-saving projects and other climate-friendly initiatives in the developing world. Lonely Planet offsets all staff and author travel.

For more information, turn to the responsible travel pages on www.lonelyplanet .com. For details on offsetting your carbon emissions and a carbon calculator, go to www .climatecare.org.

sives, flammable liquids or solids, or any other hazardous materials are prohibited. Even nonflammable liquids are restricted to 4oz in your carry-on bag; pack the big bottles of perfume in your luggage. Guards are pitiless about making you throw out whatever liquids over 4oz are in your bag at the boarding gate.

GETTING AROUND

Subway is generally the fastest, cheapest way to get around Manhattan because busy city streets get clogged by 'gridlock,' when cars sit bumper to bumper waiting for lights to change. City buses can be useful, provided that traffic is moving. Pick up a public transit map from subway ticket booths. Taxis are the most convenient mode of transportation after 1am.

TRAVEL PASSES

MetroCard (☎ 718-330-1234) is the easiest way to pay for travel on New York's public transit system.

Pick one up at any newsstand or subway entrance. The one-day Fun Pass ($8.25) is a major money saver, giving you unlimited access to subways and buses from the first swipe until 3am the next morning. The seven-day ($27) or 30-day ($89) unlimited cards are great deals, but you must let 18 minutes elapse between each swipe, making it harder for two people to share one card. Pay-per-ride options are also available – either a vending machine or subway clerk can put any dollar amount you want on your MetroCard, with bonus rides when you buy several at a time. Be aware that the single-ride cards sold from machines in subway stations expire after two hours. At print time, the single-ride fare was $2.25, though that's subject to change.

SUBWAY

The subway system (☎ 718-330-1234) runs 24 hours a day. In this

V

DIRECTORY

Travel Around New York City

	Theater District	The Met	American Museum of Natural History	Harlem	Dumbo	Coney Island	Williamsburg
Lower Manhattan	subway 10min	subway 15min	subway 15min	subway 25min	subway 10min	subway 45min	subway 30min
Upper East Side	cab 10min	cab/walk 5/10min	cab10min	subway 15min	subway 30min	subway 1hr	subway 30min
Upper West Side	cab/walk 5/10min	cab 10min	walk 5-10min	subway 10min	subway 20-25min	subway 1hr	subway 40min
Theater District	n/a	walk/ subway 15/ 10-15min	walk/subway 15/10min	subway 15min	subway 20-30min	subway 45min-1hr	subway 40min
Southern Brooklyn	subway 40min	subway 30min	subway 40min	subway 45min	subway 20min	subway 30min	subway 35min

book, the nearest subway stop is noted after the 🚇 icon in each listing. If you transfer from the subway to a bus or from a bus to the subway within 18 minutes of paying a fare, there's no double charge – free transfers are permitted. To get the latest bus and subway routes, and up-to-the-minute service changes, visit www.mta.nyc.ny.us and follow the links to NYC Transit. Other useful websites are www.hopstop.com, www.trips123.com and www.public routes.com. These for-profit sites offer free information on traveling around New York and surrounding cities via public transportation.

BUS

City buses (☎ 718-330-1234) operate 24 hours a day and generally run north–south along avenues and crosstown along the major east–west thoroughfares. You need exact coins worth $2.25 or a MetroCard to board a bus – no bills accepted. The driver will not make change.

BOAT

New York Waterway (☎ 800-533-3779; www.nywaterway.com) ferries make runs up the Hudson River Valley and from Midtown to Yankee Stadium in the Bronx. A popular commuter route goes from the New Jersey Transit train station in Hoboken to the World Financial Center in Lower Manhattan; boats leave every five to 10 minutes at peak times, and the 10-minute ride costs $6 each way.

New York Water Taxi (☎ 212-742-1969; www.nywatertaxi.com; 1 stop $5) is a new service that's really taken off in New York. These yellow taxi boats stop at various piers along Manhattan's West Side and are a wonderful way to travel to Midtown, Lower Manhattan, and parts of Brooklyn and Queens. The Water Taxi Beach (www.watertaxi beach.com) is a favorite pit stop.

TAXI
A taxi is available when the middle of its rooftop number is glowing (as opposed to when the 'off duty' lights on either side of the number are glowing). Metered fares start at $2.50, a minimum 15% tip is expected, there's a $1 tax added, and a 50¢ surcharge from 8pm to 6am. Credit cards are accepted.

CAR RENTAL
The main rental agencies in New York City include **Avis** (☎ 800-331-1212), **Budget** (☎ 800-527-0700), **Dollar** (☎ 800-800-4000), **Hertz** (☎ 800-654-3131) and **Thrifty** (☎ 800-367-2277).

PRACTICALITIES
BUSINESS HOURS
Shops are generally open Monday to Saturday from 10am to 6pm and Sunday from 11am to 6pm, with some extended hours Thursday nights; many shops close Monday. Some businesses change their operating hours with the seasons, usually resulting in shorter hours in the summer. Banks and institutional businesses keep a 9am to 5pm Monday to Friday schedule, but many also keep 9am to 3pm hours on Saturday.

Museums and art galleries are usually open Tuesday to Sunday from 10am to 5pm. On public holidays, banks, schools and government offices (including post offices) close, and transportation services operate on a Sunday schedule.

DISCOUNTS
New York CityPass (www.citypass.com), available online or at major city attractions, buys you admission into the Empire State Building, Metropolitan Museum of Art, Museum of Modern Art, Guggenheim Museum, American Museum of Natural History and a Circle Line cruise for $79 (worth $131 in value). **New York Pass** (www.newyorkpass .com) sells online cards for $75 and gives you daylong access to 40 top attractions (the UN, Statue of Liberty, Guggenheim etc), as well as discounts at 25 stores and restaurants. Two-, three- and seven-day passes are also available, and you can choose to collect them in NYC or have them sent to you before you leave home. The **Entertainment Book** (www.entertainment.com), which you can order for $35 before your arrival, is packed with passes that arm you with dining, shopping and service deals.

ELECTRICITY

Electricity in the USA is 110V and 60Hz. Plugs have two or three pins (two flat pins, often with a round 'grounding' pin). Adapters for European and South American plugs are widely available; Australians should bring adapters.

EMBASSIES & CONSULATES

The UN's presence in New York means that nearly every country in the world maintains diplomatic offices here. Most are listed in the white pages of the phone book under 'Consulates General of (country).' Embassies include the following:

Australia (☎ 212-351-6500; 150 E 42nd St btwn Lexington & Third Aves)
Canada (☎ 212-596-1783; 1251 Sixth Ave btwn 49th & 50th Sts)
Ireland (☎ 212-319-2555; 345 Park Ave btwn 51st & 52nd Sts)
New Zealand (☎ 212-832-4038; 780 Third Ave btwn 48th & 49th Sts)
South Africa (☎ 212-213-4880; 333 E 38th St btwn First & Second Aves)
UK (☎ 212-745-0202; 845 Third Ave btwn 51st & 52nd Sts)

EMERGENCIES

You can always get help by dialing 911 from any phone, including mobiles. There are also emergency-call boxes on many city corners: some look like bright orange bulbs; others are old-fashioned iron boxes

bolted to the crosswalk signals. In either case, push the button and the cavalry comes running.
Police, fire, ambulance (☎ 911)
Police information operator (☎ 212-374-5000)

GAY & LESBIAN TRAVELERS

New York doesn't differentiate much between heterosexual and homosexual – at least, not when it comes to dancing, drinking and eating. For info on the gay and lesbian scene in NYC, see p240.

INFORMATION & ORGANIZATIONS

The free magazines *HX* and *Next* are available at restaurants and bars. Look for *LGNY* and *NY Blade* in street-corner boxes. Pick up the lifestyle magazine *Metrosource* at shops and the LGBT Community Center. *Time Out* features a good events section.

Useful counseling, referral and information centers:
Gay & Lesbian Hotline (☎ 212-989-0999; glnh@glnh.org)
LGBT Community Center (Map pp106–7; ☎ 212-620-7310; www.gaycenter.org; 208 W 13th St at Seventh Ave)

HOLIDAYS

New Year's Day January 1
Martin Luther King Jr Day Third Monday in January
Presidents' Day Third Monday in February

Easter Sunday March/April
Memorial Day Last Monday in May
Independence Day July 4
Labor Day First Monday in September
Columbus Day Second Monday in October
Veterans' Day November 11
Thanksgiving Fourth Thursday in November
Christmas Day December 25

INTERNET
Public libraries offer free web access, and internet cafes are common.

INTERNET CAFES
Cyber Café (Map p163, B3; ☎ 212-333-4109; 250 W 49th St btwn Broadway & Eighth Ave; per 30min $7; ☺ 8am-11pm) High-speed computers with color printers, scanners and web cams, plus there's a coffee and wine bar.

Kinkos (Map p183, B3; ☎ 212-628-5500; www.fedex.com; 1122 Lexington Ave near 77th St; per 30 min $6; ☺ 24hr) All you need is a credit card to get online here.

LGBT Community Center (Map pp106–7; ☎ 212-620-7310; 208 W 13th St at Seventh Ave; suggested donation $3; ☺ 9am-11pm) The cyber-center here has 15 computers, open to all.

Newsbar (Map pp106–7, G1; ☎ 212-353-1246; 107 University Pl btwn 12th & 13th Sts; per 30 min $6; ☺ 8am-9pm) Has vegan coffee, lots to read and a cool vibe.

USEFUL WEBSITES
The Lonely Planet website (www.lonelyplanet.com) offers New York City information and links. Other good sites:

New York City Insider (www.theinsider.com)
New York City Search (www.newyork.city search.com)
New York Times (www.nytimes.com)
NYC & Co (www.nycvisit.com)

WI-FI
Bryant Park went wireless in 2005, and now all of New York has followed suit. **WiFi Salon** (http://wifisalon.com) has a list of locations, as does www.nyc.wireless.net.

LOST PROPERTY
Public transit (☎ 212-712-4500)
Taxi (☎ 212-692-8294)

MEDICAL SERVICES
New York Hotel Urgent Medical Services (☎ 212-737-1212) offers medical services to visitors, and doctors make 24-hour house (and hotel) calls. Expect to pay top dollar (prices begin at $200). Medical care gets very expensive very fast in the US if you don't have insurance.

DENTAL SERVICES
For tooth situations that can't wait, try **AAA Dental Care** (Map p163, D3; ☎ 212-744-3928; www.emergency dentalnyc.com; Suite 1504, 30 E 60th St).

PHARMACIES
There are a number of 24-hour pharmacies in New York City:
Duane Reade (Map p163; ☎ 212-541-9708; W 57th St at Broadway)

Duane Reade (Map pp106–7; ☎ 212-674-5357; Sixth Ave at Waverly Pl)

HOSPITALS

All hospitals have 24-hour emergency departments that must treat the uninsured.

Bellevue Hospital (off Map p151; ☎ 212-562-4141; NYU Medical Center, First Ave at E 27th St)

Lenox Hill Hospital (Map p183, B3; ☎ 212-434-2000; 100 E 77th St btwn Park & Lexington Aves)

New York Hospital (☎ 212-746-5050; 525 E 68th St btwn York Ave & Franklin D Roosevelt Dr)

....

MONEY

ATMS

You'll find 24-hour ATMs at banks and most grocery stores, but unless you are using a branch of your bank, expect to pay a $3 fee. Avoid ATMs in nightclubs and try to avoid ATMs set out on streets or in corner shops, especially if they haven't got a security camera pointed at them; many are rigged to steal your number.

CHANGING MONEY

Banks often do better deals than exchange offices, but it's always a good idea to check the rates, commissions and any other charges. Chase, a bank with 80 branches in Manhattan, has no fees.

CREDIT CARDS

Visa, MasterCard (both affiliated with European Access Cards),

American Express and Discover are widely accepted. For lost cards, contact the following:

American Express (☎ 800-528-4800)
Diners Club (☎ 800-234-6377)
Discover (☎ 800-347-2683)
MasterCard (☎ 800-826-2181)
Visa (☎ 800-336-8472)

CURRENCY

The monetary unit used is the US dollar, which is divided into 100 cents (¢). Coins come in 1¢ (penny), 5¢ (nickel), 10¢ (dime), 25¢ (quarter), 50¢ (half-dollar; rare) and $1 denominations. Notes come in $1, $2 (rare), $5, $10, $20, $50 and $100. Some shops won't accept notes higher than $20.

....

NEWSPAPERS & MAGAZINES

The *New York Times* is the nation's premier newspaper, and covers cultural events extensively in the weekend edition. The weekly *New York Observer* specializes in local media and politics. The *Daily News* and *New York Post* are popular tabloids. The *Wall Street Journal* is the daily business bible.

Time Out New York lists events, restaurants and shops; the *New Yorker* magazine covers high-brow theater, art and music events. Free street papers – such as the *Village Voice, AM New York* and *Metro New York* – offer good entertainment listings.

POST

The main post office (☎ 212-967-8585; 421 Eighth Ave at 33rd St) is open 24 hours. The post office at Rockefeller Center (p154) is open Monday to Friday from 9:30am to 5:30pm. The **Franklin D Roosevelt post office** (Map p151, C2; 909 Third Ave) is open Monday to Friday from 9am to 8pm and Saturday from 10am to 2pm.

TELEPHONE
COUNTRY & CITY AREA CODES

The US country code is 1. Manhattan phone numbers are always preceded by a three-digit area code: ☎ 212, ☎ 646 or ☎ 917, although ☎ 646 and ☎ 917 also do double duty as mobile phone and pager area codes. Even when dialing in Manhattan you must use 1 plus the entire 10-digit number. For the outer boroughs, the area codes are ☎ 718 and ☎ 347.

INTERNATIONAL CODES

Dial ☎ 00 followed by the code for the country you're calling.
Australia (☎ 61)
Canada (☎ 1)
Japan (☎ 81)
New Zealand (☎ 64)
South Africa (☎ 27)
UK (☎ 44)

USEFUL NUMBERS

City information (☎ 311)
Clubfone (☎ 212-777-2582)
Collect calls (☎ 0)
Directory assistance (☎ 411)
International access code (☎ 011)
Moviefone (☎ 212-777-3456)
Operator (☎ 0)
Operator-assisted calls (☎ 01 + the number; an operator will come on the line once you have dialed)
Time (☎ 212-976-1616)
Weather (☎ 212-976-1212)

TIME

New York is in the Eastern Standard Time (EST) zone, five hours behind Greenwich Mean Time (GMT). Daylight saving starts on the first Sunday in April (clocks are advanced an hour) and it finishes on the last Saturday in October.

At noon in New York it's 9am in San Francisco, 5pm in London, 6pm in Paris, 7pm in Cape Town and 3am the next day in Sydney.

TIPPING

Waiters work for less than minimum wage, so it is expected that satisfied customers will tip 15% to 20% of the total bill. Tips are not automatically included, but some restaurants add a 15% gratuity to the bills of parties of six or more. Standard tipping amounts:
Baggage carriers $5 for the first bag, $1 for each additional bag.
Bars At least $1 per drink (or more for faster service and stronger drinks).
Cloakroom attendants $2 per item.
Hairdressers 15%.

Hotel service personnel $2 for each service performed.

Restaurants 15% to 20% (not expected in fast-food, takeout or self-service restaurants).

Room cleaners Minimum $5 per day.

Taxis 10% to 15%.

Tour guides $20 per family/group for a full-day tour.

TOURIST INFORMATION

NYC & Co (Map p163, C2; ☎ 212-484-1222; www.nycvisit.com; 810 Seventh Ave at 53rd St; ⏲ 8:30am-6pm Mon-Fri, 9am-5pm Sat & Sun; ⊕ N, R, W, 2, 3 to 42nd St-Times Sq) operates a 24-hour toll-free line with listings of special events and reservation details. Staff are helpful and knowledgeable and the information center is comprehensive.

You'll also find information counters and centers at airports, in Times Sq (Map p163), at Grand Central Terminal (Map p151) and at Penn Station.

TRAVELERS WITH DISABILITIES

Federal laws require that all government offices have good elevator and ramp access for wheelchairs and devices to aid the hearing impaired. Almost all major venues offer good bathroom facilities for those with wheelchairs, and all city buses are able to carry wheelchair passengers. Only some subway stations are accessible (see MTA maps or call ☎ 718-596-8585).

WOMEN TRAVELERS

It's a good idea to avoid public transportation after midnight, and watch your drink at all times in a bar – just as a precaution. Carry extra money on you at night in a safe spot so you can grab a cab home, especially if you're traveling alone.

Tampons, pads and condoms are sold everywhere. The contraceptive pill and 'morning after' pill are available in local pharmacies. New York City law stipulates that rape victims be offered the 'morning after' pill while receiving treatment at hospitals, but it's not always automatically offered. If you want to take it, insist upon getting it.

>INDEX

See also separate subindexes for See (p274), Shop (p276), Eat (p277), Drink (p279) and Play (p279).

⊙ SEE

000 map pages

000 map pages

000 map pages

INDEX

000 map pages